Binding
With
Briars

So I turned to the Garden of Love
  That so many sweet flowers bore.
And I saw it was filled with graves,
  And tombstones where flowers should be;
And priests with black gowns were walking their rounds,
  And binding with briars my joys and desires.

WILLIAM BLAKE (1757-1827)

Binding With Briars

Sex and Sin in the Catholic Church

RICHARD GINDER

PRENTICE-HALL, INC., Englewood Cliffs, N.J.

*Binding With Briars: Sex and Sin in the
Catholic Church* by Richard Ginder
Copyright © 1975 by Richard Ginder

Printed in the United States of America
Prentice-Hall International, Inc., London
Prentice-Hall of Australia, Pty. Ltd., Sydney
Prentice-Hall of Canada, Ltd., Toronto
Prentice-Hall of India Private Ltd., New Delhi
Prentice-Hall of Japan, Inc., Tokyo

10   9   8   7   6   5   4   3   2   1

Library of Congress Cataloging in Publication Data

Ginder, Richard.
    Binding with briars.

    Bibliography: p.
    Includes index.
    1. Sexual ethics. 2. Sex and religion.
3. Catholic Church—Doctrinal and controversial
works—Catholic authors. I. Title.
HQ59.G56   261.8'34'17   75-11610
ISBN 0-13-076299-7

Deiparæ

FOREWORD

I am a Roman Catholic priest. My diocese is Pittsburgh. I am in good standing and celebrate the Holy Sacrifice every day.

Among my other qualifications: I was a Basselin Fellow with three years of philosophy and four of theology at the Catholic University of America. As associate editor for twenty years, I wrote a highly controversial column, "Right Or Wrong," for *Our Sunday Visitor*, in those days the most widely circulated Catholic periodical in the world, with close to a million subscribers.

I founded and for twenty-four years edited *The Priest*, a kind of trade journal for the Catholic clergy. I founded and for eleven years edited *My Daily Visitor* for shut-ins. For thirteen years I edited *The Catholic Choirmaster*. I have written altogether one hundred twenty-four pamphlets with a total sale of twenty-six million copies. I have spoken and my musical compositions have been performed on all four of the major radio networks and on CBS-TV.

I am a Fellow of the American Guild of Organists, a published author and composer, with a master's degree in philosophy and the equivalent, a licentiate, in sacred theology. For three years I taught at St. Charles College and St. Mary's Seminary, Baltimore.

I have been working on this book for twenty-five years: reading, taking notes, analyzing my own inner experience and comparing it with that of others. The seed was planted in 1949 when I first realized my sexual identity. Gradually, with the passing years, the embryo developed into a fetus, until finally last year I entered into labor. Here is the child. During all that time I was never allowed to express myself on this subject in either *The Priest* or *Our Sunday Visitor*. I was always overruled.

But once I started writing, I felt the book taking on a life of its own. It began to unfold and grow almost of itself as I thought through this whole matter of sexuality in its relationship to religion. I began the book a conservative and ended a liberal.

While writing the very first chapters, I still accepted the classical morality with which I had been inoculated: drunkenness is not much of a sin, lying is only a venial sin, and to enjoy marijuana is no sin at all; theft can usually be rationalized on grounds of need or occult compensation,* cursing and profanity are generally venial for lack of advertence, whatever you do on the Sabbath is okay so long as you get to mass—BUT that second glance at a provocative billboard is a mortal sin.

(Not, as Alex Comfort hints in *The Joy of Sex*, that we Catholics aren't playing sex as often as the rest of the world; it's just that we aren't getting nearly as much fun out of it because of what Dr. Comfort calls our "guilt hangup.")

Writing this book has forced me to rethink the whole subject of morality—rather, not to rethink but for the first time in my life to think it all the way through. As I pondered the different aspects of the subject, making them explicit in my mind, framing them in words for the reader, the classical morality on sex became increasingly implausible. I kept having to modify what I had hitherto considered my "absolutes."

If it strikes the reader that I give rather disproportionate space to the homosexuals, it is because Gay Liberation is the cutting edge of sexual liberation. If the "respectable" elements of the American community can ever come to tolerate sodomy and to welcome the gays as their peers in every way, then, *a fortiori*, they will concede anything at all to the heterosexuals. It is the gays who are the shock troops, in the front lines, on the barricades.

In dogma I remain an open-minded conservative. With Plato, Aristotle, St. Augustine, and St. Thomas, I still believe in a spiritual and "detachable" soul, in a particular judgment, and in the communion of saints. The Holy Father is the visible head of Christ's Church on earth, and the bishops in communion with him are successors of the apostles, each ruling his diocese by divine right. As a priest I have the power to forgive sins and consecrate the body of the Lord. I am not about to yield one period or comma of the Nicene Creed. I love my priesthood and my Church. I love God and I love all his creatures:

*Secretly taking one's due.

men and women, boys and girls, cats and dogs, snakes and spiders—*sed aliter et aliter*, "one one way and another another."

As for moral theology, that is something else again. My opinions may have to travel underground in the Church until popular sentiment is ready to accept them. But if you find my arguments and proofs probable, even though not conclusive, then the Church says you may form your own conscience accordingly.

For several years I was official censor of books for the Diocese of Pittsburgh. Nevertheless, it is with prayer and no little trepidation that I submit my analysis, hoping that it may bring some degree of comfort, however slight, to the reader. All my life has been a preparation for the writing of this book.

————Richard Ginder

CONTENTS

1

Christ Losing His World

"Father, why is birth control a sin?"

"Why, David, because it's the abuse of a natural faculty."

"You mean, uh, well, like standing on your head or walking on your hands?"

"But those are not sins!"

"I know, Father—so why is birth control a sin?"

Priest, impatiently: "Because the pope says so."

It would do an injustice to thousands of Catholic priests to think that they have resigned their ministry merely to acquire a wife and satisfy their sexual needs. There is that, yes—every man's instinctive yearning for a home and family of his own. Their motivation is complex, certainly, but also powerful is the consideration that Catholic moral teaching has to an almost fatal extent lost its credibility.

Sadly, too, those departing priests are only the visible representatives of thousands of the laity who feel the same way. When we hear or read of a priest just laying down his charge and vanishing into the crowd, we can take it for granted that he must represent at least ten thousand of the laity in his disaffection.

Pope John convoked Vatican Council II because he could see that the modern age had far outstripped the Church. Ours is an age much like the opening of the sixteenth century. Then, with the revival of letters, learning was no longer the exclusive property of priests and lawyers. There was the opening of the New World and the discovery of printing. There were the European wars, tearing men from their villages and sweeping them from one end of the continent to the other. In our day it is the explosion of knowledge coupled with universal education. Religion must once again submit to universal and critical inquiry.

Books on science and the arts used to be bound, stitched in leather or cloth, to last for centuries. Now they come glued into paperbacks not meant to last any longer than ten years, for by that time the knowledge they contain may be obsolete. And new knowledge alters old. Psychiatry, for instance, has isolated alcoholism and kleptomania, thus shading St. Paul's strictures on drunkenness and theft. Using tranquilizers, the new science of psychopharmacology can practically banish sins of impatience, anger, and hatred from one's conscience.

The whole world is changing, and the people in it. The pipe organ is gone. There used to be a piano in just about every parlor. Now there are few pianos and no parlors. With the coming of television, reading and writing are obsolescent among the masses.

A whole new class of people appeared during the 1940s. We have had to coin a word to cover them. We call them "teen-agers." Because of better nutrition they keep getting taller, and because of television and instant access to oceans of information, they are more precocious. The age of menarche is dropping at the rate of six months per decade.[1]

Chelsea Hospital in London is now experimenting with "test-tube babies." An egg is removed from a woman's ovaries and placed in a nutrient broth, to which male sperm is later added.[2]

Instead of conceiving naturally, a woman can now be inseminated artificially by sperm from her husband or she may choose a prospective sire from a variety of sperms labeled and stored in a "bank."

The human brain can now be separated and made to function without its body. In fact, there is a Cleveland surgeon who is confident that he can successfully transfer the head of one person to the trunk of another. A Catholic, he is waiting for clear advice from the theologians on the morality of the proposed operation.[3]

It is now possible to distinguish not just two, but seven kinds of sex: chromosomal, anatomical, legal, endocrinological, germinal, psychological, and social. Penis and vulva are rapidly losing ground as the sole determining criteria.

What is death? When the heart stops beating? The lungs functioning? The brain?

In fact, in view of current genetic experiments, we have reached the ultimate question: What, precisely, constitutes a human being?

How does moral theology solve the problems and answer the questions raised by these developments? Sadly, it doesn't. While the scientists speed forward under floodlights, the theologians are still fumbling their way with oil lamps.

For too many centuries, our moral speculation has been based not so much on the Word of God as on a confused jumble of philosophical maxims and questionable but unquestioned traditions; on correct intuitions vitiated by ignorances that are ludicrous in the light of modern science; on an intricate maze of reasoning about good and evil and on long lists of unchallenged taboos.

Like the profane sciences, moral theology studies a certain ever-present department of human experience which it tries progressively to understand and systematize. Its point of departure has been the Bible, a record of certain past experiences that cannot be repeated but which are known to us only through that record. Thus, moral theology has gradually become a police ordinance, menacing and closed in upon itself, promulgated ironically in the name of our Savior, the God who actually chose to die rather than see us go unredeemed.

Worse, we seem to have developed a double standard, a sort of two-faced morality. There is the official, formal, publicly professed morality, but then there is also the morality actually practiced and condoned by the insiders. Thus, a lie is intrinsically evil and therefore must never be used under any circumstances. This is what is preached. But only churchmen are familiar with the thesis, universally conceded by the theologians, that veracity is only a light obligation. This the churchman practices but never, never preaches. There are other instances of this double standard.

To borrow Fr. Marc Oraison's summary: "What we need is a change of method *from the bottom up*."[4]

Until the Second Vatican Council, the Church was being strangled by an arbitrary, irresponsible, and often capricious authoritarianism, by bad scholarship, suspicion of science, fear of democracy, and a self-seeking lust for power.[5] Nor has there been much change since then. Our churchmen for the most part are still missing the point—indeed, the whole point of Christianity, which is charity.

As a result of all this, the Church has lost its hold on the secular mind. For, while Dachau and Auschwitz taught the world what sin really is, the real meaning of evil, that world still sees the Catholic Church interminably preoccupied with sex, bending her energy and resources toward keeping kids and lovers from handling themselves and one another, and trying to persuade the world that all sex is wicked except, without sheath or pill, that between man and wife.

So the schoolboy asks the priest, "You mean to say that a sin of sex is as bad as murder?"

"Well," uneasily, "they're both mortal sins. . . ."

"And if I do this thing I'll go to hell, same as Hitler?"

"That's a very good question, boy. Next?"

With that, the priest has lost the class. In their minds religion has started drifting in the direction of Santa Claus and the Easter Bunny and Sister's stories about St. Hypatius of Chalcedon, who used to light his fire every morning with an icicle, St. Cuthman of Sussex, who could hang his birettum on a sunbeam, and St. Lioba, who used to float across the English Channel on an altar stone—all so much baggage to be discarded with the onset of maturity.

> We have believed
>   the beautiful false stories,
> Fed on the faiths
>   that after childhood fail. . . [6]

As far as one can judge from current sociological studies and surveys, just about everyone in the United States must be living in the state of mortal sin—according to Catholic standards, that is.

—In his study, *Adolescent Sexuality in Contemporary America,** Robert C. Sorensen found: "A substantial number of all respondents—regardless of their religious preference or lack of it —look upon the values of organized religion as being irrelevant to their sexuality." Fifteen percent of the test group agreed with the statement, "One of the reasons I stopped going to church is because churches teach that sex is sinful."[7] Thirty-six percent of the boys and twenty-one percent of the girls are currently masturbating.[8]

*Quotations by permission of Harry N. Abrams, Inc. © 1973 by Robert C. Sorensen.

Seventy-one percent of the boys and fifty-six percent of the girls have had intercourse by age fifteen.[9]

So they are starting their sex life earlier and working at it harder than their parents had supposed. Seventy-two percent of the teenagers refuse to accept the proposition: "Sex is immoral unless it's between two people who are married to each other."[10]

Which means that we have lost the kids, for our Catholic teaching is all of a piece. You can't say, "Sure, I'll take the baby—all except the left foot." It's all or nothing.

—Moving on to the next age group: *Time* reports that, "At most colleges, the sexual revolution is over; premarital sex and cohabitation among unmarried students are accepted as a matter of course. More recently, students at many campuses have become highly tolerant of homosexual and bisexual behavior. Among the most extreme avant-garde students at Berkeley and Columbia, it has become fashionable to have a homosexual or bisexual experience."[11]

So the collegians, too, have rejected Catholic moral teaching on sex.

—"On the basis of interviews with 4,000 women in every social and economic class and a comparison of the yearly rates of unwanted pregnancies by couples who do not practice birth control," says *Time,* "Charles Westoff of Princeton University's office of Population Research concludes that Americans made love more often in the five years ending in 1970 than they did in 1965. The frequency of intercourse is up 20 percent, to nearly 8.2 times a month."[12]

In view of the size and circumstances of the usual Catholic family, it would be safe to conclude that those parents are not coupling twice a week without practicing birth control.

—Statistics on the number of American homosexuals are understandably hard to come by. One knowledgable source estimates 20,000,000,[13] but another source, equally well informed, scales that figure down to 15,000,000.[14] Of American gays, 28.6 percent are Catholic.[15] (In Holland it is 44.2 percent.) That gives us at least 4,250,000 Catholics with a crucial conflict of conscience which they are all but irresistibly tempted to resolve in their own favor and against Church teaching.

—And then there are the 4,200,000 Catholics stuck with broken marriages.[16]

A recent report by the National Opinion Research Center largely verifies the foregoing statistics on sexuality:

—Since 1965 the percentage of those Catholics who approve of conjugal sex purely for pleasure has gone up from 29 to 50.
—Of those approving of remarriage between divorcees, 52 to 73.
—Approving of birth control, from 45 to 83.
—Since 1963: Of those who approve of sex between engaged couples, from 12 to 43.
—In 1963, 41 percent of all Catholics thought that parents should have as many children as possible. That percentage has dropped to 18.
—Those approving of sex education in Catholic schools: 80 percent.

As one might expect, there has been a lamentable overflow into the areas of faith and devotion. This must be due largely to the crisis of conscience forced on Catholics everywhere by the Holy Father's decision against sex in his 1968 encyclical *"Humanæ vitæ."* Over half the Catholics queried—58 percent—have lost faith in papal supremacy; they no longer believe that our Lord made St. Peter and his successors heads of his Church. In 1965 that figure was only 28 percent. Sixty-eight percent have lost faith in infallibility. What happened between 1965 and the present to so drastically reduce Catholic devotion to the Holy Father? Are we to believe that since *"Causa locuta est, Roma finita est"*?

The number of nonchurchgoers is up from 6 to 12 percent. Of those who seldom or never confess, up from 18 to 38 percent.

On the other hand, the number of weekly communicants has doubled—which could prove merely that they have somehow fixed their consciences, for it is notorious that if we do not live as we believe, we shall sooner or later come to believe as we live.[17]

Sex, admittedly, is not the whole of life and certainly not the only concern of morality. On the personal level, however, sex is so vitally important to each of us that the moral questions it provokes demand immediate responses.

We are conscious of the greater importance of other moral issues, like war, ecological preservation, violence and governmental integrity. But such great matters have only philosophical urgency, whereas personal moral problems more immediately regulate our lives.

The teaching of the institutional church is overdeveloped in the area of personal sexual morality. Like it or not, this teaching affects the daily lives of us all and deserves consideration and discussion.

Now strangely one can discuss just about anything in Catholic teaching—one could propose, say the Assumption of St. Joseph or the ordination of female bishops—and get a respectful if bored hearing. But if one even suggests for discussion lowering the price tag on sex, strange things happen. The earth quakes, thunder rolls and lightning flashes, the winds howl. It is as though you had stuck your finger in the pope's eye. Bishops and superiors, administrators, the Establishment, become terrified and fly into hysterical panic. One is, as by reflex, accused of self-interest, suspected of masturbation, dissipation, fornication, and worse. It seems we simply have to keep those teen-agers, collegians, married people, and homosexuals, estranged from God—estranged really not from God but, sadly, only from his Church—or shall we say, rather, not from the Church but only from the structure, the Establishment?

Why is this? In succeeding chapters we shall discuss the etiology of this attitude as well as the sexual problems of these several sectors of the community. We may be able to help. Perhaps not. But certainly there can be no harm in trying.

2

The "Dirty Thing"

In high school I once asked our instructor in religion, an elderly Christian Brother, if there would be sex in heaven.

"No," he replied sharply, "nor showers, nor lavatories either."

His train of thought is easily followed: in his mind, sex was associated with dirt and filth, the animal functions and limitations of the body. But in heaven our bodies will be glorified. Like the angels and devils we shall be without dirt, filth—and sex.

Our Christian heaven can seem pallid by comparison with the sexual paradise promised to his followers by Mohammed. How *could* there be a heaven without sex? Later study and meditation on my part refined St. John's imagery of harps and white robes and sempiternal hallelujah-singing before the throne of the Almighty. But the eternal enjoyment of essential Truth, Goodness, and Beauty still seemed something of a bore compared with all the robust fun of the Islamic paradise.

Here we have two cultures, the Christian and the Moslem, side by side—the one gloriously prosexual, the other dismally antisexual. Passing from one to the other, the Westerner is often disturbed by

Eastern morals. But the shock comes mainly from the openness, the sincerity and candor of Oriental freedom. It makes him acutely aware of his own concealment and falseness.[1] How did we get that way?

Christianity is a child of Judaism. Christ and St. Paul were practicing Jews, and they used the Jewish religion as the base on which to build their own. Thus, Christianity is modified Judaism —and of the thirty-six capital crimes in Mosaic law, eighteen involved sex.

It was Jesus, however, who introduced the practice of sexual abstinence as a supreme if difficult means of glorifying God. It was a novelty unknown under the Old Testament. The ideal took its place with poverty and obedience, the three evangelical counsels providing the road to perfection.

Chastity in women translates "virginity." Those who think of the virgin as an almost extinct species, mentioned only in the Bible and mythology, mistake its religious meaning. Medically and anatomically, a virgin is any female still possessed of her hymen. But that can be lost involuntarily, even unknowingly. Many a girl ruptures her hymen merely riding a bicycle or a horse. A ballet student is likely to lose it with her first *plié*.

In the religious sense, however, virginity is the determination to practice permanent sexual abstinence for the love of God, regardless of past experience. This applies to both men and women.[2]

Although, as Jesus plainly stated, virginity is not for everyone[3] (we now know that it is very largely a matter of taste and glandular urgency, or lack of it), the consecrated virgins gathered in their convents soon became the darlings of the Church, unfortunately and unfairly, with the effect of downgrading the matrons of the community together with matrimony, the sacrament of sex.

To this day, the Church frowns on second marriages. St. Paul urged widows to remain unmarried unless the single life be too dangerous.[4] Nevertheless, the second marriage was upheld as legitimate at Nicaea against the Montanists and Novatians.[5] But still they frown on the face of the Church: "A woman who has once received the solemn blessing cannot receive it again in subsequent marriages."[6]

And so, through a misinterpretation of Jesus' praise of virginity, sex began to limp in the opinion and practice of the Church. St. John canonized all virgins with his praise of the 144,000 who get special honors in heaven: "These are they which are not defiled with women; for they are virgins . . . follow the Lamb . . . redeemed among men . . . firstfruits unto God and the Lamb . . . in their mouth was found no guile . . . without fault before the throne of God."[7]

Although St. John was speaking here of male virgins, the ladies immediately appropriated the title and virginity is now commonly thought of as an exclusively feminine property which the *Catholic Encyclopedia* ranks with martyrdom in the celestial hierarchy.

Note how those words of St. John, enshrined in the New Testament, place virginity above marriage, since St. John practically says that all heterosexual contact defiles a person.

To continue with the putdown of sex in the Catholic Church, the elevation of chastity to the megavirtue and its violation to the supersin:

In choosing her Sunday Gospels, the Western Church—and I believe the Episcopalian and Lutheran Churches followed our usage here—until the last few years passed over the story of St. Mary Magdalen, the woman taken in adultery, and the Prodigal Son, so that the overwhelming majority of the laity never even heard of them. Instead, the Missal was filled out with innumerable parables of the kingdom, practically incomprehensible to the people in their proper sense.

Voltaire reports that when Mary told the angel of the annunciation to have a seat, Gabriel replied, *"Je n'ais pas de quoi."* Without bodies, the angels are incapable of sex, so purity now became "the angelic virtue." But, by the same reasoning, it could as well be "the diabolical virtue." Also, by the same reasoning, frigidity could be called "the angelic neurosis." It now became "holy purity." Why not "holy charity" or "holy truth"?

Let the apologists argue themselves black in the face to the contrary: the Church has always considered sex, all sex, pretty much of a dirty business. St. John called it a defilement. St. Paul: "I would ye were all like me" (i.e., unmarried).[8] And it was the Christian Church that formed this little cultural pocket in which we happen to have been born.

Applying this attitude, the faithful built a kind of antiseptic wall around the Blessed Mother, protecting her from all "defilement" of sex. (Hers was actually the first recorded vow of chastity.) She and St. Joseph exchanged the right to mutual sex, else theirs would not have been a valid marriage and Jesus would have been born illegitimate. They simply agreed to live together as brother and sister rather than as man and wife. Since they were such a charming couple —Joseph so handsome, she so beautiful—he would have been less than human if he had not said from time to time, "Gosh, Mary, I sure wish we could make love tonight—just this once, anyway." To which Mary might have replied, "Me, too, Joseph, but you know how it is." Now, if you find that offensive, it is because willy-nilly you still think of sex as something wicked, even between man and wife.

In sacred art, St. Joseph is invariably presented as a stooped and gray-bearded patriarch well past the age of such foolishness, lest anyone get ideas. In reality, he would have had to be fairly young and vigorous to manage all the traveling ordered by Divine Providence: from Nazareth in Galilee down to Bethlehem in Judea for the Nativity, then over to Egypt with Mary and the infant to evade Herod, then back to Galilee. That's a lot of mileage to cover on foot.

Typically, in his *Treatise on the Incarnation*, St. Athanasius (296-373) writes of our Lord that he took our body "directly from a spotless, stainless virgin, without the agency of human father—a pure body, untainted by intercourse with man." This particular homily is enshrined in the Christmas Office of the new *American Interim Breviary*.

We don't know why God chose to be born on earth of a virgin, but it certainly was not because sexual intercourse is filthy.

Celibacy began to be enforced among priests in the West until by the ninth and tenth centuries it was fairly universal: only those priests were fit to touch the Sacred Host who were not defiling themselves with women—the term is St. John's.*

The Eastern Church makes the gesture of requiring sexual abstinence from midnight on the part of those priests intending to say mass. Thus passed the habit of daily mass from the Eastern Church.

The opinions of the Fathers and Doctors of the Church (and of Calvin, too) constitute a snarling epitome of male chauvinism. Thus, Methodius spoke of women as naturally "carnal and sensuous," the "irrational half of mankind." To St. Jerome, woman was "the devil's

---

*Stephen Gardiner (1483-1555), Bishop of Winchester, which was in his day the richest diocese in Christendom with an annual income of a million dollars, had such a high regard for celibacy that although he kept two mistresses in his palace he was careful not to marry either of them. Moreover, in deference to decency and the laws of the Church, he compelled them both to wear male attire. The great Thomas Cardinal Wolsey (1475-1530) took as his mistress the sister of his confessor, which made things rather easy all around.

gateway . . . a scorpion's dart . . ." St. Clement of Alexandria: "It is shameful for [a woman] to think about what nature she has." Tertullian: Woman should make herself ugly, since her beauty "is dangerous to those who look upon it." According to St. John Chrysostom, St. Cyril of Alexandria, St. Ambrose, and Pope St. Gregory, "Woman is naïve, unstable, mentally weak, and in need of an authoritative husband."[9] For another summary, G. G. Coulton quotes a medieval couplet recorded by a Cardinal Hugues de St. Cher:

> *Femina corpus opes animam vim lumina vocem*
> *Polluit adnihilat necat eripit orbat acerbat.*
> Woman pollutes the body, drains the resources, kills the soul,
> Uproots the strength, blinds the eye, and embitters the
> voice.[10]

Now how on earth was the Church ever able to gain acceptance for such an odious and repulsive theology? The fact that most of these men have been canonized and revered for centuries throughout Christendom adds the Church's official approval to their teachings. But to teach is one thing and to gain acceptance is another, especially when that teaching opposes nature. For, to quote an authentic American folk heroine, "Sex is natural and," concluded Miss Monroe, "I'll go along with nature."

Generally speaking, one can't be sure that the official teaching was internally accepted by the people. Certainly, if it was accepted, it was never universally practiced. After all, God gave us the Ten Commandments on Mount Sinai, but that does not guarantee everyone's honesty, veracity, and marital fidelity. Readers of Chaucer and Shakespeare are well aware of the lighthearted attitude toward sex in earlier centuries.

But priests and monks were the only ones who could read, which put them away out in front. When they told the illiterate masses that the Holy Spirit guided the Church, they were believed. And how could the Church deliver God's message except through the lips of the priest? Therefore, the priest's was the voice of God, and hence the priest could not be mistaken, for God cannot err, can He? Now the priest would know better, of course, but he would naturally be reluctant to abdicate this flattering if mistaken attribute.

That was the background. Now for the particular elements that helped downgrade sex and give the virtue of chastity disproportionate emphasis.

1. To judge from the Gospels, Jesus gave very little thought to sex. He condemned wife stealing explicitly and he absolved an adulteress from her sins. But that's all. Instead, he spent his time preaching charity, forgiveness, detachment, and excoriating pride and pharisaism—sins of the spirit. James, Peter, John, and Jude scarcely mention sex in their epistles. On the contrary, the tone of the whole New Testament is mainly positive—extolling, urging, canonizing the virtues of the Master: patience, gentleness, sacrifice, truth, compassion, humility, generosity, forgiveness of injuries, and —supremely and all-inclusively—love.

It was St. Paul who staked out sins of the flesh for his very own, studying the right and wrong use of sex and then writing his findings into the New Testament. (St. Paul rates a chapter all to himself farther on in the book.) Pastors have ever since been embarrassed by our Lord's presentation of the Last Judgment, where sheep are separated from goats on the basis of charity alone. Not a mention of chastity. "Of course," priests will say, "our Lord's picture is necessarily incomplete." How do they know? Who told them? In the Book of Job, sin is equated with denial of the works of mercy. There is no mention of sex.

2. Worthy of special mention is the influence of the Irish. As Bertrand Russell once remarked, "There is the Roman Catholic Church. But then," he added thoughtfully, "there is also the Irish Catholic Church." There is a difference.

The English behaved themselves with fair decency in all their colonies and possessions except Ireland; there they were abominable. From 1534, in the reign of Henry VIII, their persecution of Irish Catholics was savage. The mass was forbidden. Priests were jailed, mutilated, killed, or—if lucky—deported. And still they said mass. There were no schools; the only education the people could get was when some priest would gather a few children behind a hedge and teach them their ABC's. This went on for three centuries, the Protestant English trying to force their religion on the Catholic Irish.

As a result, the Catholic Church became identified with the nation—as was also the case in French Canada. To be Irish was to be Catholic; to deny the Faith was to betray Ireland. The people developed a fierce loyalty to the priests who were serving them and whom they so often saw hanging at the market cross. When the English said that the capital of the Church was in London, then—by God!—every Irishman turned face and heart to Rome and the vicar of Christ in the Vatican.

To keep the Faith, they had to emphasize not the great central truths of Christianity which they held in common with the hated English—no, but those beliefs and practices which were distinctively and peculiarly Roman Catholic and hence often marginal: Friday abstinence, the Lenten observance, devotion to our Lady and particular saints, the rosary, novenas, the cult of the Blessed Sacrament (which is *not* marginal), the poor souls in purgatory, and above all the obligation of Sunday mass. Eating meat on Friday and missing mass on Sunday became just about the worst sins the Irish Catholic could commit.

(A penitent may confess the most enormous sins, but to this day his confessor will almost invariably overlook them to pounce on mass-missing and, formerly, eating meat on Friday. It is defiance of Church law. But the priority given to Church law over God's is characteristically Irish.)

With no seminaries of their own, most of the Irish boys were trained for the priesthood in nearby Paris and at Louvain where, during the seventeenth and eighteenth centuries, Jansenism was rampant. This was a dark version of Christianity that stressed the justice of God at the expense of his mercy. "Hell is crowded, heaven is half-empty"—that sort of thing. It dwelt on the most bitter and disagreeable elements of religion: "Penance, penance! We are not here to enjoy ourselves. This life is not meant to be a picnic. It is a crucifixion."

Probably the Irish seminarians did not buy the whole package, but their theology was almost certainly tainted by it. When they returned home, priests now, Jansenism gradually began to affect the quality of the Irish Faith.

Remarkably, when the Irish came to America in the middle of the last century, they found a religious climate approximating what they had just left. In America it was the WASPs of Boston and New York who turned up their nose at them and sneered at their Catholic Faith. And so we got "The Fighting Irish," the Irish-American Catholic who is aggressive about his Faith. He is proud of it. He carries a chip on his shoulder. Say anything against the pope or the Mother of God and he'll punch your face in. He never misses mass on Sunday. He is immensely respectful to all priests and nuns and contributes amply to Church support. In sum, he hews punctiliously to the letter of the law but in doing so he too often misses the spirit of the Faith. He is likely to forget all about charity.

Thus he has little but disdain for most of the Latins: "Poor Catholics; they never go to mass; they don't give to the Church," and so on. The Germans, Poles, Slavs—"can't hold a candle to the Irish."

How well I remember my dear mother: "Isn't it a *pity*, Richard, that the pope always has to be an Italian. And they're such bum Catholics!"

Anyone who has read Synge, O'Casey, and Joyce knows of Irish poverty, anger, domestic sterility, and sexual repression—in Ireland, yes, but there is where our American Church is rooted.

They are the most lovable, charming, generous, brilliant, handsome, and witty people on the face of the earth. Quick to hate, but just as quick to forgive and forget: the Church is lucky to have them. But somehow—a trauma perhaps from their national experience, or maybe just something in their Celtic blood—sex to the Irish priest is as booze to the WCTU. It has been said, and I believe it, that the Irishman is the only person in the world who will step over a naked woman to get at a bottle of whiskey. This is the island where matrimony is occasionally if facetiously defined as "a license to commit sin."

When he gets horny, where anyone else would find a woman or relieve himself, the Irishman takes a couple of drinks. If he is still horny, he finishes the bottle. The next morning he is so busy nursing his head that he forgets all about his itch of the previous evening.

I know a man of Irish blood who will announce to his circle of Irish friends, "Well, tomorrow I'm going to go out and really tie one on. I'm going to get roaring drunk and stay that way for the next three days. I won't sober up until time for work on Monday morning."

Now, by all that's holy, that fellow is proclaiming that tomorrow he intends to go out and commit a fine fat mortal sin. Yet his friends will smile indulgently and nod at one another understandingly: "That's Mickey. He's been doing that for years."

But what if Mickey were instead to make the announcement: "Well, tomorrow I'm going up to the city and get me a woman. Whenever I start vibrating like an E-string—happens about once a month—I just have to go out and get laid."

Drink and sex, both sins of frailty, the one scarcely worse than the other. But do you think his Irish friends would be so understanding and indulgent? "That's Mickey. He's been doing that for years." Not on your life! Sex is a sin! More than that, sex is *the* sin! There is indeed considerable verisimilitude in the description of the Irish as a nation of chaste alcoholics, for to them chastity has always been the megavirtue. For instance:

—Within the past year, an immigrant Irish priest confided to me that he was completely unable to understand the current "fuss over celibacy."—"Sex," he said, "is greatly overrated. A couple may"—here he flapped a hand vaguely—"you know, once, maybe even twice, during the honeymoon. But after that it's only once a year at most."

—An Irish wife will often take down the crucifix and turn the holy pictures to the wall before accommodating her husband. Granted, religion and sex seem to be mutually exclusive: but how many people say the Our Father while urinating or evacuating? And who would ever hang a picture of the Blessed Mother over the toilet? It's a simple matter of propriety.

—As the postscript to a diatribe on Hitler, I heard an Irish priest add, "But at least he was clean." I whirled on him. "Whaddya mean?" I exploded. "Why," he said, "there were no scandals during his regime."

—Sitting down to dinner with still another Irish priest, I said facetiously, "Well, shall we talk uncharitably or shall we just talk dirty today?" He looked at me over his glasses and said in all seriousness, "You know very well that it's a sin to talk dirty."

—I have never known an Irish girl named Magdalen.

These Irish priests are the people who taught their rather rigorous variety of Christianity, fuming with alcohol but oh! so chaste, to vast areas of Great Britain and Europe. Armies of Irish missionaries followed the Union Jack to every corner of the British Empire. Owing to their zeal, the color of the faith in this country too is emerald green, and two-thirds of the American bishops and an even greater percentage of the archbishops and cardinals have Irish blood in them.

Of 48,500,000 Catholics in America today, over 10,000,000 are Irish Americans. This is six times the population of Eire. To help focus those figures: there are only 6,000,000 Jews in this country. And over 10,000,000 Irish-American Catholics! In fact, our American Church is well on its way to becoming an Italo-Hibernian sect.

Irish prudery, preached and taught in church and school, was enough to give our generation a false conscience regarding sex. As a child of my mother, I know.

Combined with puritanism, the net effect on society has been —to paraphrase Pascal—that most men would gladly become whoremongers to preserve their reputation for chastity.

3. Another element implanting and cultivating this false conscience in Catholics was the obsession with sin, guilt, and punishment constantly a part of Catholic education for sixteen years from first grade all the way up through college. If you had the nuns in school, you know what I'm talking about. Seven-year-old schoolchildren were presumed capable of sin. They were lined up and marched over to the church every month for First Friday confession. Just about all our religious and moral instruction centered on sin, offending God, and showing him that we were sorry.

From a teacher's guide for second graders: This lesson aims "to develop in the child a real hatred of sin because sin offends God and hurts us." Next lesson: "We should train the children to examine their consciences frequently. . . . It is a very good means of avoiding serious sin. . . . After recognizing a fault or sin, the child should immediately turn to God, ask his pardon, and beg his mercy.. . . . God is very much displeased when his children commit sin. . . . When we sin we offend Someone who loves us very much. We offend God. And when we tell God our Father that we are sorry, we want to think only of him and how we have offended him."

As a guide for seven-year-olds preparing for confession: "Have I failed to love the Heavenly Father by: (1) Failing to turn to God, my Father, and to pray to him, especially in the morning and at night? (2) Misbehaving in church. . . . If we have not been faithful to God our Father we will pray: *God, my Father, I am sorry for having offended you. Forgive me.*"[11]

4. Living cheek-by-jowl with Protestants of every description here in America, we have had their bad influence to contend with. Says Donald Webster Cory:

> More than any other power, the United States was founded on traditions of Puritanism. The concept of sex as a necessary evil, an ugly pursuit, enjoyed by men because of the devil incarnate in the flesh, was taught by the early cultural leaders of this country. The varying and diverse elements that made up the American melting pot vied with one another to appear before the masses as pure and good, one group not to be outdone by another in the antisexual repudiation of physical desire. Thus the struggle of the Protestant Puritans to maintain a rigid and self-avowedly virtuous ban on all things sexual was strengthened by the several minorities that found conformance the road to acceptance and possibly integration into American life.[12]

5. Most theologians still contend that pleasure is always an accessory, a by-product, attached as bait to some necessary function. Thus, they say, the good Christian does not live to eat, he eats to live. And so with orgasm. The species must be continued, so the pleasure is an inducement. Presumably, if there were no fun involved, people would never have intercourse. Hence, pure self-indulgence—eating gourmet foods, for instance, or sex just for the pleasure of it—is a disorder. To salvage morality, the theological pundits say, there must always be an implicit intention somehow integrating the function with God's scheme of things.

Owing probably to our childhood training, based on the reward principle and the American work ethic and supported by religious moral teaching, there is a trace of guilt feeling in even the least unreasoned pleasure: no party without an excuse, however flimsy. The school picnic is never at the beginning but always at the end of the year. "I think I'm entitled to a little drink, now that I've finished my assignment."

6. It is too bad that the same fixtures are used both for reproduction and for carrying sewage out of the body. Despite the abundance and availability of hot water, soap, shower, bidet, douche, and enema, I daresay that much of the odium directed at sex is aesthetic rather than theological. Some people just think it's a rather sordid operation. One recalls the man at a cocktail party helping himself to a slice of tongue and the comment of the woman at his side:

"How can anyone eat something that has been in the mouth of a beast for God knows how long!"

"Madam," he said by way of reply, "would you like an egg?"

7. *"Omne animal post coitum triste."*—Every animal feels let down after sex. There is fatigue and satiety. Nature demands time to recharge the battery or, if you please, to replenish the reservoir. For any one or all of the six reasons listed above, this natural letdown is too often mistakenly translated into disgust and guilt. That could also be why mayhem and murder are so often associated with casual sex among the gays. That, too, could be why most of the sins mentioned in the confessional are those of the flesh. The natural letdown sharpens the moral guilt with which we have been indoctrinated. In twenty-five years of pastoral experience, I have yet to hear a penitent accuse himself of sins against prudence—or graft, for that matter, or grand theft, or vote stealing.

8. This may sound frivolous but it deserves at least minor consideration: The people in what are euphemistically called adult

magazines are all under thirty, whereas most older people look awful with their clothes off, and the older they get, the uglier they look. But the Church is controlled by a group of really old men, the cardinals, who have been called the Rheumatism Brigade. Now our sexual drive remains fairly constant, but it takes more and more stimulation to climax. One natural reaction is to become sexual conservatives, to favor making private sin a public crime with chastity enforced by the police, to vote for repression, reprisals, and censorship—in other words, to throw one's weight against youth. Sour grapes? I'm very much afraid that latent jealousy is at least a part of the motivation underlying the pious attitudes of self-abnegation in many of the older people.

9. Finally, there is pressure. By persuasion, moral violence, armtwisting of one kind or another, and blackmail if necessary, the rulers of the Church control debate, suppress the facts, and even distort the truth when needed to sustain the Catholic position that all sex is sinful except between man and wife with no protection of any sort against conception.

Sadly, this sort of thing comes handily to most bishops. They are descended from a long line of witchburners.

Within the Church they are in control, and no priest can fight City Hall. By the time he is experienced and mature enough to make an intelligent if critical contribution, the Church has him by the throat. He is completely dependent on the altar for his living, too old now to find employment outside the Church. He has a choice between knuckling under or starving.

Indeed, the bishops themselves are subject to control by Higher Authority. You will recall that as soon as he became pope, Paul VI told the Fathers assembled at Vatican II that priestly celibacy must remain outside the area of discussion. And so it was done.

The seminary or university instructor, priest or layman, can be summarily dismissed if he strays from the Party Line. And students, too. In *The Church and I*, Frank Sheed reports that "After a lecture in a Catholic college on Sex and Marriage, one of the students questioned me more closely about Birth Control. The following week he came to see me. He had been expelled."[13]

In his own diocese, each bishop wields political and economic power proportionate with the size of the Catholic population. If a Cardinal Cooke does not want civil rights granted to homosexuals, then, by God, the enabling legislation is defeated at the polls! A bishop is forever acquiring real estate. The insurance on every parish edifice in the diocese is usually written by whomever the bishop chooses. Building contracts are not commonly thrown open to bids. The bishop decides who gets them. A cooperative district attorney (bingo, gambling at parish affairs, priests in trouble) can be made a Knight of St. Gregory, and the governor (anti-abortion legislation) a Knight of the Holy Sepulcher.

The faithful are soon informed through the editorial columns of the diocesan paper which candidates should be voted in or out of office, for the bishops are not content with directing the sex lives of their subjects by spiritual arguments alone. They would like to remove all possibility of ethical choices, to create a world of spiritual luxury without freedom. They would make everyone, the whole community—not just Catholics, but Protestants and Jews as well —conform to conventional patterns of sexuality by penalties, spiritual, physical and social, by threats and curses—if necessary, by calling in the police and urging them to use their truncheons and coercive hardware in enforcing what they see as the will of our gentle Savior.

That is how, in this great land of ours, one finds policemen detailed to solicit and entrap homosexuals, to loiter in public lavatories. One finds them sneaking up to cars parked in the dark and peeking in to see if anything sinful is going on.

In his epochal little book, *The Time Has Come*, Dr. John Rock describes the final session of the American Birth Control League's first national conference. It was to be a public meeting at Town Hall, a privately owned property in New York City. The date was November 13, 1921. Margaret Sanger was to speak on "Birth Control: Is It Moral?" The hall had been reserved and paid for.

"But," writes Dr. Rock, "when Mrs. Sanger arrived she was confronted by closed doors and by policemen who told her, 'You can't go in this place tonight.' "

Well, Mrs. Sanger finally did get in amid great disorder, indeed, a near riot between the audience and the police. After long and considerable tumult, the police officer in charge handed the chairman of the proposed meeting a statement which the chairman read to the audience: "I, Captain Thomas Donahue of the 26th Precinct, at the order of Monsignor Joseph F. Dineen, Secretary to Archbishop Hayes, have ordered the meeting closed."[14]

In his *Letters to a Young Catholic*, the contemporary German novelist, Heinrich Böll, recalls that the Vatican was the first foreign state to seek an understanding with Hitler. He says further that the religious instruction he himself received as a conscript was concerned

entirely with sex, not once mentioning the *real* moral dangers
threatening young Germans drafted into the service of an evil totalitarian state: "Not a word about Hitler, not a word about anti-
Semitism, about a possible conflict between orders and conscience."

How was the German Church able to ignore the transcendent
problems of Hitlerism, to fuss over a comparative trifle like sex, while
the Nazi party was busily at work on all sides murdering a total of
50,000,000 human beings, the greater number of them Catholics?
How were the priests able to continue lecturing the recruits on the use
and abuse of the penis, their voices all but drowned out by the
anguished screams of the tortured and dying?

"Den Kern, den wirft man weg." The Church is so busy polishing
the shell that she throws away the kernel or, more familiarly, the baby
is thrown out with the bath water.

Recently I proposed to a friend—half-joke, whole-earnest, as the
Irish say—that the two of us start a church in which charity should be
revered and practiced as the supreme virtue.

It's already been tried," he said sadly, "and if Christ failed, what
chance would we have?"

Chastity is certainly a comparatively minor virtue, not one of the
leaders but rather trailing along as a *sine qua non*. The big three are
faith, hope, and charity, "and," says St. Paul, "the greatest of these is
charity." Those are the theological virtues. The moral or cardinal
virtues are prudence, justice, fortitude, and temperance. Temperance
then is the genus of which chastity is one species: a habit or grace of
soul, empowering us to control our sexual impulses.

Oh, the Church does preach and practice charity, but there is no
record of a person's being roasted alive for lack of it. The Code of
Canon Law enacts all kinds of penalties against unchaste ecclesiastics,
none against the uncharitable. Of two men being considered for a
bishopric, the one unchaste, the other uncharitable, you can safely
put your money on the uncharitable priest for the miter.

In this chapter we have seen something of how the order of the
virtues came to be subverted, with charity overthrown in favor of
chastity, such that, as Böll says, we are forever straining out the gnat
and swallowing the camel.

Having seen How, in later chapters we shall try to discover Why
this disorder came about and Why it is maintained and defended to
this day.

3

"The Highway Code"

Over the years we Catholics have always boasted rather smugly that the teachings of our Church never change. This has been true of the great central dogmas contained in the Apostles' and the Nicene Creed—mostly, I should think, because belief here doesn't cost us anything. There is so little in them that affects our daily lives—that lowers the price of gasoline, for instance, or helps cure a hangover. People are just not interested enough to challenge them. Mary was conceived without sin? "If you say so, Father." Who cares, anyway?

In 1950 Pius XII proclaimed it divinely revealed that our Blessed Mother was taken bodily into heaven. In 1968 Paul VI condemned certain sexual practices. In the first case, there was scarcely a ripple of disapproval. Few cared. But in 1968 the uproar threatened to split the Church. The assumption of our Lady was a matter of dogma, whereas birth control was in the field of moral theology. While holding fast to the certainties of revelation, then, we must not ignore the certainties of science. Morality is the area of significance right now.

Moral theology takes the rules enunciated by Scripture, tradition, and reason and applies them to the changing circumstances of our daily life. The difficulty is precisely that the circumstances of daily life are in constant flux, forever shifting. This has become increasingly obvious with technology constantly presenting us with fresh wonders: telephone, automobile, movies, radio, television, miracle drugs that have lengthened our life expectancy by decades and practically eliminated infant mortality—and much else. The world has been explored and mapped from pole to pole. Computers process the data being poured in by anthropologists and sociologists. Public opinion polls can take the pulse and temperature of the community on any given issue within a matter of hours.

An earlier theologian could rather grandly declare, for instance, that incest must be contrary to the natural law, because "All men have always and everywhere abominated the practice." But our contemporary moralist must walk on eggs, always aware that his data may be completely reversed by tomorrow morning's paper. Formerly, principles were sacrosanct: the nature of law, for example, and the basic determinants of morality. But the partial emergence of the Church from its earlier condition as a kind of ecclesiastical police state has encouraged Catholic thinkers, philosophers, and theologians to step forward with fresh insights and conclusions which they had previously suppressed for fear of reprisals.* I write of this emergence as being only partial, because the hierarchy are still trying to abort any discussion of sexual morality unless the conclusion favors the present discipline.

It is a mistake to think that the Church never changes, for she does. It is the truth that never changes. The Church takes about two hundred years to reverse a position, moving slowly to ease the shock, but it does happen. The taking of interest on money is a case in point. Condemned until the nineteenth century (1821), it is now the foundation of capitalism and the Vatican itself has an endowment matching

---

*Back in the late forties while *The Priest* was still an infant, we hazarded an article by the late Fr. H. A. Reinhold advocating the introduction of at least a little English into the liturgy. A friend on the staff of the Apostolic Delegation warned us that the subject was taboo in Rome and we were inviting suppression of our little magazine.

Ten years later we ventured a few good-natured witticisms at the expense of the Rt. Rev. Monsignori. Came a prompt letter of rebuke from the Apostolic Delegate bidding us lay off, since the prelature was—of all things!—"a legitimate source of revenue to the Holy See." It seems that on his nomination, each lucky prelate is privileged to send five hundred dollars to His Holiness. Surely inflation has since increased the privilege.

that of Harvard University. Witches have gone commercial. Heretics are no longer burned. As recently as fifty years ago, under the Fourth Commandment, our catechisms obliged Catholics to "be content with their state in life." You don't see that any more. Gone is the Roman Index of forbidden books. The Eucharistic fast has all but vanished. At death we now have a choice between burial or incineration. These last rules were disciplinary, true, but always taught as "touching on revealed truth."

To insert a word on "natural law"—a fact often denied but more often misunderstood: there is undoubtedly a natural law obtaining among all men everywhere. One must not confuse this with the "law of nature," the natural physical law, which is the proper object of the physical sciences: physics, chemistry, biology, astronomy, and the like. We do not choose, for instance, to digest our food, to lengthen our hair and nails, to grow tall, to be either heterosexual or homosexual, whereas we do have a choice when it comes to observing or flouting the natural moral law, which governs the free or moral actions of human beings. The difference between natural law and the law of nature is the same as that between winking and blinking.

All moralities agree in imposing a behavior which their adherents fail to practice. All men stand condemned by their own ethics, a code at once approved and disobeyed. Hence, all men are conscious of guilt. This natural law is a sort of universal Gallup Poll on what C. S. Lewis refers to as Decent Behavior. He says that, for instance, no one anywhere is ever going to pin a medal on a soldier for running away. The double cross is similarly odious. While it is true that polygamy does not offend natural law, you must keep your hot hands off your neighbor's wife.

The trouble is that Catholic moralists have tended to extend the scope of natural law far beyond common sense, stretching it to cover almost every offense from shoplifting to distractions in prayer, whereas the anthropologists tell us that in reality the Ten Commandments are a pretty fair summary of the law. It reduces to a very few tribal taboos against murder, wifestealing, kidnapping, and robbing one's own clansmen. Sex is not otherwise mentioned.

From the fact as recorded in Scripture that God himself dispensed the first human beings from incest and ordered the Israelites to despoil their Egyptian oppressors on the night of their deliverance, we conclude that incest and forcibly recovering one's own are not opposed at least to the primary precepts of the natural law.

It is universally recognized that there is a "Thing Above" to be worshipped and placated. But otherwise every time you think you have something definitely banned by natural law, it slips away from you. You hear of a case or a custom that would seem to indicate otherwise.

—As to infanticide: A Franciscan friar who has been working with natives for the last twenty years told me that certain tribes regard multiple births as an evil omen, so they somehow never occur. The first one out is saved, but the rest go into the rubbish. Or so it was until the mothers started calling in outside help and going to the hospital to have their babies.

—As to modesty: The Montagnards, a tribe of valiant aborigines who fought on our side in Vietnam, considered it immodest to cover their backside, so by custom the men at least are supposed to leave it bare from cradle to grave. Again by custom Chinese women were to hide their feet, but could show their *yoni*.

—Surely the animals are bound to follow nature? But apes masturbate and play bisexual games.

—If anything were incontrovertibly opposed to natural law it should be sodomy, buggery,* "that wicked and unnatural sin that cries to heaven for vengeance, never to be mentioned among men." But it turns out that we Western Christians are the only ones who think so, and we are only a minuscule parenthesis in the geographic spread and the two-million-year history of mankind on earth. A discussion guide of the Sex Information and Education Council of the United States (SIECUS) on homosexuality has pointed out that the majority of the human societies studied by the Council—forty-nine out of seventy-six, other than our own—have condoned or even encouraged homosexual behavior for at least some members of the society.

The gay tourist finds that generally speaking the farther east he travels, the more relaxed is the attitude toward pederasty and sodomy. The Moslem influence in North Africa is benign. André Gide used to duck over to Tangier for occasional relief. He preferred rather young boys, fifteen, and in Tangier the "chicken hawk" can have them as

---

*"Buggery" is the English legal term. "Bugger" is a corruption of "Bulgar," for it is reported that the natives of Bulgaria had once enjoyed an international reputation for their dexterity in this matter.

young as twelve if it suits his pleasure. Tangier is a veritable mecca for the international gay set. Thailand, India, Singapore, Hongkong, Tokyo—all are tolerant of boy love to a greater or lesser degree.

Apparently St. Paul, and with him the whole Western Church, acquired a horror of sodomy not from Jesus but as a heritage from the Old Testament, where it is recorded that God wanted the Jews to increase and fill the land.

So it would seem that sodomy is not against the natural law.

There is a word in the English language that cannot be understood except in terms of a law that is somehow respected by all men. Oddly, it has no equivalent in French or German. They have to borrow our term. That word is the adjective "fair" and its noun "fair play."

When I say "That's not fair!" you know exactly what I mean. I am appealing to C. S. Lewis's Universal Standard of Decent Behavior. Whether it is inborn or acquired, I don't know. We first begin to grasp the concept when someone cheats in our childhood games, or perhaps when the teacher chooses a "pet" in our class and starts favoring him.

Whenever you hear some wiseacre denying the existence of a natural law, then, just think of that word "fair." Without a natural law it has no meaning. So there is a natural law. We may not know all its particulars, but it's there anyway. We can deny it, but it won't go away.

Now to summarize the classical teaching of the Church on sex. Remember that I am not necessarily defending it. At this point I am only making a noncommittal statement.

All sin is a violation of God's law. It can be formal or subjective: an action is wrong and we know it, or it's all right but we think it's wrong and do it anyway. It can be merely material or objective: the action is wrong, but we don't know it. It can be mortal or venial, grave or slight, i.e., a felony or a misdemeanor.

The first, and just about the only, principle on sex is that a man's seed is for his wife's vagina, and any deliberate spilling of the seed outside that vagina is a mortal sin. In fact, the Catholic can do only one thing lawfully: "normal" coitus in marriage.

All sins of sex are grave at least objectively. There are no misdemeanors in this area. Every offense is a felony. This is based on the presumed inevitability of escalation. No man can say to himself, for instance, "I'll stop with a kiss." There is an old saying that "An erection has no conscience." Once a person starts, there's no stopping him. Or so they say.* Merely to kiss a girl's breast is as wicked as to cut it off. Both sinners go to hell—although the one may go a little deeper.

But I consider this a false and mischievous assumption. We have all read Freud, after all, and we know that practically all gestures of affection are sexual at base. As a parish priest I would often find a beautiful child waiting in the sacristy to serve my mass. And I couldn't help myself. I had to make contact in some way. But an adult just doesn't shake hands with a child. I could only tousle his hair or give him a playful slap on the bottom. Harmless, but sexual at base; so, according to our theologians, I had just unfitted myself for mass. I was in the state of mortal sin. Rubbish!

Another consideration: you might as well hang for a sheep as for a lamb. If lover-boy thinks he has already committed a mortal sin by just kissing his girl, he might as well push right through to the end. When the mouse finds himself caged in the trap, he might as well eat the cheese.

Some sins are worse than others. Fornication is apparently the least of them. Perhaps in your innocence you had thought that masturbation was at the foot of the scale. No, say the theologians, self-sex is a worse sin than fornication because it involves wasting the seed.

Adultery offends not only against chastity but also against justice in violating the rights of the innocent spouse. Incest is another doubleheader. The son who uses his own mother sexually is offending perhaps less against chastity than against "piety," or the reverence we owe our parents under the Fourth Commandment. This rather implies again that sex is a Dirty Thing, to be had only between husband and wife on a contract basis. But at least these sins are "natural." The seed is going into a vagina.

Buggery, copulation by mouth, sex with animals, manual orgasm, and all other such variations, are against nature because they involve spilling the seed. Along with murder, oppressing the poor, and defrauding the laborer of his pay, sodomy "cries to heaven for vengeance."

Lascivious thoughts or daydreams if willful are mortally sinful.

*Except Sanchez, A. Adam, and J. Stelzenberger (in Hans Küng. *Truthfulness* (New York: Sheed, 1968), p. 29n. By order of Claude Acquaviva, fourth successor of St. Ignatius, this absurd opinion was officially sponsored by the Society of Jesus in 1612.

Specific desires, i.e., directed at some particular person, are as evil as the act desired. Porno mags and films would be classified as thoughts, to be judged by the same principles.

Obscene speech is ordinarily sinful only if used deliberately to make another person horny.*

The theologians distinguish between and are divided in their estimation of oral and anal sodomy. Some call anal "perfect" and oral "imperfect" sodomy, one worse than the other. Others contend that it's imperfect if done with a woman, perfect if done with a man.

In the confessional, the penitent must make specific mention of anal sodomy. Thus, the gay penitent would say, "I had sex (or committed sodomy) ten times: seven times with one man, one time with each of the others." If it's anything less than buggery, he would tell it as "impure touches with other men." But I mean to discuss confession at greater length in a later chapter.

The authors of the textbooks generally do not go into the refinements of sex such as one finds developed for instance in the classified ads of the Los Angeles *Free Press* and the Berkeley *Barb*. Those things are reserved for discussion in the more scholarly clergy journals such as *The American Ecclesiastical Review, The Thomist, Cross Currents,* and *Theological Studies*. I must say too that, judging from my own experience in the confessional, knowledge of such refinements is not at all necessary for the usual parish priest. In over twenty-five years of hearing confessions under all circumstances, I won't say that I rarely, I'll say that I never heard mention of such things as spanking, fetishism, S/M, F.F., bondage, the dildo, partialism, rimming, and cross dressing. I suppose that, depending on the circumstances, the confessor would classify them either as self-abuse or impure touches.

Now this is all pretty heady stuff, for it is the application of general principles to particular situations. Chipping away the concrete, however, and getting back to the abstract, the normative syllogism comes out like this:

First, the definition of lust (*luxuria*): It is any "inordinate use of the power of generation."

Major premise: A human act which contradicts the purpose of that action as established by God is intrinsically evil when the act is not subordinated in the divine scheme to some higher purpose.

Minor premise: The sin of lust is such an act.

---

*An old Capuchin, when I would confess lascivious conversation, would murmur, half to himself, "Better to talk about it than do it."

Conclusion: Therefore the sin of lust is both grave and intrinsically evil.

In proof of the major: By its nature as constituted by God, every natural act is ordered to a particular end: e.g., eating is for nourishment. Hence, man sins whenever he deliberately frustrates such a purpose, built in and intended by the Almighty.

Extramarital sex goes against the procreative intent built by God into the function, hence it is *ipso facto* disordered and "intrinsically" evil. Apart from the supposed inevitability of escalation, such an action puts the good of the individual above the good of the species,* and hence it is always gravely wrong—even if the act is incomplete (as with the man who stimulates himself, stopping short of climax) or merely internal (sexual thoughts).

Later on, I'll have a great deal to say about all this, but since this chapter belongs to Aristotle and the classical theologians, it seems the logical place for the syllogistic statement of their reasoning. Incidentally, you are never likely to find a better example of abstract, irrefutable ratiocination opposing common sense and human experience.

So much for the "matter," or material sin. Now for the formal, subjective element, the only factor that can diminish the guilt of a sin against purity and turn it from mortal to venial.

First there is the matter of deliberation. Did the man know what he was doing? Did he plan the sin? Did he leave home that night with the intention of batting out a home run? Or was it a sin of surprise? Did he just kind of slip into it?

Then, most important but most complex, the matter of freedom—not just physical but more especially psychological: pot seems to lower resistance; booze definitely does. Temperament, heredity, environment. Homosexuality. The girl in the hotel lobby may be stony broke and so hungry that she is morally unable to resist the hospitality she is offered.

From even these few pages one can draw certain conclusions about moral theology, at least as it has existed from Trent to Vatican II.

—It is a dangerous field, the science of minimums, of casuistry rather than love. Moral theology does not speak of God's grace and love, of generous and total surrender to our Holy Redeemer. It studies

*And, pray, what has the species ever done for us?

rather how to give least and still get by. It is a stingy, pettifogging science.

—Moral theology has so far been "act-centered," taking single actions out of context and studying them one by one under a glass bell in a vacuum, concentrating on the objective and playing down the subjective aspect. Sure, Don made it with Alice last Tuesday night; that fact is crucial. But it is perhaps just as important to know that Don had been a randy bachelor for at least twenty years, he had lost his job that day and was contemplating suicide until he ran into Alice, who was not only pretty and charming, and built like Cleopatra, but sympathetic and—oh, happy night!—a nymph who worked him to exhaustion. They had had a few drinks together, and then things started to happen—fast.

Well, the experience did Don a world of good. It quite literally saved his life. It relaxed him and helped him forget his troubles. In fact, he enjoyed it so much that now he can just barely summon enough imperfect contrition to validate the sacrament of penance.

—All of which would indicate that in their ivory towers the moralists have been speculating, ratiocinating, and excogitating an unreal brand of theology, in many cases widely divorced from the circumstances of everyday life.

4

The Fundamental Option

I wonder how many people still think of God as a glorified book-keeper operating a kind of cosmic computer that keeps track of all our actions, good and bad. According to this notion—casuistry—at judgment God just punches the tabulator key and our final score emerges, plus or minus, heaven or hell. Then he might say, "Tough situation, George! Three more points and you'd've made it. Just one more Hail Mary. Well, *c'est la morte* . . ." Or, conversely, "Congratulations, Al! It was that last aspiration that saved your neck. Put you right over the top!"

My picture is overdrawn, I know, something of a caricature, but can you blame me? That's the way our generation was brought up. First, in the nursery, we were told about the recording angel and we were shown pictures of him with his long beard, writing with a quill in a big book. He kept track of our good and naughty actions and struck a balance each night.

At school and on retreat we were urged to examine our conscience every night at bedtime to see if we were still friends with God (as if one wouldn't know), and then to make an act of contrition as a hedge against overnight death. If we omitted that particular scrutiny, there was our periodic examination of conscience before confession.

During our seminary days we priests made an additional fifteen-minute examination every day on some particular virtue or vice. Some of the men literally kept book on their sins and faults, entering their daily offenses against particular virtues in a kind of spiritual laundry list.

Whatever its drawbacks, I am not going to belittle this practice of examining one's conscience regularly and systematically, for that is a part of how thousands—no, millions—of Christians achieved holiness and saved their souls. So keep on using it if you like, and God bless you!

The trouble with all this spiritual nitpicking—concentrating on our unworthy thoughts, words, deeds, and omissions—is that it tends to color everything either white or black: you are either in the state of grace or in mortal sin, all good or all bad. To cite a truism, there is some good in the worst of us, some bad in the best of us. But in the nitpicking system, the "act-centered" method, a boy might think, "Well, no sense getting up for mass today. I jacked off last night. State of mortal sin. Going to hell anyway." And so he practically hands himself over to the Devil until he either makes an act of perfect contrition (which he has been taught is next to impossible) or gets to confession.

In fact, it is my impression that moral theology conveys approximately that idea. The soul in mortal sin is supernaturally dead. Certainly, the Christian may carry on with his usual routine of piety: grace before and after meals, handouts to moochers, kind words to troubled souls—but, the theologians say, these are now "dead" works, the fruit of habit and merely natural virtue, untouched by charity and therefore of no supernatural account. A person might as well not bother.

In his own defense, the theologian might say, "Ah, but you misread me. It has to be nothing less than a grave sin, a complete turning from God as our last end, and, as you well know, we theologians have always contended that that is a very hard thing to do: to commit a mortal sin. I should say that our friend's masturbation was wrong, but not sinful. In any event, his grace at meals implicitly reestablished diplomatic relations with the Deity."

But, sadly, that is not the way it looks to the rest of us.

(I once made an east-west crossing on the old *Queen Elizabeth* with the late Lord Beaverbrook, the English publishing tycoon. As a devout Presbyterian, he was a firm believer in predestination, but unlike the rest of his coreligionists, Beaverbrook knew with all the certainty of his own firm faith that he was booked for hell rather than heaven, so—enjoying his exemption from righteousness—he spent most of his free time praising God and chasing skirts.)

In a large parish where I was once an assistant, our leading layman was what we priests sometimes call a "church mouse." He was in his late sixties, retired, and it seemed that he only left the Blessed Sacrament to take his meals and sleep. He heard mass and received daily. He was active in the St Vincent de Paul and Holy Name societies. He had a good wife, a nice home, and his children had married and moved out. Not pushy or aggressive, either, but rather unobtrusive. We all liked him. I was there when he died and was buried with solemn honors.

Some years later his son confided to me that after the old man's death the family had opened a locked closet and found it stacked from floor to ceiling with erotic and paperback pornographic novels of the most moronic type.

Question: Our little church mouse was not all white, that's for sure, but was he all black? What effect did those books have on his eternal destiny? Is he in heaven right now or in hell? Can anyone be at the same time half-good and half-bad? I rather think so. But I also think that our little church mouse was more good than bad, and that at this moment he is smiling down on all of us.

A similar but vastly more complex instance: The English modernist, Baron Anatole von Hügel, an otherwise pious and right-living Catholic, could be writing a polemic undermining the divinity of our Lord. Then he would interrupt his work to spend an hour on his knees before the Blessed Sacrament. It looks as though he was gifted—or afflicted?—with "doublethink," defined by George Orwell as "the power of holding two contradictory beliefs in one's mind simultaneously, and accepting both of them."

In *The Thomist*, Fr. Charles E. Curran of the Catholic University of America, helps resolve our problem by reminding us that not everything wrong is sinful—which is only a more simple way of drawing the distinction between objective and subjective sin. Thus, artificial birth control is always wrong, but circumstances may exempt a particular person from guilt, as I am now convinced they must have done in the case of so many good wives and mothers with whom I used to do battle in the confessional.

With much hemming and hawing and many a qualification, Fr. Curran applies his reasoning even to the gay scene. It is generous of him because he is on the theological faculty of the university with a position to hold, and the front-line troops are the ones that suffer most, as he himself found out in 1968 when his contract was dropped and it took a student strike and a brace of lawyers to get him reinstated.

Fr. Curran believes that moral theology has for too long tended to study the action apart from the agent. This is known as "casuistry." But it is time we moved away from this act-centered way of thinking. We should put the act back in the whole picture and see how it fits. [1]

Thus, according to traditional Catholic doctrine, masturbation is objectively wrong. No priest would preach a sermon urging self-sex. But here we are confronted by the teen-agers, at the peak of their sex drive and still too young to marry. Common sense would indicate that when they masturbate they are more driven than free agents. In their case, then, it is wrong, but it is not a sin.

According to William James, in *Varieties of Religious Experience*, most people once in their life experience "conversion," a psychological crisis in which they reject all thought of sin and make a definite election of God as their savior and the ultimate purpose of their existence. [2] The evangelical sects stimulate individual conversions by means of revival meetings. Billy Graham's rallies, for instance, are directed toward conversions. This election of salvation is a serious matter. For the rest of his life the convert will associate it with that glorious sunburst of joy, the feeling of release from all sin, when he walked to the front of the tabernacle and gave himself entirely to Jesus.

But we Catholics were four hundred years ahead of them. Quite early, in his *Exercises*, St. Ignatius Loyola, founder of the Jesuits, presents the Christian soul with Jesus confronting Satan, each at the head of an army. St. Ignatius paints a vivid picture, appealing to both intellect and imagination as he lists the advantages and disadvantages of service under either captain. Finally, he steps back and says, "Now make your choice. But remember that once you have chosen, you can never go back." [3]

In *The Church*, Fr. Hans Küng speaks of this election as "a radical decision for God. The choice is clear," he says, "either God and his reign or the world and its reign." (This is St. Ignatius all over again.) "Each one individually is confronted with a radical decision: where in the last analysis does his heart lie—with God or with the goods of this world? . . .

"Thus the decision for God is irrevocable: 'No one who puts his hand to the plow and looks back is fit for the kingdom of God.'—'Whoever does the will of God is my brother, my sister, my mother.' And what does the will of God demand? Not merely the negative rejection of the world, but a positive commitment; not the fulfillment of a vast number of commandments, but basically only one thing: love."[4]

This decision for God is called "the fundamental option." On reaching the age of reason, every Catholic has made his fundamental option at least implicitly and ratified it again and again in his thanksgivings after Communion. Now, if we think of it as citizenship, if we compare it with our loyalty to the flag, then grave sin becomes the religious equivalent of treason. And one can exceed the speed limit, chisel on taxes, and prevaricate on official forms, but one does not lightly sell nuclear secrets to the enemy. We may fudge in our dealings with Uncle Sam, we may gripe about the government, but our basic loyalty is firm and when the chips are down our heart is in the right place and we would sell our bridgework if necessary to defend our country.

The parallel with religion is clear. Mortal sin is treason, a complete and deliberate sellout of Almighty God. Now here is Greg, a good boy, in high school, reverent, dutiful, respectful, pious—he has everything going for him, except that every other night or so he just has to masturbate before sleep. He is immediately repentant and tries to make an act of perfect contrition before dozing off. Since Father is in the confessional only once a week, Greg is not a daily communicant. But he does receive every Sunday.

Think of Greg's situation now in terms of our present-day act-centered moral theology. We are to believe that the boy drops his basic commitment, renounces his loyalty to God and his heavenly citizenship, and then picks it right up again, sliding in and out of the state of grace no less than three, sometimes four times a week, or over one hundred fifty times a year. Surely it takes more deliberation than that to abandon a basic commitment? Wouldn't it take at least as much thought as we give to buying a new car or taking out an endowment policy?

I would say, and most priests would agree, that Greg's excesses are venial sins at worst, and that he need not hesitate to receive Holy Communion daily.

A man never expresses himself in a single act. It is the pattern that counts. Hence the judgment of a shrewd old saint that "No one ever drops dead spiritually." When we see or hear of a man doing something completely out of harmony with his previous life—Pope Paul a suicide, for instance—we can be practically certain that there was no sin. In fact, when you get right down to it, most sins of the committed Catholic are accidents.

Society makes constant use of this pattern judgment in hiring people and sharing responsibility. Aspiring to the priesthood, the young man goes to the seminary, a live-in college, where experienced judges of character observe him for at least four years. They are looking for a stable pattern of right living and good judgment. Once they are convinced of the man's stability, they have no hesitation in recommending him for ordination.

That, too, is the basis of courtship: the boy and girl are studying each other to see if their present daze has a foundation in reality.

We hear gossip of someone we know very well and our first reaction (and it is trustworthy) is to exlaim, "Oh, John would never do a thing like that!" But if John did, you see, it means that he was not himself. It was not the action of the real John.

According to the late Bishop W. M. Bekkers, "Heroism is not an everyday occurrence. Our unspectacular daily lives give little encouragement for heroism, but indicate instead the path of gradual development."[5]

As another example of a fundamental option in the natural order, take the man who sets himself the goal of a college education. Everything else yields. He measures his every expenditure against the need for it and the dent it will make in his savings. There may be occasional extravagances, but in the main he steers his course straight to the registrar's office.

(I have heard a college chaplain growling about being routed out three or four times a week to absolve some particular student from his imagined sin of masturbation. What that priest should do is call the boy in and give him an hour's instruction on the fundamental option.)

This explanation of our supernatural life has such verisimilitude that one must wonder why it was not more widely taught before this. To run through it again, let us go back to St. Ignatius's figure of Christ recruiting an army. It is a cross-section of humanity. The men have all the varying strong points and weaknesses of human beings everywhere. As in the United States Army, there are lazy colonels, forgetful captains, drinking lieutenants, horny sergeants, and a vast multitude of profane, hard-fisted, brawling privates. That army includes you and me.

Now, with all our faults, we are basically loyal. Despite occasional lapses in discipline and breaches of army regulations, *we are on His side.* We are wearing His uniform and when we get our marching orders, we snap into it and get things done. Every once in a while a real s.o.b. turns up in the ranks. He has to be court-martialed and dishonorably discharged—maybe even hanged. But that doesn't happen often.

Now can you see the meaning of the fundamental option? Very few American soldiers collaborated with or defected to the enemy. Sadly, it did happen now and then, but still it was comparatively rare. And that is the moral equivalent of mortal sin: the total reversal of allegiance.

Was it Ben Franklin or Chairman Mao who said it?—"Sow an action, reap a habit. Sow a habit, reap a character. Sow a character, reap a destiny." But the action is not the destiny. We shall be judged on our character, on what we *are*, what we have made of ourselves —not on our very last action before dropping dead.[6]

There are three kinds of sin according as they spring from ignorance, frailty, or malice. Sins of ignorance are no sins at all. Ignorance of the law is a perfectly valid excuse before God.

Sins of frailty originate in the bodily appetites: intemperance, impurity, sloth, for instance. Sexual offenses may well be among the least of all sins because we have both the temptation and the opportunity always with us. It is as though the alcoholic had a bottle built into his pocket. For the nature of temptation and yielding to sex, imagine a healthy, hungry person seated at a banquet and told that he may not eat. Would you hold him much to blame if he broke down and helped himself?

Sins of malice are the worst. While our Lord just sort of waved sex aside like a pesky mosquito, he cursed and bitterly denounced sins of malice: cold, calculating hatred, vengeance, slander, pharisaism, the cynical corruption of the innocent.

Think of the reporter or editor gloating over a job of character assassination that could well drive his victim to suicide. Of the man who nurses his appetite for revenge, sometimes for years, until he finds the opportunity to move in and break his victim's heart. Of the people who generously gave the Indians blankets—after first polluting them with smallpox germs. Of the jealous people in all the professions scheming to keep a colleague from getting his just due.

These are all sins of malice. Sins of the flesh are small beer by comparison. The malicious sinner stews over his project, envisioning the anguish of his victim beforehand and then recalling it afterward with glee.

Compare such a monster, plunging his knife into the back of a rival—compare him with poor little Greg masturbating miserably between the sheets. Greg succumbed only after at least a token struggle; there was instant sorrow and no victim. You can see the difference: the infamous wickedness in sins of malice—the understandable weakness and utter lack of damage in the other.

There is again the consideration that "futile sex," as I'll call it, is neither abortion nor infanticide but only a wasted potential. The first time I dropped the seed as a young teen-ager, I confessed that I had killed a baby. The priest naturally asked for an explanation. I explained. Then he explained. "But it's the same thing, isn't it?" I asked. "Not by a long chalk," he said. So then he did some more explaining.

A wasted potential in "futile sex"? It just might be a good thing. Think of the ten trillion spermatazoa thrown off by only one man in the average lifetime. (Who counted them, by the way, and how?) All 10,000,000,000,000 clamoring for eggs to fertilize. It's just a good thing that approximately 9,999,999,999,995 never got there.

About this basic choice, this fundamental option, this decision for Christ: From observation and personal experience I have an idea that it is not greatly affected by our everyday failures in virtue—our lies of convenience, catty remarks, neglect of prayer, intemperance, sexual lapses. On the contrary, our subsequent sorrow and reception of the sacraments may make us even better off than we were before we committed our peccadilloes.

5

The Priest and Sex

The Latin Church is the great reality that overshadows modern civilization and the history of the Western world—not Jerusalem nor Alexandria, not Constantinople nor Moscow, but Rome, with its inexhaustible arsenal of moral power. Other movements rise and fall: feudalism, chivalry, the Renaissance, the Enlightenment—they come and they go. But ever working through it all with resolute purpose and combined effort, regardless of place or circumstance, is the imposing mechanism of the Catholic Establishment.

In the cloister, the monk is forming the minds of the youth who will one day control the destinies of their age, while his monastery is the harbor of the desolate and the home of the stranger. At law, the priest is resisting the baron, extending his more humane and equitable code over the whims of custom and feudal law as administered by a class of ignorant and arbitrary tyrants.

In the palaces of kings and emperors, the hand of the churchman, often invisible, is guiding the ship of state. Rich with gold and territory, and fortified by the supernatural mystique of their high office, cardinals and archbishops make war and peace, owing allegiance to no one except the emperor whom they have elected and the pope who first anointed and then crowned that emperor.

Far above all men, from his pontifical throne, the Vicar of Christ claims all of Europe as his domain and dictates terms to kings. At the other end of society, the lowly minister of the altar, with his power over the body of Christ and his power of absolution, moves among the serfs and peasants, promulgating and enforcing the decrees of his superiors.

Reinforcing the structure are the cathedrals with their radiant windows scattering jewels over the pavement, the solemn plainchant and glorious counterpoint, the sumptuous vestments enhancing stately ceremonies in the sonorous language of the Caesars. In those days there were no movies, no radio or television; these were the theaters of the masses.

To the secular historian it is a problem. To the Catholic it is a miracle, an extension of the incarnation, the continuing presence of Christ in his world. "How many divisions has the pope?" asked the cynical Stalin.

None. The Church operates through an organization perfected through two millennia, wielding wide and absolute authority through moral power alone, touching all things with its influence, walking unarmed through deadly strife, advancing with renewed strength after every setback, conquering alike the savagery of the barbarians and the apathy of the effete Romans, fusing discordant races and hostile nations into one vast brotherhood of belief. This was the Establishment: pope, cardinals, archbishops, bishops, and priests in hundreds of thousands. It is still with us. It will be waiting to greet Christ on doomsday.

From village pastor all the way up to the Holy Father in the Vatican, each is basically a priest, as was Christ, set apart from the rest of society by the sacrament of holy orders. So let us look more closely at this hallowed personage—this priest:

He always presents a challenge. He perplexes people. Outwardly a man like everyone else, he mingles with the crowd, and still there is something elusive about him. Although he may be in the midst of them, he yet remains inaccessible. However open and candid, he remains a man of mystery. Men think they understand him, yet definitions fail when they come to speak of him.

He is adaptable, and yet in an age of change his principles and his character remain changeless. He converses with his fellowmen without yielding to their pressures or being influenced by them. A strange man—yet not a stranger!

"If the world hates you, remember that it hated me before you. If you belonged to the world, the world would love you as its own; but because you do not belong to the world, because my choice withdrew you from the world, therefore the world hates you."[1]

The priest and the world: he is ever its adversary. He will never be forgiven for daily bringing back to earth Him whom they thought they had forever sealed in a tomb, suppressed forever.

A fatherly adviser? A good-natured citizen? That is the least of it. He is like God. He is a fighting man and he can terrify the Evil One. Like St. Michael, he challenges the Dragon, driving him from the souls of men and then healing their hearts.

There he is, the priest, in every century, in every nation since the time of Christ, an enigmatic and mysterious reality—beloved, feared, hated: a man, and yet more than a man.

This is the man whom the great and compassionate Voltaire wanted to strangle; he was hanged by Bloody Bess; he traveled with Chaucer to the cathedral at Canterbury, which he had built; it was he who taught Alfred the Great how to read, who first showed Europe how to farm the land. This man. This priest.

Nations rise and fall, conquerors come and go—through wars and revolutions, the priesthood remains, changeless, eternal. It goes on, generation after generation, outwardly humble, but with the nobility of an imperial dynasty that has never known interruption.

The priest is indeed a strange man. The world hoots at him, calling him the survivor of a day that has passed, a witch doctor dedicated to the perpetuation of silly superstitions. The world says he is reactionary when in fact he is ahead of his time. He looks to the future and by scanning the present predicts what is to come. He anticipates and prepares for it. He transcends all progress and secular humanism by always showing men Christ, the new Adam, and begetting in them the life of a world above nature. But because he speaks in the accents of eternity, the world considers him a bore.

This is the eternal paradox of the priest. In a world gone out of control he stands aloof, giving the lie to all who say that continence is impossible. He has given up his own life to reconcile man with God. Poor and weak, he is without political power, without money or the arms with which others make their will prevail. Indeed, is there anyone weaker than a priest?

And yet his very weakness is his strength, for "he can do all things in Him who strengthens him."[2] His special concern are the weakest of all men: those who suffer, the ignorant, those who fall.

In him, our Lord's prediction of hatred and persecution, made at the Last Supper, is constantly being fulfilled. In all history there has been no institution more often belittled, more blindly misunderstood, more savagely attacked than the Catholic priesthood. And never more so than at this moment, and—one writes in tears—never more subtly, more effectively, than by those of our own household, by Catholic priests themselves.

"Yea, mine own familiar friend, in whom I trusted, which did eat of my bread, hath lifted up his heel against me."[3]

And yet it is only before a priest that people will kneel. They know it well—God's enemies—and it infuriates them. Until the end of time the priest will be the most beloved and the most hated of men, the dearest brother of some, the archenemy of others. His mystery remains a holy enigma even to himself. But it will stand, a witness of the invisible kingdom, until this world slides into the abyss. Priests know that when they go up to the altar for the first time. They are not unaware of the fact that until death they will be "a sign of contradiction"—a light for the children of light, darkness for the sons of the night.

The priest is chosen by our Lord himself: "You have not chosen me, but I have chosen you, and have appointed you that you should go and bear fruit, and that your fruit should remain."[4] The candidate is called and ordained by some particular bishop, to whom he swears lifelong reverence and obedience. In return, the bishop guarantees his support.

The sacrament imprints an indelible character on the soul, marking the man as a priest forever. Holy orders cannot be repeated. It is permanent.

The Western Church will ordain no one who has not freely taken an oath of lifelong celibacy.

So much for the juridical facts.

The laity and even some priests with them are sometimes uncertain as to the nature and obligations of priestly celibacy. They know we are literally incapable of sacramental marriage. By declaration of the Church, sacred orders, together with solemn vows and the simple vow of the Jesuits, invalidate any subsequent attempt at marriage. The Holy See can always dispense, of course.

But the informed layman also knows that there is more to it than psychological castration. The priest has the added guilt of sacrilege. Shortly before being ordained a deacon, the seminarian swears before witnesses and signs his oath averring that he is a completely free agent, that he is fully aware of what he is doing and of its nature, and that he forever renounces marriage and all use of sex, "so help me God and these his holy Gospels on which I rest my hand."

I used to marvel at priests presuming to ask the Holy Father for a dispensation on grounds of ignorance: "I did not know, understand, apprehend, what I was signing." How could that be possible, I wondered, after at least six years of previous deliberation. But now I think I know.

I was ordained in 1940, and I can safely say that the priests of my own class and those ahead of me are or were unbelieveably innocent about sex. We spent a whole year studying justice but less than a month in the study of sex. Our instructor was afraid of telling too much and perhaps inflaming our imaginations. He was bashful, self-conscious, rather like a father fumbling his way through "the facts of life" for his young son. Sensing the tension, we students were too shy to ask many questions. There was no mention of the female orgasm, hence of female masturbation, must less of lesbianism. Sodomy, oral and anal—well, I guess all of us had heard talk of such "abominations" back in high school and college, but to us they were in a class with idolatry and murder.

I got my own special course in the Blue Book—as we seminarians called the tract on sex—from the original German of Krafft-Ebing, with the hardcore episodes turned into Latin, which made them all the more provocative. I had found the book misplaced in the stacks of the university library.

Most priests can see no very valid reason for a continuing curiosity about sex—indeed, they would consider it rather prurient and unbecoming—so after leaving the seminary they scarcely give it another thought. One result is that they know only as much as and often less than the white-collar men and college graduates whose confessions they are hearing. They don't get *Playboy*. For the most part they know only what they see in the paper, *Reader's Digest*, and the news magazines. But if at first glance the heading and content of an article appear sensational, illustrated, perhaps, with lurid art, modesty may lead them to skip over the article without reading it. They will not want to risk getting upset and thus jeopardizing their oath of celibacy.

When I signed the oath I was so hopped up with enthusiasm and holy zeal that I would have signed away my right arm on demand. I had not yet fully realized my sexual identity. Did I think I could keep such a vow?

Certainly, *provided* I was constantly in the company of more than a hundred chaste and idealistic men of my own age; *provided* I was kept from booze, pills, radio (there was no television), newspapers, and periodicals, except for relatively rare occasions; *provided* there was a spiritual program involving morning prayers, meditation and two masses before breakfast, a fifteen-minute particular examen before dinner, half-hour sermon before supper, and night prayers before bed; *provided* there was a fine choir carrying out the full liturgical program of Solemn High Mass, vespers, and compline every Sunday and holy-day; *provided* I had access to a pipe organ, a comprehensive library, occasional symphony concerts . . .

Why, certainly, if I had all that as I had had it for the past seven years, along with a friendly and understanding superior, I anticipated no trouble at all in keeping chaste.

But then the whole thing was pulled right out from under me with my first assignment as a priest, when I found myself alone with a paranoid pastor—a failed Sulpician—in a shabby rectory, in a little country town, without choir or organ, an hour's drive from the nearest library and concert hall, at $33.33 a month and no mass intentions.

A priest friend has dictated his own history into a tape recorder for quotation in this book. While it is pathetic, it is also edifying in a Graham Greene sort of way, exemplifying the struggle between flesh and spirit in the soul of a sensitive idealist and ending apparently with the final triumph of divine grace:

> After years, yea! decades of struggle with temptation against my vow, I finally settled on the theological axiom: *"Ad impossibile nemo tenetur"*—"No one is obliged to do the impossible." So I just stopped fighting and relaxed. And curiously at that point the Devil seemed to lose interest. I am not tempted nearly so violently now as in my youth. Or can it be that, God help us! growing older, I am losing virility?
>
> The transition from seminary to rectory drastically reduced my inspirational motivation. As my student days receded farther and farther into the past, the oath of celibacy also became a dim and only half-remembered obligation shouldered by a naïve young man very little like the man of today. Once,

under heavy temptation, I remember shouting back at the
priest-counselor who was patiently reminding me of my
obligation: "Certainly I swore it back in 1943, but I'm no
longer the same person"—for that was just how I felt.

It makes a man wonder if in these hectic times it is still possible
for anyone at all to make a lifetime commitment. Is the perpetual vow
still feasible? Apparently the American public no longer considers
marriage a lifelong contract. And the thousands of defecting priests,
many of them attempting marriage without a dispensation—they
seem to take rather a light view of their oath of perpetual celibacy.

So by the time I was thirty-five I found myself in an
impossible position. I had solemnly, publicly, and with
considerable applause committed myself to a lifetime of sexual
abstinence, which I now discovered I was morally and almost
physically incapable of keeping. My daily garb, the Roman
collar, the reverence of the parishioners—all were constant
tributes to the man who was brave and strong and loved God
enough to shut sex completely out of his life. The first time I
sinned I naturally felt like a heel and rushed right off to
confession. But then sin gradually wears a groove in the soul
and after a time one moves over to make room for it in his life.
I "adjusted."

What was I to do on discovering this seemingly
invincible libido of mine?

I honestly believe that we overestimate the oath of celibacy. We
Catholics tend to think of it as though it were 90 percent of our
priesthood, when in reality it is just something added on, with no
intrinsic relationship to the sacrament. The married clergy are commonplace in the Catholic Oriental rites.

I had looked forward to priestly work for twenty years and
had been especially and expensively trained for it. I liked it. I
enjoyed helping people and was busy at it day and night:
visiting the sick; taking care of the state hospital in our parish
with its three thousand patients; instructing converts; teaching
catechism in the school; regularizing marriages; rounding up
delinquents for baptism and confirmation; raising money for a
new school; and much more. There was no end to it. Now, was
I to ditch all that just because every once in a while I had to, I
just had to, slip off and relax my sexual tensions? "Nobody has
to commit sin." I had so often said it myself to penitents and

converts. But there were times when I had to have release or go
nuts. So if I was to salvage the principle, the only possible
conclusion was that in those circumstances I was not sinning.

But it is also an important article of our faith that each of the
sacraments confers its own proper grace; otherwise our Lord would not
have bothered instituting seven separate rites. Marriage and the
priesthood confer what is called "grace of state," a continuing title to
all the help needed in carrying out one's duties.

For years I used to wonder if my "grace of orders" was
just a pious fiction dreamed up by the theologians to pull them
out of a hole. I was thinking of it as something from on high
coming at me several times a day to shove me out of harm's
way, inspiring me in the pulpit, whispering advice for my
penitents. But I had never experienced that sort of thing.
Then came Pope John's Vatican Council followed
immediately by the stampede of priests in tens of thousands
out of the rectories, friaries, and monasteries. Even bishops.
Where was their grace of state?

He has a point. The number of divorces has doubled in the past
twenty-five years. Grace of state? If anywhere in the world there is a
sacramental country it has to be Italy, whereas Scandinavia, broadly
speaking, has no sacraments at all. Yet by comparison Scandinavia is a
vast area of civic calm, while Italy—well, statistically, there is a petty
theft every 71 seconds; a pocket picked every 42 minutes; a substantial robbery, usually armed, every 2 hours 40 minutes; a murder every
8 hours 56 minutes; a bomb going off every 67 hours 26 minutes; and
a kidnapping every 5 days.[5] What becomes of all that sacramental
grace presumably beamed down on Italy at the invocation of
thousands of priests and bishops baptizing, anointing, absolving, and
communicating practically every Italian on the peninsula?
Pope Clement VII, a Medici bastard, was succeeded in the Holy
See by Paul III, who had imprisoned his own mother and sold his
handsome sister to Alexander Borgia, alias Pope Alexander VI. Thus
he became rich and a cardinal. In his old age he doted on his bastard
son, whom he wished to make a prince. Emperor Charles V promised
him Parma for the boy in return for his alliance. Grace of state? We're
talking about successors of St. Peter, Vicars of Christ, and Heads of
His Mystical Body on earth. But let us continue with our case history:

The solution came to me just recently. We are only now beginning to realize that salvation is not so much a matter of individual acts as the overview of a man's whole life. We are only now beginning to realize that infallibility and the divine assistance were not meant to cover every single pronunciamento of all the popes; rather assures us that at this moment we can depend on the Church for all the guidance needed to save our souls.

So with sacramental grace. Every man's life is a drama that ends only with death. We can't know how each one's play is going to turn out until just before the curtain falls. So that sacramental grace need not be a series of impulses adjusted to each of our acts. It can be a general direction, like the beam that guides airplanes to their destination in safety.

I sat asking myself the other day: "Where was your grace of orders? What became of your confirmation with its 'strength to become a strong and perfect Christian and soldier of Jesus Christ'? What of your baptism?" And then came the thought: "Well, you're in the state of grace. You're still in the Church. You said mass this morning, and if you dropped dead this minute you'd have moral certainty of salvation. What more do you want?" God's grace can do no more.

Since celibacy is so difficult (indeed, for the average person perpetual continence is naturally impossible), why does the Latin Church continue to insist on it for all her priests?

For reasons of spirituality. Provided it be made "with a great heart and a willing mind," the sacrifice of hearth and family is the greatest gift one can offer to God. The apostles "left everything" to follow Christ. In those first days, the price of admission to the Church was high. The very first Christians gave everything they had to the congregation—remember Ananias and Saphira?—considering their earthly possessions cheap by comparison with the priceless treasures of heaven. But besides giving up earthly things they were apt to express their fervor by mortifying the flesh and sacrificing their passions and affections. This would certainly be the tendency of the stronger natures, the born leaders among their fellows. And appreciation of their superior virtue and fortitude would eventually endow them with a reputation for holiness which would make them doubly influential.

Since the priest is different from the rest of men, his life-style must also be different. He must be a man set apart from his fellows, consecrated to the one holy purpose, reverenced by the world as being superior to human passions and frailties, devoted soul and body to the interests of the Church, and distracted by no temporal cares and anxieties foreign to the welfare of the great corporation of which he is an employee.

By demanding celibacy, the Church successfully affirms its right to command the entire life of the clergy and to break every bond that might beckon to a divided allegiance.

Thus celibacy separates priest and people as the communion rail separates tabernacle and sanctuary from the congregation.

Commenting on the triumphant progress of the Latin Church through the centuries, Henry Charles Lea, no friendly witness, writes:

> It was by no means the least of the factors in the conquering career of the Church that it required of all to whom it granted the supernatural powers conferred in holy orders that they should surrender themselves to it unreservedly and irrevocably, that they should sunder all human ties, should have no aspirations beyond its service, no family affections to distract their loyalty, no family duties on which to waste its substance, and no ambitions save for the rewards which it alone could bestow.[6]

In fact it was by plowing resolutely through every one of Lea's finely printed six hundred pages, loaded with page-long paragraphs, that I reached increased appreciation and reverence for my own celibacy. Lea sets out to discredit the practice by listing every violation in the recorded history of nineteen centuries—with, Fr. Herbert Thurston wryly maintained, "ten palpable blunders in any ten consecutive pages."[7] But what comes through is an invincible firmness on the part of popes and bishops. Despite their own lapses, often notorious and scandalous, they never yielded in principle. No pope ever bedded a wife in the Vatican. Until recent centuries, there was almost constant resistance on the part of the lower clergy. Turmoil. Proclamations by local and ecumenical councils. Episcopal visitations. Courts of inquiry.

Here, for instance, is Lea's comment on thirteenth-century England: "The rule was now fairly established and generally acknowledged: concubinage, though still prevalent—nay, in fact almost universal—was not defended as a right, but was practiced with what concealment was possible, and was the object of unremitting assault from councils and prelates."[8] Because even Henry VIII would not tolerate a married clergy, Cranmer had to smuggle his wife over from Germany in a barrel.

Toward the end, Lea is reluctantly conceding that "In Ireland, for instance, we rarely hear of immoral priests, though such cases would be relentlessly exposed by the interests adverse to Catholicism. . . . In the United States, also, troubles of this kind only come occasionally to public view; but here again the Church is surrounded by antagonistic Churches. . . . Ernest Renan, a witness of unquestionable impartiality, whose clerical training gave him every opportunity of observation, declares emphatically that he has known no priests but good priests, and that he has never seen even the shadow of a scandal."[9]

Such agelong indomitability can only have been inspired from on high, and Pope Paul has declared that he is not about to abrogate a law which—perhaps through the anguish of its subjects—has drawn down such blessings upon the Church.

Now for a few final comments on celibacy: It is all too easy to limit chastity to continence, to make the two terms equivalent, an error which would make SS. Anne and Joachim unchaste. Chastity is defined as "properly ordered behavior with regard to sex." Between man and wife, chastity "integrates sex with the purpose and dignity of the whole man and his personal human relationship with the other partner." For the unmarried, "chastity means deliberate renunciation of all voluntary use of one's power of generation."[10]

It is not only an unfortunate but a false posture when Catholic apologists try to defend celibacy by sneering at sex as something beastly. Typically, according to one such author:

> Surrender to the physical passions is a debasement for men. But among these passions the one that works the greatest havoc is the sex passion, and the reaction against it finds expression in the idea of impurity: all that relates to the sex passion has something dangerous and degrading about it.[11]

This author contends that defilement is the end product of *all* sex, inside or outside of marriage, even though the seminal effusion be involuntary. What does that make your parents and mine?

If there is a feeling among many people that sex and religion do not mix, there is an opposite feeling among even more people that sex and religion do indeed mix. One recalls that religious book of the

Hindus, the *Kama Sutra*, and the erotic carvings on the facades of Indian temples; the houris of the Moslem paradise; the sacred prostitutes of Alexandria; the cults of Priapus, Eros, and Aphrodite; the Saturnalia and Lupercalia of the Romans—whole liturgies of sex in which huge images of the phallus were paraded around the town with divine honors, and sex was revered as sacred and regarded with life itself as the greatest gift of the gods.

In fact, outside the Catholic Church, who has ever regarded intercourse between a groom and his bride as a "defilement"? Indeed, how can any Catholic dare to classify the consummation of a sacrament as a "pollution"?

No—the reason for celibacy is mainly spiritual, ascetic, mystical. Christ went the whole way. He offered his life in sacrifice to the Father. Few of us priests are called to that ultimate expression of latria. In its place we offer the greatest gift within our power: a home and children of our own, together with the greatest pleasure known to our race: the pleasure of sex.

Any lesser argument is not only an insult to the married priests of the Catholic Oriental rites—the Ukrainians, Ruthenians, Romanians, and others—but it is canceled out by their experience and that of the Lutheran and Episcopalian clergy, all of whom have demonstrated over the centuries that, from the institutional point of view at least, a married clergy is feasible. It works.

For the Latin Church, however, abrogation of celibacy would likely cause at least fifty years of confusion. Some of the laity would be pushing their priests toward matrimony, while others would have nothing to do with a married priest. Bishops would tend to prefer the celibate for advancement, and all clergy appointments would be governed by the size of the rectory available.

Whenever there is an attempt to dissolve the priesthood, the dissidents aim at three objectives, the three elements which throughout history have separated priest from layman:

1. They want the vernacular to replace the priestly language in the liturgy;

2. They want communion in both kinds, the way the priest has it;

3. They want the priest to have a wife, as they do.

The first two objectives have been achieved. In the years ahead we can expect ever-increasing pressure toward the abrogation of celibacy.

6

The Organizer

It has been said facetiously that if Jesus had not founded the Church, St. Paul would have. But our Lord certainly did found the Church. The seminal texts constituting its charter are all to be found in the Gospels. One can there descry the rudiments of a hierarchy: diversification of function among the apostles.

Ten years younger than our Lord, St. Paul was converted in his early twenties and beheaded at fifty-seven. St. Luke tells us that he had relatives: it was his sister's boy who saved him from the conspirators in Jerusalem. He must have been homely and he likely had a stammer. He was probably nearsighted, for he first insulted the High Priest and then apologized on the score that he had not recognized him. He recalls that the Galatians would have given him their own eyes if that were possible, and at the end of that epistle he says that he wrote it in his own hand with large letters. His trade was tentmaking and he spoke both Greek and Hebrew besides the Aramaic of the common people which our Lord generally used, although St. Paul said that our Lord could also speak Hebrew.

According to the *Acts of St. Thecla*, accepted as authentic by SS.

Jerome and Cyprian, St. Paul was "fat, short, broad-shouldered; his black eyebrows joined over an aquiline nose, his legs were crooked, his head was bald, and he was filled with the grace of the Lord."

To judge from the poverty of imagery in his writings, he had little imagination. Did he have personal magnetism? Force, dynamism, certainly, but hardly the charm of our Lord. By comparison St. Paul was a rather angular personality with a one-track mind. Our Lord got along beautifully with all his followers, but St. Paul's relations with his traveling companion, John Mark, deteriorated to the point that they finally had to split up.

Our whole life long, we have heard the epistle and the Gospel, St. Paul and Jesus, placed on the same level at mass. The Church accords St. Paul the authority and veracity of God himself. And yet St. Paul never really knew Jesus. He did not live with him day in and day out for three years as did the Twelve. Ask St. Paul if Jesus snored and he would not know. Was Jesus a good swimmer? Did he like lots of pepper on his eggs? How did he like his fish?—fried or broiled? Even Judas would have known. But not St. Paul.

It was he who institutionalized the teachings of Jesus, transforming Christianity from a Jewish sect like the Essenes and Pharisees, modifying it, adjusting and adapting it to make it not just acceptable but downright attractive to the Greeks, Romans, and subject peoples of the Empire. Had it not been for St. Paul, you and I would likely not be Christians today—although the Church of our day would certainly astonish Jesus and perhaps even St. Paul.

At first, Christianity was preached by Jews to Jews as fulfilled Messianism. St. James and St. Peter would have let it go at that, but St. Paul was determined to admit the gentiles, exempt from circumcision and the Mosaic Law. Can you imagine the reaction of a Roman gentleman inquiring into Christianity and being told that as a first requisite he would have to be circumcised with the usual stone knife and with only wine as anesthetic? And then the dietary restrictions: separate sets of dishes for meat and dairy products, no more ham, pork, bacon, oysters, shrimp, lobster, clams, snails—and other meats and fowl only if kosher. These two considerations alone would have made it all but impossible for the Jewish religion to become universal. What St. Paul did was to keep what was attractive in Judaism while dropping what the non-Jews would find hard to accept.

Thanks largely to St. Paul, then, during the first century of its existence Christianity was a miraculous success. The Church became increasingly gentile, abandoning its Hebrew background and expanding into the Greco-Roman world with its many philosophies. Persecution by the Jews and Romans only seemed to help. But in proportion as it became hellenized, it became theological.

The Jewish had always been a simple theology. Their original tribal deity gradually developed into Yahweh, the sole omnipotent God, creator of heaven and earth. If divine justice did not confer earthly prosperity upon the virtuous, logic necessarily transferred it to heaven, which entailed belief in immortality. But there was never anything complicated or metaphysical about the Jewish creed. There were no mysteries. Every Jew could understand it.

We find this same simplicity in the synoptic Gospels, but it disappears in St. John where our Lord is already identified with the Platonic-Stoic Logos. St. Paul's epistles, too, are loaded with theology. He was imbued with Greek philosophy and its dualism between spirit and matter—the one good, the other evil. Hence he often contrasts the "flesh" with the "spirit." By "flesh" he means "sinful man," but it was taken to mean the human body.

However, with St. Paul, philosophy and theology were necessities rather than luxuries. He had to protect his converts against the ideas of Gnosticism. This was a confused but influential sect combining Oriental, Greek, and Jewish currents of thought to produce the notion that salvation was to be had by sharing in a "mystery" or by possessing a certain esoteric "knowledge" (*gnosis*). Since according to the Gnostics the body was evil, they forbade all sex and idealized virginity. This was to stop procreation. "Liberal" Gnostics, however, held that "spiritual" men were above all laws and that sex was permissible so long as one was careful to avoid conception.

Because Gnosticism thus made a fetish of virginity, because it honored our Lord and thought ill of the Jews, it was becoming a sort of halfway house between philosophical paganism and Christianity. St. Paul was well aware of this threat to his converts. There is a hint of his concern where he advises young widows to marry again and have more children,[1] a counsel directly opposed to the Gnostic ban on marriage and procreation. But with St. Paul, sex is to be used only between husband and wife, and then mostly as a matter of duty, i.e., to satisfy the "debt," to quench the fire of "concupiscence."

He could have gotten this idea from the Stoics, who believed that sex was a necessary evil. Any yielding to passion in sex or marriage was to be resisted as irrational. Man had control over only one thing—his will. The will was therefore the supreme human value, while the emotions were the supreme evil.

The Stoics saw this as a universe fettered by cosmic determinism. The only virtue was a will in harmony with nature. A man had perfect freedom only when he rid himself of worldly desires. It was not only the bad passions—hatred, avarice, gluttony—but all the passions that were condemned.

One must remember that the Church was still very young. There had not yet been time enough to establish an intellectual stance. It had no cultural tradition to fall back on, and Stoicism was certainly more compatible with the doctrine of Christianity than was Gnosticism. It was mainly Stoicism, then, that provided intellectual support for the Church's condemnation of abortion, infanticide, the abuse and neglect of children, divorce, and the several varieties of sexual experience apart from marital intercourse. With Stoicism, churchmen like St. Paul could refute Gnostic rejection of marriage without denying the ideal of virginity. But with Stoicism, Christianity also came to regard sex as low, degrading, and beastly.

It looks, too, as though St. Paul borrowed some little from the Cynics, especially for the foundation of a Christian ascesis.[2] The first Cynic, Antisthenes, had lived in Athens as an aristocrat until after the death of Socrates, when he became disillusioned with the things he had formerly valued and came to despise them. Henceforth he would practice only simple goodness. He went to live with the poor and dressed like them. He held that all complicated philosophy was worthless. What could be known must be plain to the common man. While he was by no means an ascetic, he rejected luxury and all pampering of the body. Diogenes was a disciple of his. Because Diogenes decided to live like a dog, he was called a "cynic," Greek for "canine."

With Stoicism and Cynicism, a negative and repressive element was introduced into the teaching of our Lord, which had hitherto been characterized by its cheerful philosophy of self-acceptance. While St. Paul may have considered these Greek philosophies merely a crutch to help gain acceptance for Christianity among the pagans, a crutch to be discarded later, the crutch became integrated with the system when the elements borrowed from Stoicism and Cynicism were forever frozen into Christianity by the doctrine of biblical inspiration.

And thus the plaint put by Swinburne in the mouth of the dying apostate Julian: "Thou hast conquered, O pale Galilean; the world has grown grey from thy breath."

But did Jesus actually intend a gray world? A world of anathemas, excommunications, suspensions, interdicts, and curses, where "this" is forbidden under pain of mortal sin, and the least smidgen of "that" is grave matter, where it is a sin for a boy to kiss a girl, a world of blossoms and rivulets nevertheless so menacing that it is most safely viewed from behind the bars of cloister or convent? Does true religion actually consist in flight from the world? In the beginning, God looked upon his creation and saw that it was good. Has it since turned evil that we must reject it?

It is easy to love our Lord but not St. Paul. We can admire him, but—thank God—we don't have to love him. He is just too stern.

While Jesus was a small-town boy educated only by his mother and St. Joseph, St. Paul by comparison was a big-time operator, sophisticated, student and protégé of Rabbi Gamaliel, who was the most learned man in Israel.

Except for his trip to Egypt as an infant, there is no hint that Jesus was ever outside Judea. He never saw a chariot race, never a gladiatorial combat, for there was neither sport, nor slavery, nor open debauchery in Judea.

Jesus was strictly "country." The Gospels are alive with birds, sheep, wolves, dogs, pigs, and fish. With him we are out in the sunshine and fresh air, on the water, up in the mountains. We meet all kinds of people: officers and enlisted men, snobs, good women and loose women, rich men and no-accounts, the sick and the well.

(And how Jesus loved the soldiers, those romantic adventurers, ambassadors from the outside world—from Rome, and Britain, and Spain—with their tales of strange peoples, animals, and fruits.)

By contrast, St. Paul in the course of his travels became familiar with the great cities of the Mediterranean world. He watched the races at Antioch and the spectacles of the Circus Maximus in Rome. He saw the painted women of Alexandria, applauded and wept at the dramas of Sophocles and Euripides in Athens. With the first-century equivalent of a graduate degree in philosophy, he could debate on equal terms with kings, consuls, and rabbis.

But just as our Lord was by temperament a positive thinker, St. Paul was negative. The words of our Lord fill the reader with a sense of peace and tranquillity. He is so anxious to crowd all of us into the kingdom of heaven, whereas with St. Paul it is just the reverse: he seems to be in a perpetual tantrum, furiously compiling endless lists—not, like our Lord, of those who are going to be saved, but rather of those who are on the highroad to hell.

Jesus opens his public ministry with the exquisitely lovely Sermon on the Mount, including the beatitudes and the counsels of perfection. Then he goes on to preach the love of enemies and he gives us the Golden Rule.

But our very first experience of St. Paul plunges us immediately into a savage excoriation of the very people he hopes to convert, with a denunciation of idolatry which, by some peculiar logic, he says is "punished" by delivering the sinners over to the voluptuous delights of cunnilingus and anal and oral sex. This is punishment? Certainly not for most healthy people today. Besides being abandoned by the Almighty to "disgraceful passions," the idolaters are filled with "every kind of wickedness," to wit—

Maliciousness, greed, ill will, envy, murder, bickering, deceit, craftiness, gossip, hatred of God, insolence, pride, vanity, disobedience.

Idolaters, furthermore, are without conscience, loyalty, affection, and pity.

One simply cannot imagine our Lord expressing himself in that vein. But St. Paul seems almost to enjoy compiling his rather tiresome lists of people who are to be turned away from the pearly gates. In his letter to the Galatians he cites no less than fifteen vices—most of them sins of weakness—that incur damnation.[3] There is a similar list of fourteen in his epistle to St. Timothy.[4]

The converts at Ephesus must have been enjoying what is now called the Play Function of sex, frowned on by the Stoics, Cynics, and after them by the Christians, for St. Paul felt called on to remind them that fornicators and "unclean or lustful persons" will be shut out of the kingdom: "These are sins that bring God's wrath down on the disobedient; therefore have nothing to do with them."[5] Lewd conduct, promiscuousness, and lust of any sort are not even to be mentioned. Obscene, silly, and suggestive talk is "out of place."

Now compare that with our Lord's preaching. He indicates it is true a final separation of sheep from goats, but always for hardness of heart and never for sins of weakness, i.e., for sins of the flesh. Rather, where St. Paul is so ready to curse and damn priceless souls bought by God's own sweat and blood, it is as though Jesus—about to foot the bill out of his own pocket, so to speak—has a keener realization of their value.

Where St. Paul preaches a vengeful God of strict justice by pointing out fifteen roads to hell for the Galatians,[6] Jesus tells us of the good shepherd who leaves his flock to go after the one lost sheep: "There will be more rejoicing in heaven over one repentant sinner than over ninety-nine virtuous men who have no need of repentance."[7] And perhaps the most moving story in all the Gospels, the prodigal son—one sinner—whose joyous father ran out to meet him, "clasped him in his arms and kissed him tenderly," and then told his servants, " 'Quick! Bring out the best robe and put it on him; put a ring on his finger and sandals on his feet. Bring the calf we have been fattening, and kill it; we are going to have a feast, a celebration, because this son of mine was dead and has come back to life; he was lost and is found.' And they began to celebrate."[8] And there is the woman who kissed and anointed His feet at table: "Because she hath loved much, much is forgiven her."[9] Our Lord just cannot bring himself to reject anyone completely. Thus, "It is *hard* for the rich to enter the kingdom of God."[10] (But they do enter.) People who do such and such "shall be called *least* in the kingdom."[11] (But at least they get there.) He who holds his brother in contempt *"risks* the fires of Gehenna."[12] (In other words, he has a chance.) The unjust steward will not be released from prison *"until* he has paid the last penny."[13] (But he will be released.)

More positively, those who leave all things "will enter the kingdom of God," a passage soon followed by an exposition of the great commandment of love.[14]

Our Lord gives us only one catalog of sins: "From the mind stem evil designs," he says—"murder, adulterous conduct, fornication, stealing, false witness, blasphemy. These are the things that make a man impure."[15]

Compare that with St. Paul's ten classes of supernatural "rejects" listed in his first letter to the Corinthians.[16]

As countervalence, of course, there is that soaring chapter on charity in First Corinthians[17]—one chapter out of exactly eighty-seven in thirteen epistles.

Although there are passages in which St. Paul—after the manner of Uriah Heep: "I'm an 'umble, 'umble man"—almost brags about his sins, like the priest confessing his guilt before mass, he is careful never to specify. It is, however, safe to surmise that the great saint avoided the more vicious sins such as hatred, detraction, cruelty, and lying, confining himself to the usual sins of the traveling man, the lesser ones of drunkenness, gluttony, fornication, and similar sins of human frailty. (To judge from the epistles, St. Paul did not consider masturbation a sin. He never once mentions it.)

His thirteen epistles have always provided a happy hunting ground for Christian deviationists. Two of the greatest bodies of Protestant Christianity—the Lutherans and the Presbyterians—quit the Apostolic Church because their interpretation of the letter to the Romans differed not just from the Catholic but from each other's.

St. Paul wrote in such volume—more than any other author in the New Testament; by that alone he is vulnerable. He was always in a hurry, hardly unpacked at Ephesus before he was writing back to Corinth, then dictating a letter to the Galatians between conferences at Salonika.

And he was like a physician, not writing a newspaper column for the general public, but treating individual patients by mail: people have been getting overheated with wine at Divine Services in Corinth; the people at Salonika think the world is going to end next week; some claim they have already seen the Antichrist; that chap in Corinth who married one of his in-laws . . .

These and many more like them were special problems that had to be set straight with special advice. The temptation over the ages—and 1,900 years is a very long time—has always been to take a command or suggestion of St. Paul's out of context, and then either to generalize or to make a wrong application: the prescription for an adult with cancer is applied to a child with mumps; or the remedies for leprosy are applied to every ailment that comes down the pike; or the drastic measures required to check an epidemic are all brought to bear on one isolated case.

In fact, so much trouble and misery has come into the world through misreadings of St. Paul that one could believe we would all be better off if he had never written a word. But, strangely, no such evils have ever sprung from the words of our Lord. To be sure, in the beginning there was much controversy and expenditure of wind over the number of persons, natures, and wills in Jesus, but there was little if any actual bloodshed. Comparing our Lord with St. Paul in this respect:

Our Lord had ordered the apostles to teach the world "to observe all things whatsoever I have commanded you . . . He that believeth not shall be condemned."[18] If thy brother will not hear the Church, "Let him be to thee as the heathen and the publican."[19]

"Condemnation" here refers not to this world but to the next. It is God who will judge and condemn. To say that someone is to a Christian as "the heathen and the publican" is simply to say that he is outside the fold, a non-Christian. Jesus mingled with the heathens and the publicans of his day just as we mix with the atheists, Moslems, Jews, and every other variety of non-Christian in our own day.

But now comes St. Paul with a seemingly discordant command to St. Titus, Bishop of Crete: "A man that is a heretic, after the first and second admonition, avoid."[20]

(Webster defines a heretic as "one who, having made a.profession of Christian belief, deliberately upholds a doctrine varying from that of his church, or rejects one prescribed by his church.")

These words of St. Paul to St. Titus introduced the practice of Shunning into the Christian community. There must have been a special situation over there in Crete; the faith must have been weak on that island, the first Christians easily demoralized. St. Paul judged it wiser for them to stick together for purposes of morale. But later generations would develop that single imperative "Avoid!" into a complicated structure of interdicts and excommunications aimed at punishing the nonconformist rather than protecting the faithful, when it was actually the protection of the faithful that St. Paul intended.

Catholic fanatics pushed even farther into error with an impossibly broad misinterpretation of St. Paul's words to the Corinthians. After rebuking them on several matters, he concludes, "Which do you prefer, that I come to you with a rod, or with love and a gentle spirit?"[21] Now plainly St. Paul was only asking his converts to choose between praise and blame. The "rod" was purely figurative. But zealots in later centuries took it literally, concluding that the Church had the right to beat nonconformists, and still later zealots argued and assumed the right (the *"jus gladii"*), using St. Paul's "rod," to beat the offenders to death.* Poor St. Paul!

Hence the Sacred Inquisition of the Holy Office, which, in Spain alone, from 1484 to its dissolution in 1820, roasted alive altogether 1,394 "heretics." Thus, typically:

—Around 1530, Alonca de Vargas in the Canary Islands was prosecuted as having smiled when she heard mention of the Blessed Virgin.

---

*As recently as 1931, the late Fr. John L. Bazinet, S. S. was denied his doctorate in Rome because he refused to defend the *"jus gladii."*

—Also in 1530, Alonso de Jaén was held for urinating against a church wall; and Gonçales Ruis, who told his opponent over the card table, "Even with God as your partner, you can't win this game."

—In 1635, Pedro Ginesta of Barcelona, over eighty years old, was accused of having forgotten and eaten bacon and onions on a Friday.

—One poor devil was to be liquidated for purely political reasons, but of course a "heresy" of some sort had to be dug up as a pretext. The worst they could find in his case was a quondam facetious oath, "by God's nose," sworn by the prisoner. One of the more learned inquisitors finally identified this as a prime instance of Patrisomatism—the heresy teaching that God the Father has a body. Well, the prisoner admitted having said it but denied any intention of heresy. Standing finally bound hand and foot to the stake, he cried out that he was sorry about the whole affair—indeed, he had good reason for sorrow!—and begged God's mercy on his soul. Whereupon, as a boon, he was allowed to be strangled before the faggots were kindled.[22]

Apparently St. Paul thought his technique of Shunning should be practiced on moral as well as doctrinal delinquents, in Corinth as well as Crete, for he tells the Corinthians:[23]

> I wrote to you in my letter not to associate with immoral persons. I was not speaking of association with immoral people in this world, or the covetous or thieves or idolaters. To avoid them, you would have to leave the world! What I really wrote about was your not associating with anyone who bears the title "brother" if he is immoral, covetous, an idolater, an abusive person, a drunkard, or a thief. It is clear that you must not eat with such a man. . . . "Expel the wicked man from your midst."[24]

He reverts to the same theme in his second letter to the Thessalonians: "We command you, brothers, in the name of the Lord Jesus Christ, to avoid any brother who wanders from the straight path and does not follow the tradition you received from us."[25]

(The reader will note that when St. Paul speaks of "immoral" people, like our own generation he is narrowing the whole field of morality down to sex. With St. Paul, when we call a man "immoral," we do not mean that he is a grafter or a liar. We mean that he is sexually irresponsible.)

St. Paul was insistent on this idea of Shunning. It was an important part of his strategy for protecting the faith of his converts. They were to stick together in their own little ghetto. Later in the same epistle to the Corinthians, he quotes from Menander's *Thaïs*: "Bad friends ruin the noblest people."[26] And he warns the Ephesians to stay away from "fornicators, unclean, and lustful people": "Have nothing to do with them."[27] He certainly had sex on the brain.

Now let us examine more closely St. Paul's practice of pious ostracism, for in ages to come, a misapplication of it would produce decidedly wicked and unchristian results:

Any decision as to who in the community or parish is "immoral, unclean, lustful, a fornicator, miser, or a thief" calls for a judgment, and yet if our Lord insisted on anything it was precisely on the duty to refrain from judging others:

> Judge not, that you may not be judged; because the judgments you give are the judgments you will get, and the amount you measure out is the amount you will be given. Why do you observe the splinter in your brother's eye and never notice the plank in your own? How dare you say to your brother, "Let me take the splinter out of your eye," when all the time there is a plank in your own? Hypocrite! Take the plank out of your own eye first, and then you will see clearly enough to take the splinter out of your brother's eye.[28]

(Of course, now, St. Paul had never read that passage, nor anything at all of the four Gospels. They had not yet been written.)

The same commandment is repeated in Mark and Luke. In St. John's Gospel it occurs as the rescue of the woman taken in sin: "Let him who is without sin cast the first stone."[29]

In our day, the practice of Shunning has become nothing less than systematized hypocrisy with the sanction of both Church and secular society. It is what we know as the Code of Respectability. Why call it "hypocrisy"? Because, as we all know, the respectable person is merely the one who has not yet been caught at it. Respectability judges by externals: the embezzler is respectable; all are respectable who operate in the dark or behind closed doors.

But let some naïve shopgirl get pregnant without a husband and all the respectable people in the parish will tilt their nose, avert their head, and pick up their skirts lest they be contaminated as they pass—the respectable people, that is: the uncharitable, the secret drinkers, the grafters and vote stealers, the mental adulterers, to say nothing of the white-collar criminals. They will cite St. Paul (but not our Lord) in defense of their attitude. They will take to themselves the sacrilegious prayer of the Pharisee: "O God, I thank thee that I am not like the rest of men—grasping, crooked, adulterous—or even like this tax collector." But the other man kept his distance, "not even daring to raise his eyes to heaven. All he did was thump his chest and say, 'O God, be merciful to me, a sinner.' Believe me," our Lord said, "this man went home from the temple justified, but the other did not."[30]

What this does, you see, this business of judging and shunning, is to sanctify a religion of purely external observance, to hallow it by a system of rewards and penalties, of social approval and disapproval—a sort of religion that Jesus abominated: "Hypocrites! Whitewashed sepulchers full of dead men's bones! This people worship me with their lips but their hearts are far from me."[31] The widow's penny was more acceptable than the rich man's fiver.[32]

It is a theme that like charity informs the entire Gospel: external conduct has meaning only insofar as it reflects the condition of the heart. "Washing one's hands before meals is not all that important, for it is not what goes into the body that matters but what comes out of it from the heart."[33] One of the several strictures against Jesus on the part of his contemporaries was that he consorted with the disreputable: "This man eats with sinners."[34]

As with every contravention of our Lord's precepts, the results have been calamitous. We have seen how the Holy Inquisition followed the practice of Shunning to its logical extremity: they not only judged their fellow Christians, but they forever removed the "undesirables" from the community by strangling or burning them—"heretics," fornicators, homosexuals, witches . . . thousands and thousands of them, and not just in Spain but all over Europe.

Instead of being welcomed into the parish like every other child of God, the illegitimate became a "sin child," barred from the priesthood and destined all his life to be several notches below the rest of the community in "respectability." As for the unmarried mother, she would forever curse herself for not having murdered the child in her womb. Thus, "respectability" becomes an inducement to feticide. By the mortal sin of abortion, she keeps the respect of the parish; but by refusing to offend God, she loses it.

Besides the son or daughter shunned by his parents for marrying outside the Church, there is the child born or developed into a homosexual. But these are the very people, the gays and those in spiritual straits, who need all possible love and compassion. They should not be rejected, not by anyone, but least of all by their own kin. All avenues should be kept open—with the hope of reclaiming those outside the Church; out of Christian love and piety toward the gay, who will suffer insult and humiliation enough without being ostracized by his own family.

Jesus drew no distinction between the "deserving" and the "undeserving" poor. All the poor are "deserving." That distinction comes from a misinterpretation of St. Paul's advice to the Church at Salonika. During the first few decades after the ascension of our Lord, the Christians entered into voluntary communism, and as everyone knows who has ever lived in a commune, each member must pull at least his own weight. No one dissolves morale like the slacker. If you want your breakfast, you get up and help fix it. If you sit at table, you help with the dishes. Now it seems that at Salonika some of the converts were fudging. So St. Paul advised the Church there: "If any man will not work, let him not eat."[35]

It was the Protestants who took those words out of context and added a steady job to the Code of Respectability. The temperamentally unstable, the Bohemian, the artist during his lean season between commissions, joined the "undeserving" poor. He got no Christmas basket. But the Catholic Church realized from the start that St. Paul's was special advice for a particular situation. Applied otherwise, since there is no record of his ever having punched a time clock, our Lord himself certainly would have starved. And during the Middle Ages, Christendom swarmed with mendicant friars—1,400,000 in Germany alone on the eve of the Reformation[36]—priests and brothers who wandered from place to place preaching, praying, and begging. Luther himself was one of them.

To summarize: While our Lord founded Christianity, St. Paul systematized and shaped it up for acceptance throughout the world of non-Jews. It was largely under his influence that Christianity took a rather bleak view of our life on earth with its joys and its pleasures. Jesus was a positive, St. Paul a negative, thinker. An extension of his advice—surely intended only for the special circumstances of the infant Church in the first century—the practice of Shunning, carried on and intensified through the ages, spawned a number of abuses including the Inquisition and the mischievous and thoroughly unchristian concept and code of "respectability."

In a later chapter we shall look more closely at the forty or so classes of people destined for hell in the epistles of St. Paul. And we shall see that recent findings, especially in the behavioral sciences, can contribute much toward softening the seeming severity of the great Apostle to the Gentiles.

7

Truth by Fiat

If any of the recent popes had a stormy pontificate, it was Pius IX. Only two years after his coronation in 1846, his first minister, Count Rossi, was assassinated. Two days later a threatening mob assembled in the square of the Quirinal all set to lynch him. He escaped to Gaeta and a republic was proclaimed in Rome, the capital of the Holy Father's own province, his for the previous fifteen hundred years. In 1849 the French recovered Rome for him and the papal government was reestablished. In 1860 he lost a great part of his territory by plebiscite to Victor Emmanuel of Sardinia.

A liberal in the first few years of his reign, his troubles turned him into a determined reactionary. He personally proclaimed the Immaculate Conception in 1854 and ten years later promulgated his encyclical *"Quanta cura"* with its syllabus of errors, an incredibly inept statement which had the effect of alienating the world of science and scholarship for the next one hundred years.

Now, strangely, while he was devoutly hated in Rome, "Pio Nono" was loved and venerated by the rest of the Catholic world.

There are popes like Pius XI and Pius XII—aloof, distant, chilly; and there are the warm, friendly popes: John XXIII and, to some degree, Pius IX. He was the pontiff who started the Cult of Personality, a highly emotional and sentimental "Veneration of the Pope." Before his time the popes had had little appreciation of public relations. Nowadays we are used to reading of mass pilgrimages to St. Peter's, and if we go to Rome we certainly hope to have at least a public audience with His Holiness. It was not always thus. Pio Nono started it.

In 1869 he convened the first Vatican Council, which declared him personally infallible. The Council was adjourned informally, its business unfinished, when the soldiers of Victor Emmanuel entered the city and the pope withdrew to the Vatican, where he and his successors lived as voluntary "prisoners" until the establishment of Vatican City by Mussolini in 1929.

It would not be exactly correct to say that the definition of papal infallibility was an opportunistic measure calculated to shore up the disastrously sinking prestige of the Holy See, but the Holy Father's troubles did win the prayers and sympathy of Catholics all over the world, with the sentiment, "If he wants it, give it to the poor man!"

Now when you think of it, this method of getting at a question of fact by vote is hardly scientific. One thinks of the children who found a hamster in the schoolyard. They took it into the classroom and asked Sister, "Is it a boy or a girl hamster? How can we tell?" The nun got red in the face and began to stammer in confusion until the class genius spoke up. "I know how we can tell," he said. "We'll take a vote on it." So—is the pope infallible or is he not? It is a matter of fact, not of expediency or of the wiser course. But—"We'll take a vote on it."

It might be appropriate to remark here that the Council Fathers had only the vaguest notions of Church history. They were chosen as bishops, among other reasons, for their obedience to Church law, which law included the Roman Index of forbidden books, which Index always promptly banned any straightforward account of the bad popes. Thus, the Fathers at Vatican I had not even read Gibbon. Pastor and Ranke had not yet written their histories of the papacy. It was not until some decades later that Leo XIII opened the Vatican Archives with the simple injunction to all historians: "Tell the truth!" And so they did, but it was too late. The damage had already been done. Papal infallibility had already been affirmed: an error committed by a presumably infallible ecumenical council. For instance:

—Immediately following the *Synodus horrenda* of March, 896, seven popes and one antipope ruled in a little over six years. Within only one year, four popes clambered up onto the blood-stained throne of St. Peter, hung on precariously for a few weeks—or days, before being stabbed or poisoned and hurled into the grave.

—Count Gregory of Tusculum had each of his three sons in turn elected pope. In the fall of 1032, having run out of sons, he turned to his fourteen-year-old grandson, who was elected and crowned as Benedict XI. What a charming if preposterous picture—an eighth-grader solemnly presiding over councils of mature and learned men, trading off an archbishopric for a hunting knife or a bowl of marzipan, excommunicating his playmates for outrunning him in a race! The vast and lofty machinery of Christ's Church under the sole control of a young boy! It would make a wonderful novel, but it hardly supports the dogma of papal infallibility.

—Pope St. Celestine V, elected 1294 in his eighties, resigned after only fifteen weeks. A recluse through his entire life, he was confused and bewildered in the Vatican, with no idea of the rich gifts he could dispense, handing them out casually on request. Blank bulls began appearing, peddled by unscrupulous officials of the Curia, to be filled in as desired by the purchaser. He was easily persuaded to retire, after which his successor kept him locked up.

—For seventy years, 1378-1448, no one knew who the real pope was. In 1409 there was a pope in Rome and one at Avignon. French and Italian cardinals joined to depose both and elect a successor. But both popes refused to step down. So now there were three popes, with all of Christendom excommunicate, for each of the two or three popes, following his installation, would immediately excommunicate all the followers of his competitors.

—This multiplicity of popes was not without precedent. In 1046, twenty months after Giovanni Gratiano had *bought* the See of Peter, three popes ruled in Rome simultaneously: Gregory VI, John XII, and Sylvester III, each claiming sole possession of the keys of the kingdom, each powerless to eject the others. Which one would have been infallible?[1]

Even so, there was acrimonious controversy both inside and outside Vatican I. Most of the Austro-Hungarian bishops were against infallibility, as well as nearly half the American and about one-third of the French bishops. Among the American opposition were Archbishops Kenrick of St. Louis and Purcell of Cincinnati, Bishops

Vérot of St. Augustine, Fitzgerald of Little Rock, Domenec of Pittsburgh, McQuaid of Rochester, McCloskey of New York, and Archbishop Connolly of Halifax. Cardinal Newman was also opposed, but on grounds of expediency rather than belief.

A number of German Catholics went into schism and formed the sect of Old Catholics. After over a hundred years they are still with us and with valid orders, now settled mainly in Holland —although the *World Almanac* reports some 63,000 of them right here in the United States. They never consecrate a bishop without sending proper notice to the Holy See. In Switzerland the opponents of the council united in a sect called Christian Catholics.

Among the minority opposing infallibility there were many "heavy hitters"—grave, prudent, and scholarly bishops. It took plenty of courage to debate against the personal interest of the Holy Father, but they had their reasons.

Because the matter of the Holy Father's personal infallibility has become academic since its definition in 1870, there is no practical reason to examine the arguments on either side. Pio Nono used the attribute only once, i.e., when in 1854 he defined the Immaculate Conception. Leo XIII never used it. Nor did St. Pius X. Nor Benedict XV. Nor Pius XI. Pius XII used it in 1950, defining the assumption. Following his election, Pope John said he would never make an infallible statement. And he never did. Nor to date has Pope Paul.

(Canonizations are infallible, but rarely if ever controversial. Canonization is defined [jocosely?] as a device for proclaiming that Italians are in heaven: Sarto, Galgani, Goretti, Cabrini, Savio, et al.)

Now in the last century there has been only one infallible statement: the Assumption. All the rest have been fallible. But many of the laity have a "feeling," an impression of partial, a kind of percentile, infallibility, based perhaps on the gravity of the issue under discussion.

One will say to such a person, "It's not infallible, you know." And he will begin, "Yes, but—" What remains unsaid is "it's practically infallible," or maybe "it's about 90 percent infallible." But this is wrong. Either it is or it isn't. God must operate perfectly. Either he moves in with his protection or he doesn't, but the one thing he does not do is extend his protection on a percentile basis.

As principal theologian and chief teacher of the Church, the pope enjoys a special charism, a grace suited to his high office. But as we have already seen, we don't know how such a grace operates. There was the case of the priest in a previous chapter, and the facts on the bad popes, which I have just related.

A papal statement then enjoys not infallibility but a certain degree of authority, which is defined as "a right to obedience." Thus, when the pope lengthens or shortens the Eucharistic fast, when he modifies dietary legislation or changes the ceremonies of the mass, there is question only of authority. But when he gets into something of really vital concern, such as the liceity of torture, slavery, capital punishment, the use of sex, capitalism, and so on, then, since obedience may be a matter of agonizing difficulty, we have a right to examine his reasoning—for unreasoned obedience is not piety but fanaticism.

So we check out the statements of previous popes (rather, the theologians do it for us), of the bishops' conferences, of outstanding individual bishops, and of the universal teaching of the theologians. Then we may conclude that the matter under consideration has been taught universally as binding under grave sin, is an expression of the Church's *"magisterium,"** and hence is an equivalently infallible doctrinal statement. Or perhaps otherwise.

However, it is contended that not only the Holy Father personally but the Universal Church collectively is infallible. Now if the Holy Father presents a problem to the public relations experts of the Church, the apologists, when he makes a mistake, the difficulty increases exponentially whenever the Holy Spirit changes his mind and the whole Church has to backtrack on some official teaching. The theologians slide out from under, if they can, with the excuse that the conditions necessary for infallibility were not verified. But surely it is time for us either drastically to qualify this dogma or to drop the baggage entirely. It is improbable, unnecessary, impractical, embarrassing, and an obstacle to reunion with our non-Catholic Christian neighbors.

1. Improbable.—The Church's claim to infallibility must rest on the historical evidence, if any, in the New Testament. Revelation closed c. 100 A.D. The key texts, it is supposed, imply the corporate infallibility of the Church. Thus—

---

*"(It) has the meaning, sometimes of teaching, sometimes of the teaching function and competence to teach, and sometimes finally—and this is new—of the body of prelates who possess public teaching authority: the magisterium."—Yves Congar, *apud* Hans Küng, *Infallibility?* (Garden City, N.Y.: Doubleday, 1971), p. 222. The word was not much heard of before Vatican I.

"Thou art 'Rock,' and upon this rock I will build my Church; and the gates of hell shall not prevail against it."[2]

"Know that I am with you always; yes, to the end of time."[3]

"I will ask the Father and he will give you another Paraclete—to be with you always."[4]

"When he comes, however, being the Spirit of truth, he will guide you to all truth."[5]

". . . God's household, the church of the living God, the pillar and bulwark of truth."[6]

Now those texts neither imply nor prove infallibility. All they tell us is that our Lord wants his followers to teach his Gospel and that they have certain knowledge of what to teach. But the texts do not tell us how they are to arrive at that certainty. Of course the apostles had *natural* certainty. They had been on the scene, in person, eyewitnesses to the crucial events.

These first witnesses have long been gone, but before leaving us they wrote down their testimony. It is still with us, the word of our Lord and the miracles that within decades made converts in tens of thousands.

The Holy Spirit will "remind" the apostles of all that Jesus has said to them. Now Bishop Leonard of Pittsburgh is a successor of the apostles in the collegiate sense. But how can the Spirit possibly remind him of all that Jesus has said to him?*

However, as seen, we know from that very last verse of St. Matthew's Gospel that Jesus will be with his Church to the end of time. But how? Is it necessary to postulate an infallible Church—"infallible" as the term is now understood? Couldn't it be just the ordinary divine assistance that will underwrite the survival of the Church with the preservation of all the truths needed by men to save their souls? In fact, this promised presence of Jesus could as easily refer to the Blessed Eucharist.

"In Church history," says Bishop Francis Simon, "we must shed the myth (as we have already shed it in other fields) that God continuously enters into the chain of secondary causes."[7] It is an accepted principle of exegesis that if it is available you take the ordinary natural explanation rather than reaching out for an extraordinary, supernatural, miraculous intervention.

2. Unnecessary. We just don't need infallibility. We have the New Testament. Infallibility can add nothing to its certainty, for

*If you talk to Jesus, you're pious. But if Jesus ever talks to you, you're nuts.

infallibility is not self-evident but itself rests on the Bible for proof. We have the magnetic personality of Jesus Christ with his solution of life's greatest problems and the gathering of his followers into one worldwide communion. The Jews don't have it, and they have been around almost twice as long as we Catholics, their religion still substantially intact. Islam is a great and going concern after thirteen centuries—without infallibility. Buddhism and Hinduism have survived for a much longer time than Christianity—without infallibility. So who needs it?

3. Infallibility is impractical. Vatican I defined faith as the assent to belief in a divinely revealed truth because of, and solely because of, the authority of God revealing. In other words, we give our assent not to Church or pope but to Almighty God himself. And it is not the Church's understanding of the revelation that is the final and permanent norm, but the available evidence itself.

There are cases where the hierarchical magisterium has been wrong in the past and there is no reason to think it could not be wrong again. Infallibility not only allows the Church to proclaim certainties even apart from the existence of satisfactory evidence, but it also leaves no room for errors and changes even in those cases where she has exceeded the evidence, and thus infallible teachings, even when based on insufficient evidence, become a permanent norm of belief. In a word, infallibility becomes a substitute for proof.

Now in every other area of everyday life, all solutions to current problems are provisional, based on the available evidence, but always open to correction. In religion, too, our solutions should, indeed must, be provisional and open to revision, based on the conviction founded on what the records prove, that the substance of the Gospel will never be overthrown. For the Gospel is the only divine indispensable leaven; all the rest is dough exposed to its working.

But belief in infallibility mistakes interim for final solutions, as will be abundantly demonstrated. [8]

The bishops have no authority to go beyond the Gospel nor to *im*pose, but only to *pro*pose, revealed truth. The listener's obligation to accept is motivated not by the authority of the hierarchy but by the recognition of Christ's Gospel in their teaching. We submit not to authority but to the truth; not to the teachers, but to the Gospel.

(Of course, the individual must always be willing to submit private opinion to the final judgment of the community, with Christian love on both sides.)

Practically speaking, can we Catholics honestly say that the infallibility of our Church has been its principal guarantee of unity, the most effective preservative of the Gospel substance?

I don't think so. Our sister communion, the Orthodox Church, has to this day kept the faith without benefit of infallibility, and the major Protestant bodies still adhere to the great central mysteries of Christianity, belief in the Trinity and the Godhead of our Lord. So evidently it is not infallibility that keeps the Gospel intact from age to age, but rather fidelity to Christ as he is portrayed in the authentic Gospel accounts.

Because of their greater tolerance, the Protestant churches include many communicants who seem to have lost all belief in the supernatural, but we have excommunicated perhaps an equal number. Even with infallibility, Catholics are dropping out in the hundreds of thousands because of our inadequate response to such vexing problems of our day as birth control, divorce, and homosexuality.

4. Infallibility is an embarrassment. It is the kind of reasoning that drives Catholic thinkers right up the wall, tieing their hands with *a priori* commitments, limiting their research and speculation by decisions long since discredited. No wonder secular scholars tend to bracket our theology with phrenology and astrology as a pseudo-science.

The boast is made: "The past is our teacher." All right. But let's not become abject prisoners of our past, saddled with all the mistakes our ancestors made in the mystical name of infallibility. Now here are some instances in which "infallible, irreformable" doctrines proved not only mistaken but were changed or even canceled out. Remember now that even only one such example is enough to invalidate, to disprove the dogma of infallibility.

—Cardinal Newman once said that "To live is to change." St. Augustine wrote, "Even the earlier plenary councils are often corrected by later ones, if as a result of practical experience something that was closed is opened, something that was hidden becomes known." For example, according to Fr. John L. McKenzie, "A few years ago a theologian made a survey of theological manuals written in 1880-1900. He found that of some twenty-five manuals, all but three or four censured the theory of evolution as heresy." "Their misjudgment can be pardoned," says Fr. McKenzie; "their assurance in their misjudgment cannot."[9] Pope Vigilius was excommunicated at the fifth ecumenical council of Constantinople in 553; Pope Honorius I at the sixth ecumenical council of Constantinople in 681, a condemnation affirmed also by the seventh and eighth ecumenical councils, affirmed also by Pope Leo II, and confirmed by subsequent popes.[10]

—The Church no longer claims temporal power and the need of a large state within which to operate. Vatican II presents the Church as a spiritual power, here in the world not to rule but to serve.

—St. John Vianney, the Curé of Ars, had a fervent devotion to St. Philomena and claimed that he had obtained many favors through her intercession. Her cult became something of a fad during the early 1900s. Just about every diocese in the country had at least one parish dedicated to her. But in the early 1950s it was discovered that she had never existed. "St. Philomena" had been an archaeological mistake.

—Slavery, the actual physical ownership of one person by another, was accepted as legitimate by the Church until the middle of the fifteenth century when, in 1462, Pius II declared it to be "a great crime."[11]

—Before Constantine the Great (274-337) the Church was pacifist according to the formula, "The Church abhors blood." But with Church and State united in the fifth century, service in the army became practically a religious duty in defense of Christendom. The principle became more and more firmly rooted until by the time of the Crusades, the *Decretum* of Gratian adopted Mohammed's doctrine that to fall in battle against the infidel was to merit heaven.

But in recent decades we have gone back to the pacifism of the early Christians with Paul VI in October 1965, crying out to the United Nations: "No more war! No more war! No more war!" Now, mind you, the whole Church moved as a unit in this doubly reversed position: the pope, the hierarchical magisterium, and the consensus of the faithful.

—The record of the Church is especially scandalous as regards Jews and homosexuals. Hitler could have studied our Christian record for techniques on handling the "kikes" and "faggots."

Innocent III and Lateran IV banned Jews from holding public office, since it was "absurd" for a Jew to have authority over Christians. In the fifteenth century, the Roman Jews were ordered to wear yellow hats, but with brilliant ingenuity they gradually added a little orange to the dye, then a bit of red, until the original yellow had become a beautiful deep red hue and all Jews began to look like cardinals.[12]

It was Justinian in 529 who made sodomy a crime against the

state as being the chief cause of earthquakes. Guilty gays had their heads chopped off. Later they were hanged. Still later, they were strangled. Last of all, they were burned alive—as was Jacques de Molay, last Grand Master of the Templars, so that Philip the Fair of France could confiscate the wealth of the order. Even as the flames were shriveling his flesh and singeing his hair, De Molay cursed both Philip and Boniface VIII, Philip's accomplice, predicting that they three would meet before the judgment seat of Almighty God before the year was out. And so they did.

And the witches: Just because some poor old granny could turn herself into a black cat, the Church would have her roasted alive.

—The Church has only recently come to recognize the fact that the man accused of crime has any rights at all. From 700 to 1200 the ordeal, with hot iron, molten lead, and boiling water, was accepted by many bishops as a legitimate means of discovering "the judgment of God."

In 866 Nicholas I condemned the ordeal as immoral, but Innocent IV reversed this, allowing torture in questioning a defendant. Until publication of the new Code of Canon Law in 1918, the Church had no "Fifth Amendment" principle against self-incrimination. Under the influence of "a persistent, contrary theological opinion and a dramatic change in the civil law," Canon 1743, No. 1 made an abrupt change in Church law.[13]

5. That infallibility, both papal and ecclesiastical, is an obstacle to reunion is self-evident. Where all the heads of the several Christian communions should walk abreast, perhaps allowing the Holy Father one pace in advance as first among equals, infallibility runs the Catholic flag right up to the top of the pole with all the rest arranged somehow beneath them.

From the foregoing with all its evidence of infallible decrees canceling out irreformable dogmas which are again revived by inerrant proclamations, can anyone reasonably believe in infallibility? In all those tergiversations of the Holy Spirit? Of course that is a libel on the Paraclete, for it is not he who is responsible. It is rather the course over the ages of weak, sinful men fumbling their uncertain way toward the true Light of Light. The Spirit is there helping, to be sure, but not as the principal cause and instrument of their utterances.

The fact that so many venerable convictions have proved wrong makes it impossible for us any longer to accept past beliefs as such without proof. In our sophisticated nuclear age, the concept of "truth by fiat" is becoming increasingly frivolous. It is only the *probabile*—what can be proved—that is assured of a future.

The Church does for a certainty pass along the whole of Christ's revelation, but not necessarily truth only, as we saw in the numerous instances cited above. She teaches without fail all the revealed truths, but there will always be in addition a number of human opinions and errors which she mistakes for revealed truth, e.g., the cult of St. Philomena.

Hence the popularly held notion of a detailed and verbal infallibility is not only childish but embarrassing to the Church. It invites the invidious question: "Can infallibility verify what is demonstrably false?" It occasions the conclusion (in itself a fallacy): "False in one thing, false in everything." And its corollary: "Fool me once, shame on you; fool me twice, shame on me."

What, then, is infallibility? According to Fr. Hans Küng, it is "a basic persistence of the Church in truth, which is not destroyed by errors in detail."[14] It was not meant to cover every single utterance of popes and councils. Rather, it assures the Catholic that at this particular moment he can depend on the Church for everything needed to save his soul.

8

Catching Up

It was around 1700 that religion moved from center stage into the wings of the human scene, to be summoned back onstage if at all only once a week. It was then that housewives transferred their pious images from the parlor to the bedrooms, the family Bible was removed from the hall table, and businessmen took down the crucifix that had hung in their office. And if persecution ceased it was not so much from a new spirit of tolerance as from boredom. For what difference could religious belief possibly make in the really vital affairs of daily living? Where formerly Christianity had been the cake with Scholastic philosophy as the icing, Science now became the cake iced with a dab of religion.

The Renaissance had brought with it a reaction against asceticism and other-worldliness, turning men's minds to human life as it could be lived here on earth. Western Europe once again resumed the way of scientific discovery where the Alexandrian Greeks had left it a thousand years before.

But it was not humanism, not the Reformation, that would revolutionize the beliefs of man; it was science. Science would build a whole new world for humanity. Applying power to the production of consumer goods, it would transform the feudal world into the sprawling civilization of our day. As a serious factor in men's beliefs and actions, science did not make its appearance until the eighteenth century.

First there was the Copernican and then the Cartesian revolution; Isaac Newton's world-machine; the success of the mathematical interpretation of nature; Newton's mathematical synthesis; the development of the experimental method; the empiricists' attack on tradition.

(How remote this all sounds from infallibility, final-formal-material causality, hylomorphism, primary and secondary causes intended by—or attributed to?—the Creator.)

Along with science came the growth of religious rationalism, the deistic attack on revelation, the critique of prophecy and miracles, the rationalist attack on deism, and then skepticism and atheism.

In the science of human nature, Auguste Comte founded sociology (if indeed it can be called a science); the deductive mechanical method was developed; environment became practically omnipotent in its influence on behavior.

The science of society brought political economy, social physics, and *laissez faire,* Adam Smith, and the wretched science of the factory system.

The science of government saw the decline of absolute monarchy and the rise of modern constitutionalism: John Locke, Rousseau, John Stuart Mill, Thomas Jefferson, Andrew Jackson; democracy on the basis of natural right.

Outside the Church, morality became "ethics," dropped religion and founded itself rather on the humanitarian ideal; religious tolerance finally prevailed, while cosmopolitanism is still fighting it out with pacifism ("interventionism" versus "isolationism").

And over all streams the proud banner of a "progress" that, thanks to Darwin and his theory of evolution, (still only theoretical) is inevitable.[1]

But though the world moved on, the Church stood still—not with Christ in the first century, but with Augustine in the fourth—an outmoded antique, venerable, fascinating certainly—but then people turned away from it as being impractical and returned to the affairs of their daily lives, the things that really mattered. Xavier Rynne was depressed by it all as he watched the entrance of Pope Paul to close the second session of Vatican II.

Preceded by the college of cardinals robed in white copes and miters, he says:

> "a fifth of whom seemed to be pitifully aged figures
> hardly able to hobble along, the Pope himself appeared carried
> high on the sedia gestatoria. He seemed acutely conscious of
> the tawdriness of all this faded splendor and perhaps even sorry
> that he had not decided to make a more appropriate entrance
> by walking the length of the nave on foot. As he passed down
> the central nave, the Pope scarcely looked to right or to left to
> acknowledge the fitful applause from the episcopal benches.
> Everything suddenly seemed to have a worn-out look about it,
> the vestments, the uniforms, the damask-draped tribunals.[2]

The Church has been slow, hesitant, fearful, turned toward the past rather than the future, regarding the three crucial developments that have shaped the modern world:

1. Modern science and industrialism;
2. The rise of democratic liberties; and
3. The social breakthrough: the end of a privileged hereditary aristocracy and the elevation of the lower classes.

And, sadly, through their resolute conservatism, churchmen have almost always managed to back the wrong horse. By sticking with the *ancien régime* in France, they lost the Church her eldest daughter.

It was this inveterate reactionism that gave rise to a bitterly hostile Freemasonry in the Latin countries.

Nowadays, however, the alliances seem to be reversed and the Church is likely to find her greatest loyalty and most numerous support among the non-college educated, religiously devout, politically conservative, blue-collar people, as against the educated, non-devout, liberal, white-collar class.

Because of their conservatism—it comes down to that: an inability or refusal on the part of churchmen to come up with solutions for the great central problems of present-day morality—the Church of our day is still losing its customers in droves and the faithful are making their confession not to their parish priest but to the pollster. Religion advances or declines in direct proportion with its relevance. In just the last ten years, the number of priests in France alone has dropped from 40,000 to 30,000.[3]

Why, then, do practically all churchmen tend to support and justify the status quo? Why this unconscionable zeal for, or at the least, tolerance of, the political establishment, whether in Mussolini's Italy, Franco's Spain, or even in Red Czechoslovakia and Hungary?

Well, for one thing, since the time of St. Ambrose, Church and State have always worked together in procuring the spiritual and temporal welfare of the governed. With us it is a habit.

Again, the Church of Christ is a visible organization with visible, sensible, perceptible sacraments, five of them conferred only by priests under the direction of a hierarchy. The structure must be secure, episcopal authority maintained, priests left free to offer the Holy Sacrifice, hear confessions, and bring the sacraments to the dying. And these considerations are jeopardized under a regime that is hostile.

But apart from essential considerations of religion, there is money, power, and prestige involved. Who would not want to be a bishop! Who would not be tempted by the powers of the office? He has the best of both worlds. He signs his name with a little plus sign before it. He lives in a palace, rides in a limousine, is treated like a medieval prince, and it is wonderful how a little lace and a few red ribbons can inflate a vacant personality.

His salary: $5,000—$10,000? Don't be silly! To be consecrated bishop is to be made in effect a wealthy man. As the head of a diocese, he is accountable to no one. If he has enough pull in Rome, he can have an auxiliary appointed to take care of the more tedious functions such as confirmations and graduations—which leaves him free to review his irregular Greek verbs or, more likely, watch television. Priests and laymen flutter about his person, for besides the awarding of lucrative pastorates and contracts, he has the power to create a sort of minor nobility in the form of monsignori, papal counts, and Knights of the Holy Sepulcher. Thus he can reward his friends and punish his enemies.

Amidst all this splendor, as a successor of the apostles, he is *ipso facto* accounted a holy man and, like the *staretz* of Old Russia, he is regarded by the laity with a reverence amounting almost to a holy fear. Is it any wonder that the first rule of all bishops from the top down is: Don't rock the boat! Don't shake the plum tree! But how can you be disinterested in controversy when you are getting an unlimited salary tax-free and want to keep it? But then one must ask whether the interests of religion and truth are identical with the temporal advantages of the hierarchy.

It is a combination of advanced years, great wealth, a swelled head, and the necessity to believe in the heaven-decreed righteousness of a system which has permitted him to possess such power that turns a bishop's head.*

It is not hard to understand, then, why most churchmen submit when confronted with implacable force. Think of Henry VIII and his bishops, of Hitler in Germany and Austria. Cardinal Innitzer, Archbishop of Vienna, in those heady years, actually wrote a letter to Pius XI ending with "Heil Hitler!" over his signature (and was immediately ordered to Rome, where he was properly snubbed by the pope, for by that time Pius XI had taken the true measure of Adolf Hitler and his Nazi followers). Now, most recently, we have Paul VI's desertion of Cardinal Mindszenty.

Even discounting the advantage of hindsight, diplomatic relations between the Vatican and Hitler were not just ill-advised, but scandalous as well. The Holy See was the first of the foreign powers to recognize Nazi Germany, and the Concordat of 1933 broke the back of the German Catholic resistance. At that time the Cardinal Secretary of State was Eugenio Pacelli, who would succeed to the papacy in 1938. As apostolic nuncio, Pacelli had lived through the Communist *putsch* of 1923 in Munich; he never forgot it. And apparently ten years later he could see fascism as nothing worse than martial law against Communism.

A few months earlier, in 1933, Hitler had blackmailed Pius XI into ordering the dissolution of Germany's Catholic Center Party, thus removing the last obstacle to his control of the Reichstag and ultimately of all Germany. Hitler threatened to publish the fact that certain cardinals of the Roman Curia had heavy investments in European munitions factories. Sadly, neither Pacelli nor Pius XI could have seen that by their actions—misjudgment in the one, weakness in the other—they were consigning the Catholics of Central and Eastern Europe by the tens of millions to Hitler's infamous KZ's.[4]

One could easily be disillusioned at this, at how the Church always manages to adjust in the face of relentless power. The Germans call it *Realpolitik*: acceptance of a present situation, however disagreeable, rather than holding out at whatever cost for an ideal that might never eventuate.

---

*While the layman sees his bishop through a haze of reverence that tends to obscure his faults, the attitude of the clergy is usually casual, jocose, sometimes critical. The Fathers draw a distinction between the man and his office with its supernatural powers. And there is a great deal of faith underlying this quasi-familial relationship: "The bishop may be an s.o.b. but—by God!—he's *our* s.o.b. and we won't let any outsider put him down."

Thus we rarely see our bishops or priests leading a crusade, marching, picketing, making a noise for any cause however worthy. They kept their mouths shut about slavery before the Civil War and have had precious little to say on the subject of integration since then; nothing to say on women's suffrage; very little on child labor, except in 1924 when Cardinal O'Connell of Boston came out bravely denouncing the Child Labor Amendment as "this Soviet legislation." (If that smug old curmudgeon is not in heaven right now he must be forever astonished.)

In social action, Catholic churchmen generally do not lead; they let the others go to the front, and then only after those others have won the battle do they move in to help enjoy the victory and share the spoils. But they themselves take no chances on getting shot down in defense of an ideal that is still unpopular.

Although our Lord clearly preached separation of Church and State with his imperative: "Give to Caesar what is Caesar's, but give to God what is God's,"[5] the union of both proved just too tempting both to pope and Caesar, and they began moving together with the conversion of Constantine less than three hundred years after the ascension of our Lord. Churchmen actually seem to prefer governmentally guaranteed privileges to freedom from the ambiguous demands made in exchange for them. They actually prefer to act on men in society by external force, rather than win their hearts by spiritual means.

So there was an exchange of "benefits" between Church and State. The bishops would impose patriotism and loyalty to Caesar as binding in conscience. In return, Caesar would support the Church and exempt it from taxes, pay all salaries, and offer his militia for the enforcement of Christian morality, control of the Jews, and the destruction of heretics, gays, witches, and similar undesirables.

But surely the bishops could see that a person is not a thing to be manipulated from the outside, that pressure of any kind encroaches on the integrity of the human person as a free agent? What does coercion contribute to the working out of human salvation? If such pressure is needed to get results, then the results are worthless. External religious observance under pressure is not a religious act. Assent to truth under pressure is not assent to truth at all.[6]

However, with the union of Church and State, the terms "sin" and "crime" became interchangeable. Thus, in 529, the Emperor Justinian made sodomy a capital crime as the chief cause of earthquakes. The offense eventually passed to the jurisdiction of the Church until 1533, when the English King Henry VIII, to harass the bishops and trim back their authority, took sodomy away from the Church courts and returned it to civil jurisdiction.

Traces of this theological orientation in the philosophy of government remain in all the Western nations, even in the democracies. Indeed, this matter of using police and public monies to prevent sin poses a nice problem here in America, where all the churches and sects function on an equal footing. In the area of censorship, for instance, what standards shall we follow—Presbyterian, Baptist, Methodist, or Catholic? Indeed, why should there by any censorship at all? Why not let the individual follow his own standards?*

There is a developing consensus that sin is no affair of the State, that crimes without victims are not really crimes at all: gambling, for instance, and the use of pills, booze, and sex—that the police should devote their time exclusively to enforcing the laws against violence. My philosophy here is that of John Stuart Mill:

> The sole end for which mankind are warranted, individually or collectively, in interfering with the liberty of action of any one of their number, is self-protection. The only purpose for which power can be rightfully exercised over any member of a civilized community against his will, is to prevent harm to others. His own good, either physical or moral, is not a sufficient warrant. . .
>
> The only part of the conduct of anyone, for which he is answerable to society, is that which concerns others. In the part which merely concerns himself, his independence is, of right, absolute. Here advice, instruction, persuasion, and avoidance by other people if thought necessary by them for their own good, are the only measures by which society can justifiably express its dislike or disapprobation of his conduct. [7]

St. Augustine, by no means a laxist, reluctantly conceded that in his ideal City of God there had better be brothels to save the wives and daughters from rape. Our society more or less tolerates them as a source of income to the police. Following Mill, and on the principle that free will includes the right to commit sin, we should have licensed prostitution and not just for the heteros but for the gays as well.

When Senator Smoot argued for federal censorship of imports, Senator Millard Tydings of Maryland reduced his appeal to the absurd: "Let us close every church from now on," he said, "and make the

*A readable and authoritative treatise was written on precisely this subject by the late Fr. John Courtney Murray, S.J.: *We Hold These Truths* (New York: Sheed, 1960).

Ten Commandments statutory. Let us call out the Army and make righteousness compulsory."*

Objection: "But the State has to protect herself against the bad morals of her citizens. Look at what happened to Greece and Rome."

Response: What are "bad morals"? Those that do not conform with our own, whether Jewish, Moslem, Christian Scientist, Mormon, Roman, or Irish Catholic. Is there possibility of a consensus? And if there were, would Christ approve of enforcing morality by means of guns, clubs, shackles, and poison gas? There is no discernible connection between "bad morals" and the fall of Greece, Rome, the Holy Roman Empire, Spain, the Third Reich, and, most recently, the British Empire.

To recapitulate: We have seen that although the secular world has moved on from the Renaissance through the Enlightenment to the age of science, the Church has obstinately refused to keep pace, to assimilate the new learning and adapt it to the Gospel of Christ. Why?

Because the bishops, established in power and affluence, are enamored of the *status quo*. As they see it, any change can only be for the worse.

Hence, union of Church and State is their ideal, even though it involves shabby compromises, the employment of physical violence to keep the People of God in line, and even though it seems to contravene the express command of our Lord.

Traces of this tradition remain to plague the rest of us— Protestants, Catholics, and Jews—right here in our democratic American republic, and right now in this last quarter of the twentieth century: morality enacted in Congress and State House. Now let's look at the philosophy behind this morality, at least so far as sexuality is concerned.

---

*Doubtless the most infamous example of this confusion between public and private morality is the Connecticut birth-control statute, passed under Protestant pressure in 1879:

"Use of drugs or instruments to prevent conception. Any person who shall use any drug, medical article or instrument for the purpose of preventing conception shall be fined not less than fifty dollars or imprisoned not less than sixty days nor more than one year or be both fined and imprisoned."

This statute quite blatantly confuses the moral with the legal, transposing a private sin into a public crime. The criminal act here is the private use of contraception.

9

The Church and Sex

IX.

The Church and Sex

Three centuries after the resurrection, God raised up three men, each a genius in his field, who were to determine the thought and history of Christianity from their time right down to ours. They were all contemporaries, all born within a span of fifteen years:

St. Ambrose (340-397), "the last of the Romans," fixed the ecclesiastical concept of Church and State;

St. Jerome (345-420) gave the Western Church its Latin Bible and was eminently influential in the development of monasticism;

St. Augustine (354-430) fixed Christian theology until the Reformation, and both Luther and Calvin borrowed heavily from his teachings. It is impossible to overestimate the influence of St. Augustine on Christianity, and it is his bleak view of sex that both repels us and yet of necessity holds our interest.

Born in northern Africa, this man began life as a playboy. He never married. Instead, he kept a mistress who bore him a son, Adeodatus—"Gift of God." Nevertheless, his was a religious nature and the vocation was in his blood, so he looked into Christianity, the religion of his mother, St. Monica, but his fastidious good taste rebelled against the barbarous Latin of the Bible. He turned instead to the cult of Mani (216-276)—the Manichaeans.

Manichaeism combined Christian, Gnostic, and Zoroastrian elements: Evil is a positive principle embodied in matter, while the good principle is contained in spirit. It thus established a conflict of

Light vs. dark
Good vs. evil
Soul vs. body

It condemned meat eating and all use of sex, even in marriage. It sounds eccentric to us now, but it was an intermediate creed that attracted many cultivated people of the day, including the youthful Augustine, despite his mistress. Now Augustine's experience with Manichaeism was no mere flirtation. He was immersed in the stuff for nine long years, from the time he was nineteen until he was twenty-eight. Those are the years the young man of today spends in the seminary: four years of college with perhaps a postgraduate year of philosophy, then four more years in the study of the sacred sciences. For the intellectual, these are the sensitive, the formative years.

Now if after completing his seminary education, an intellectual genius decides that the Catholic religion is not his cup of tea—if instead, for instance, he decides to become a Moslem, he is bound to carry with him into Islam many of the opinions, judgments, insights, and habits of mind acquired in the seminary. He can't help it; it would be morally impossible for him, however he might wish it, however hard he tried, to wash his mind clean of Christianity.

And so it was with St. Augustine. He left his sect but carried with him into Christianity the Manichaean, dualist, antilife, antisex cast of mind. And this he could not help but write into his theology, which became normative and has so remained until this day.

He left Africa in 384 and settled in Milan, where he came to know, indeed to love, the local bishop, St. Ambrose. It was under his influence that Augustine renounced his past and at thirty-nine became an ardent Christian. He was a man who never stopped writing, dictating to two secretaries simultaneously. His works come to twenty-one fat volumes octavo. His doctrine on sexuality can be found most systematically expounded in his *City of God*.

Sex in marriage is not sinful, he says, provided the couple intend to make a baby. Yet, even in marriage, people are ashamed of sex as shown by their desire for privacy.* What is shameful about lust is its independence of the will. Orgasm simply overwhelms human reason for the moment.**

Virtue demands complete control of the will over the body, but such control is not enough to make the sex act possible. Hence the sex act seems inconsistent with the perfectly virtuous life.

Concupiscence ("horniness") is an irrational drive whose chief characteristic is insatiability. Children are born from the power of concupiscence and inherit both the reality and the guilt of this shameful drive. Children are evil not because they are human, but because they are concupiscent. Since this evil is transmitted by sex, intercourse itself is evil and can be allowed only to make babies.

In consequence, according to St. Augustine, sex during pregnancy or in old age is illicit. But, oddly, sex between man and wife for pleasure instead of procreation is a lesser evil and hence a lesser sin than adultery.

He sternly forbade abortion, exposure of unwanted babies, and every kind of birth control. In his treatise on the morals of the Manichaeans, he even condemned what today is known as rhythm. This idea of his, centered on the supreme importance of begetting, was to be for sixteen hundred years the official doctrine of the Christian Church in the West. He would be quoted time after time against the condom, the diaphragm, and the pill. It was certainly an overreaction to the loose living of his salad days, but none the less effective as a scourge of Christian generations to come. Why, he even judged it at least venially sinful for a man to ask his wife for sex to avoid adultery. And, within a few centuries, the churchmen of Western Europe were interpreting his teaching with ever-increasing strictness.

—In his *Pastoral Rule* Pope St. Gregory the Great (540-604) warned married couples that pleasure is not a fit purpose for intercourse, that if any pleasure entered in, the couple had "transgressed the law of marriage." "Their pleasures" had "befouled" their intercourse. He instructed St. Augustine (d. 604), first Archbishop of Canterbury, that married couples could not receive holy communion after intercourse. It was as impossible to couple without sin, he said,

---

*I find this argument invalid. People don't exactly go public, either, when moving their bowels, urinating, scrubbing their dentures, or paring their toenails. Sex is only one of many personal functions demanding privacy.

**As does, say, a pint of vodka?

as to fall into a fire and not burn. Only a miracle could save one in either case. But the Church no longer agrees with Pope St. Gregory the Great.

—The imposition of celibacy on the clergy was accompanied by a host of "proofs" from Scripture and tradition that the sexual act was inherently unworthy. At the same time, the still-legitimate marriages and wives of clerics were gradually put down and degraded. According to St. Peter Damian (d. 1072), "We may rightly call them not spouses, but concubines or whores."

—In the twelfth century, Huguccio, Gratian's chief commentator, taught that coitus "can never be without sin." Innocent III (1160-1216; pope, 1198), himself an expert theologian, accepted this verdict without question. St. Augustine's doctrine on reproductive intention to free intercourse from sin was commonly accepted by the twelfth century, strongly affirmed by the theologians and canonists of the thirteenth century, and was held throughout the fourteenth and fifteenth centuries.

—For centuries it was the common opinion of the theologians that intercourse during menstruation was a sin.

—Until Vatican II the procreation and education of children was regarded as the first purpose of marriage.*

How many people could be in hell for deliberately violating these norms, which today are recognized as blunders of the magisterium, but which in the best faith they mistook for the utterance of the Spirit of God himself? There are so many other instances, too, where the Church has changed not just the periphery but the very substance of her authoritative teaching on morality.

Right now there are at least three compelling problems confronting the Church with the force of emergency, disaster, panic: birth control, divorce, and homosexuality. Catholics are turning from the Church by the millions, scandalized at the impossible and to them seemingly cynical counsels offered in their distress, at the indifference of churchmen who shrug their shoulders and in effect say, simply, *"Débrouillez vous!"* or, "God's grace, my dears."

---

*And it is still regarded as something more than a meritorious hobby. But do not our contemporary moralists perhaps inflate beyond common sense the content of "education"? It certainly refers to religious and moral rather than academic training. ("Society needs plumbers as well as doctors," Bishop Boyle used to say, "shoemakers as well as lawyers.") The parent is bound to give his child at least the minimum in the way of catechizing and good example needed to save his soul. Any more than that is supererogatory.

The Metropolitan Community Church, organized in 1968 for gays in Los Angeles by the Reverend Troy Perry, already has over 20,000 communicants with daughter churches all over this country and in Europe. Homosexuality is an urban phenomenon and we Catholics are an urban people, gathered beneath the shadow of church and school. So, many thousands of Mr. Perry's membership are bound to be our Catholic lambs grazing now in an alien pasture.

"You're Catholic, of course?" I said to a gay Chicano not long ago. He was in his early twenties.

"I am . . . I was," he said defiantly, "but now I *hate* my Church, or what *was* my Church. Oh," he said sadly, "you know what I'm trying to say."

"Yes, I think I do."—And I too was sad.

The Church will change, but Catholics—people, persons, individuals, immortal souls redeemed by the sweat and blood of Christ—can't wait, nor should they have to wait.* In the meantime, by all we have believed, they are tumbling into hell like an Alpine avalanche for disobeying Church and pope.

"They are not tumbling into hell"? Certainly not. But there we have another inconsistency, one more crack in our sclerotic moral theology, still another loss in its credibility and function.

Our Lord came to teach us the truth and thus set us free. He preached no sermons on sex. Indeed, he barely mentioned the subject. He was only thirty-three when he died—with no credits at all in theology.

But then came the scribes and Pharisees of the New Law, proving that to the professedly pure all things are impure. They took Jesus' simple ban on wife stealing and developed it into an intricate commentary on kissing, intercourse, buggery, transvestism, fetishism, bestiality, fellatio, incest, pedophilia, sadism, masochism, masturbation, analingus, cunnilingus, dirty pictures, posing in the buff, scant bathing suits, sex dreams with and without climax ("If it happens, don't enjoy it!"), erections voluntary and otherwise.

With a fine feeling for semantics, they have devised a terminol-

*"There are no specialists able to restore opportunities to an aged person who has foregone his chances for erotic experience, together with its enrichments, and is now dying. . . .The truth, that the experts were only guessing, can sometimes emerge too late—and along with it, the horrendous implication that too much was staked on the conjectures of other people."—George Weinberg, *Society and the Healthy Homosexual* (New York: St. Martin, 1972), p. 139.

ogy that begs the question in practically every instance. The moral theologians know no such neutral word as "sex" unless synonomous with "gender," for in their opinion sex as an indifferent act simply does not exist. With them it has to be either "purity" or "impurity." To the rest of the country "pollution" is an ecological term, but every time the professional Catholic sees the word he automatically thinks of orgasm. Intercourse is invariably "the marriage act." One's first encounter with sex is "seduction." The body is divided into zones that are "decent," "less decent," and "indecent," e.g., the hands, the arms, and the breasts respectively. All sins of sex are mortal. So it seems at times that the phallus is dominating the whole of moral theology and a man would rather be thought uncharitable than unchaste. (You can sue a man if he says that you are unchaste, but not if he "merely" says that you are uncharitable.) Good Christ, what have they done to your Gospel!

"Woe to you lawyers! because you have taken away the key of knowledge; you have not entered yourselves and those who are entering you have hindered."[1]

Said the late Bishop Bekkers, "When demands are made that exceed the power of the people, whose is the fault? With the people or with the bishops' interpretation of God's law? Do they not perhaps exaggerate God's commands? Are they not perhaps the latter-day Pharisees, who lay burdens on the people's shoulders and thus alienate them from God and his love?"[2]

Now, while the Church is giving us a new deal all around, surely it is time to "demythify" sex. We are well rid of the Roman Index of Forbidden Books: positive law, yes, but "based on divine law," the moralists insisted. A mistake corrected, but the damage done first: a venial sin if you read only a paragraph or so, but a mortal sin if more than two pages. Cardinal Newman wondered how any boy could be properly educated without reading Gibbon's *Decline and Fall of the Roman Empire*. Why, only to keep it in your house overnight, you had to have a license from the Apostolic Delegate. I have confessed my own share of sins against this particular canon. And now it's gone.

The Eucharistic fast: again, positive law but, again, "based on the divine law of respect for the Blessed Sacrament"—this despite the fact that the apostles received their first holy communion on a bellyful of roast lamb! Another mistake corrected. But how many of the faithful were kept from holy communion by a snowflake on the lips, a postage stamp thoughtlessly licked? And how many committed mortal sin by receiving in bad faith on a broken fast?

Now that Scholasticism is no longer the required method in theology, now that we can start with Scripture instead, can't we rethink this whole matter of sex—getting away from Aristotle and St. Thomas, whose analysis of morality is based, after all, on an interpretation of the universe that is no longer valid? We have learned so much from Freud and Kinsey, from the insights of the social sciences, of medicine, biology, genetics. The population explosion, for instance, has thrown a new light over the whole problem. When the world needed populating, God permitted incest, polygamy, divorce, cutting the red tape right and left. So now that population limits are being exceeded, wouldn't God expect us to use common sense and impose the appropriate controls?

Ironically, the present position of Jews and Catholics is just the reverse of what Jesus intended. At his coming, the Jews were still loaded down with all the judicial, ceremonial, dietary, and sex laws of Leviticus and Deuteronomy.* Jesus meant to rid us of all that. Instead, a tribe of guilt-peddling theologians rose up within the Church and now, in this twentieth century after our Lord, we find ourselves in worse fare than were the Jews of our Lord's day.

In the meantime, the Jews have been set free of the Old Law not by Jesus Christ but by Moses Mendelssohn (1729-1786), the Orthodox "Father of Reform Judaism," so that actually their present state is what Christ intended for us.

And what do the Jews think of birth control? Of sex, generally? For they could well be our tutors in this matter. They, too, are under the divine command to "increase and multiply," as indeed they have done. But to attribute Catholic morality to the Jews, even to associate them with it, is an outrage. "Judaeo-Christian," indeed!

—The concept of any sexual act being, like the lie, "intrinsically" evil, such that it could never under any circumstances be justified, has long been obsolete among our fellow Christians and is being challenged more and more often by Catholic moralists.

> A relativist world-view has been substituted for an absolute one in the physical sciences. A dynamic, processive, existentialist philosophy dominates the humanities and behavioral sciences. Is it any wonder that any attempt today to base an ethic upon static, absolutist concepts not only fails to motivate people, but cannot even be understood?[3]

*By the time of our Lord, many of the judicial and sex laws were obsolescent.

—What is "natural" and what is "unnatural" in sex? Whatever is in conformity with nature. But whose nature? A man is physically incapable of acting against his own sexual nature and thus doing what is for him "unnatural," because he can't be aroused for such an act. For lack of opportunity, the hetero may be able to pervert his natural appetite for girls and take on a man instead, as in prison, but the true gay could never substitute a female. So "if you can do it, it's natural."

—There is no divinely ordained position for coupling. It is genital anatomy for the most part that determines which positions are best for a given couple. Face-to-face can be harmful in the later stages of pregnancy. Fat people (and the quadrupeds) do it from the rear. For the rest, the most pleasurable is the best position.

—Seismologists assure us that sodomy has nothing at all to do with earthquakes. Since that was the reason impelling Justinian to list it in the civil code as a crime, and since that reason is now discredited, why not strike sodomy from the penal code? Unless, of course, the Church wants the secular arm to continue burning her heretics, buggers, and witches for her!

—"Homosexuality is a sin." It is not. Sodomy could be a sin, but homosexuality is a condition, a biological temperament. Of the estimated 15,000,000 gays in this country, certainly at least one-third of them—including many priests, monks, and nuns—must be continent. Semantic imprecision betrays a lack either of accurate information or of clear thinking.

—As every priest knows, it is not hatred, nor slander, nor rash judgment, nor vengeance, nor any of the really vicious sins against Christ, but it is the comparatively small change of fornication, birth control, and adolescent masturbation, "fun sins," that are the curse of the confessional. In fact, the people confess hardly anything else. But I mean to write on these subjects in a later chapter.

One has the feeling that if our Lord were to advise the bishops right now he would urge them to tighten up on charity and loosen up on sex. Charity is somehow kin to sex, and love lurks even in lust. There was great wisdom in the young people's advice back in the late sixties, to "Make love, not war," for sex, even wrong sex, is a unitive force, whereas hatred is divisive.

If the bishops could only recall the anguish caused in a teen-ager by scrupulosity, always over sex—and by his false conscience on masturbation!

Asked about her views on sex, the wonderful Alice Roosevelt

Longworth once said, "Let people do what they want, so long as they don't do it in the street and frighten the horses." And that, I think, is closer to the mind of Christ than our present stringent control, with everything banned "under penalty of mortal sin" except procreative acts between man and wife.

As our Lord predicted, there will always be conflict between him and the world. But in urging a review and revision of Catholic moral teaching on sex, we are not acting from self-interest nor lining ourselves up with the world, for we are not of the world. We are on His side, trying to reduce the volume of sin in the Church, arguing for that peace of mind and heart which is his will on our behalf.

This world *is* improving after all, and improvement will continue if all of us will only keep working at it. Slavery—in the sense of one person actually owning another—has pretty well been abolished throughout the world. Savagery has given place to kindness, selfishness to philanthropy. Men are no longer hanged for slight offenses, nor legally permitted to be tortured to make them give evidence. We have enlightened wage standards, and at least in civilized areas no one starves. Children are barred from working in factories and coal mines. Women finally did get the vote. And at last we have a Church that is slowly opening up to free discussion without danger of reprisal, that is gradually putting aside its fear of the facts.

10

Why Sex?

"Do you think masturbation is a common release from daily tensions?" Private and public responses to this question are almost always affirmative. Informed and even militant Catholics who generally seem to have the facts on dogma, moral and Church history at their fingertips, see another purpose—relief of tension—to be sufficient reason for engaging in sexual activity. Such Catholics have apparently and unconsciously abandoned as untenable the Catholic teaching that masturbation is a sin. They may know that a principal purpose of sex is generation, but they see other purposes as equally justifying.

Apart from considerations of sentiment and morality: When stimulated by friction of one kind or another, the human sex organs produce pleasure, relieve boredom, relax visceral tension, and tranquilize the nerves. In cooperation with a companion, the process can foster love and can even, on comparatively rare occasions and if a lot of bothersome but necessary conditions are brought together—it can even be used to make a baby. Bach did this twenty-two times, wearing out two successive wives; but most couples nowadays are content to make at most two or three babies in their lifetime.

Now what is unique about sex is that, except for reproduction, all these things happen simultaneously. Pregnancy may or may not result, but the fun, the pleasure, is there every time. As to pregnancy, by using our God-given intelligence, we have a choice when it comes to reproduction; it is now optional.

But even so, if you want to create a child with your orgasm, you really have to put your mind to it. You must marry a woman who will not mind nine months of pregnancy with all the awkwardness involved, the pains of childbirth, suckling the infant, washing and changing diapers. Both of you must be fertile and the sex act must coincide with the few days in the month when she is ovulating. You should have a regular job and a home of your own for privacy and later for the child to grow up in. Looking ahead, too, you can see twenty-one years of supporting that child through college at an overall estimated cost of $78,000. It is obviously something that can and should be done only a few times in a person's life.

But the strange thing is that, unlike the animals, human beings are always able to have sex. In fact, one might say that the man at least is always ready and eager for orgasm. He could impregnate a different woman every day for sixty years, which would give him 21,915 children, and it wouldn't hurt him in the least. On the contrary, the continual production of hormones would benefit his health. A few of the Moslem rulers have actually sired up to four hundred children. In a single orgasm an estimated 350,000,000 male sperm cells are ejaculated, of which at most only one is effective.

Viewing man, then, only as animal, procreation is the main purpose of sex, as it is with the beasts. But had God meant human sexuality only or even principally for reproduction, he would have set us up like the animals, the woman like a bitch capable of coupling only when in heat. So, taking the whole man as human being with mind, memory, and imagination, and his attendant anxieties and worries, one very important purpose of sex becomes relaxation of tensions. Because we always have them with us—our tensions—that is why a benign Providence has enabled man and woman to procure orgasm, alone or with another, any time at all.

As a tranquilizer, the orgasm beats Thorazine. A dose of Thorazine stuns one like a thump on the skull with a mallet, but orgasm is followed by a sense of delicious relaxation when everything feels grand.

One of the melancholy phenomena of our times is "nerves." In other days people were expected to go in for bodily austerities great and small, but in those times nerves were minimal; they are a product of our era. By striking down most of her laws on fasting and abstinence, the Church implicitly concedes that nerves are the austerities of our day and she urges us to bear with ourselves, our depression, gloom, moods, variability of temper. To bear with oneself is an act of great virtue. But when we are on the point of chewing out everyone in sight and making them miserable, perhaps telling off the boss and losing our job, an act of sex can settle the nerves like a snap of the fingers.

In college I had a classmate who used to get so tense at exam time that study became impossible. The only way he could quiet his nerves for study was by masturbation. He is a priest, now, and I don't know anything about his personal habits but I do know that he seems to be doing great work with no signs of tension.

Dr. Robert C. Sorensen reports, further, that "Hostilities toward others can be satisfied sexually through masturbation, as can desires for experiences people do not want to have in reality. . . . Some young people relieve their doubts and insecurities through the medium of masturbation."[1]

Sex also offers an interval of relief from boredom to people confined by circumstances to a limited area: prisoners, the military, students. Again, "Make love, not war." Wars come ultimately from a sort of universal boredom.

I have tried over the years and prayed for the grace to see something subjectively significant in orgasm, but for the life of me I can't. It does provide a catharsis of sorts, discharging all one's fantasies and half-formed desires, but what is that? It means only that orgasm is no more than a mental sneeze, a psychic release from pressure of the spirit. Others feel that orgasm lifts the spirit, bringing one closer to God; Nature; Knowledge.

For almost two thousand years the Church has taught that the only purpose of sex is procreation. But deep in the jungles of New Guinea there is an incredibly primitive tribe of aborigines. These poor people have been copulating through millions of years, thousands of generations since their Ur-grandparents, Adam and Eve, and they still don't know what it is that starts a baby. They have no idea what it is that gets a woman pregnant. Oh, they have intercourse, all right. They do that right handily. But why? For the pleasure of it. Just for the fun of it.

65141

How can we blame their ignorance? Pleasure is inevitable with copulation, whereas conception is a rather hit-or-miss affair because it depends on so many contingencies. How many people have tried and tried without success to have a child? But they certainly had sexual pleasure with each attempt.

What seems to stultify this insistence on procreation is the projected worldwide population; it looks as though we'll be standing hip-deep in babies before this decade is out. World population continues to increase at the rate of 93,000,000 people a year.[2] Latin America doubles its population every twenty-four years, Africa every twenty-seven years, and Southeast Asia every thirty years.[3] The whole world, America included, is on the way to becoming like India—one vast privy, steaming with urine and reeking of feces.

Originally a blessing, human fertility is now a curse. In *Sex in Our Time* (London, 1973), Chapman Pincher points out that the average man's lifelong output is forty-three pints of semen containing ten trillion spermatozoa, each capable of fertilizing an egg and thus producing another human being. By comparison, *The World Almanac* estimates the present population of the whole world at only three and one-half billion. With reference to the pope's recent ban on contraception: amidst all those riches of vitality, surely a few orgasms would not be missed? But the moralists waggle a prohibitive finger, and that is one more instance of where moral theology falls flat on its logical face.

The last time you climaxed, were you thinking of having a child? No, and neither will any of the approximately 27,000,000 boys and girls who will manipulate themselves before sleep tonight, and precious few of their 65,000,000 elders who will be sleeping together at the same time. No, we use our sex organs as God gave them to us: to drain the bladder, to express mutual love, occasionally just for the pleasure of climax, and to relieve tension or boredom. During intercourse we just might beget a child—but then again we might not.

The two most pressing of our biological drives are, first, self- and then race-preservation. First we must have food, water, warmth, and a secure place for sleep. But then as soon as we are safely snuggled in, we begin looking for a sexually compatible companion. Love is a pleasant but by no means essential accessory. Historically, the concept of romantic love did not develop, at least in Western civilization, until the late Middle Ages and early Renaissance. Conjugal love has always been at most a little flavoring added to the mixture. Basic was the orderly satisfaction of desire, protection and inheritance of property, and continuation of the family or dynasty.

Catholic philosophy sees it self-evident that there is no human appetite without its licit satisfaction, both of them, appetite and satisfaction, conferred on us by our loving Father in heaven. This is one of the arguments used in demonstrating human immortality. We get hungry; God has provided food. We thirst; there is drink. We are exhausted; we sleep. We get horny; we marry.* Because it's only human wanting to live forever, we aspire to immortality, we wish it were so, we hope it is so; therefore, it must be so. Not as conclusive as the metaphysical proof of St. Thomas—a suasion, an argument *ex convenientia* as the Scholastics would evaluate it—but it has its place.

The guiding star of my young years, Bishop Boyle,** was talking one night about his predecessor, a man who refused to dispense anyone at all for a mixed marriage.

"You know," the bishop said, "he was actually making a priest inaccessible to them just as surely as though they were alone on a desert island. Had they only known it, they could have exchanged consent before witnesses and it would have been a valid marriage even without the priest."

Now here we have a man and woman who have married because they want to enjoy the greatest possible intimacy with each other. They want to get naked and press skin against skin, belly to belly, and become two in one flesh. Prudence forbids their having a child for any one of a dozen possible good reasons. But the Holy Father says that they may not prevent conception by pill, condom,*** or IUD. What the pope has done has been to make that wife morally inaccessible to her husband—something he has no right to do: "What God hath joined together, let no man put asunder."[4]

When that man and his wife get hungry, they eat. When thirsty, they drink. When tired, they sleep. But when they get horny and their systems crawl with desire, the pope raises an admonitory finger, taking away their God-given right to intercourse. They can express their love and relax their tensions only by mutual masturba-

*I should have explained long before this that "horny" is an ancient and honorable word formed from the "horn," which was one of Old England's terms for the penis.

**Hugh C. Boyle, Bishop of Pittsburgh, 1921-1950.

***The rubber sheath covering the penis to preclude insemination, supposedly invented by a seventeenth-century Col. Condom of the British Grenadier Guards.

tion or perhaps by sodomy, oral or anal. But that would be a greater sin than birth control. Or would it?

Lo! the dilemma: a natural appetite that can't be gratified. Oh, it can be, all right, except that for this couple it would be, objectively at least, a heinous sin, whether contraception, masturbation, or sodomy. So at least says the Holy Father.

But if he is correct, then God is at fault. He blundered. He has made a dreadful mistake and left quite a long loose end flapping about in his creation: a natural appetite that can't be satisfied short of sin. Now God can't make a mistake, but the Holy Father can. His pencil has an eraser on it, just like ours. So therefore it must be the Holy Father who is mistaken, and therefore married couples can appease their sexual appetite any time at all and not only without sin but even virtuously.

Can anyone fault my logic?

Necessity knows no law. One does not sin merely by doing what one has to do. It is not theft when *in extremis* the destitute person helps himself to such food and raiment as he needs for survival.

As Cain and Abel matured, the only women available were their mother and their sisters. "We'll have to commit incest," they might have told each other, "and let the theologians straighten it out later."

As indeed the theologians did. They said that in the very beginning of the race God had no choice. He had to permit incest if the species was to continue. He also allowed polygamy. And divorce, "because of the hardness of your hearts," as our Lord explained to the Jews.[5] But then God tightened up.

Now there is no record in Scripture of God sending an angel to his people with these several messages and dispensations. He expected them to use their own common sense, starting with the need to populate the earth. "There are not enough men to go around? Well, then let one man service a plurality of women."

So God adapts his law to the needs of the current situation and the people accept the change.

Does not the same reasoning apply to our particular married couple? Like Cain and Abel, they look around for sexual relief but all they can see are forbidden means—pills, condoms, diaphragms—just as all that Cain and Abel had available were their mother and their sisters. There was, there is, no choice. Our couple have to use the forbidden means just as did Cain and Abel. May they not be equally confident of a dispensation?

As we shall see, the Holy Father's letter of July 29, 1968, *"Humanæ vitæ,"* was an authoritative but not an infallible document; he could have been wrong. If one is convinced that the pope was mistaken, then birth control is no more than a sin of disobedience. But if one becomes convinced, further, that the pope exceeded his authority in thus separating man and wife, then it's no sin at all.

As we have already seen, the dogmatic source of our guilt hang-up on sex is the traces of Gnosticism, Stoicism, and Cynicism which crept into the teaching of St. Paul and were then canonized by the Church, according to which all flesh is evil and sex is therefore suspect. Then came St. Augustine with his heritage of Manichaeism, reaffirming St. Paul's characterization of the body as evil. Theirs was the influence that formed our Catholic conscience on sex—yours and mine.

While it is true that guilt "is not a feeling but always a *conviction* of the mind—an often cold-blooded awareness of having transgressed the law of God in some way,"[6] such statements are more easily written and read than implemented. Our early training, "inoculation," has its roots deep in our emotions, and the emotions are notoriously evasive, in almost constant revolt against the intellect.

To rebut my reasoning that necessity knows no law, it will certainly be argued that in addition to intercourse with condom, the pill, sodomy, and masturbation, there is another way—that of continence with the help of God's grace.

True, the married couple have a claim on the grace of the sacrament, but grace is an intangible something that should be ruled out of discussions in moral theology. In practice we pray as though everything depended on God, but we think, speak, and act, as though everything depended on ourselves. We don't figure grace in as a ponderable factor. So far as I have felt or known it, I have never had an actual grace in my life—or if I did, I never recognized it.

So the problems of the Church with sex are not likely to be solved by invoking grace as a kind of *"deus ex machina."* It is also unreal to ask the advice of Aristotle (d. 322 B. C.) as interpreted by Aquinas (d. 1274), or to consult the fourth-century St. Augustine on behavioral problems of the twentieth century; for the terms of the problem (as well as Church teaching) have substantially changed. Rather, on the uncomplicated data of Scripture, we must shine the clear light of reason, common sense, and the intuitive knowledge of experience, aided by all the findings of the physical, psychological, and the behavioral sciences.

11

July 29, 1968

There is such an accumulation of superstition, suspicion, and official prejudice against sex within the Catholic Church that the possibility of liberating it seems hopeless. Fear, shame, and guilt are woven into our training through childhood and adolescence, at home and in school. It is implicit in the devotional attitudes of the Church, in the assumptions of hagiography and liturgy, in our official ascesis, re-stated by Pope Paul VI as recently as 1968 in his encyclical on birth control, *"Humanæ vitæ."* And who or what is to blame? Did the Church impose her morality on Western civilization or was it the other way around? Did Greco-Roman culture force her philosophies on the infant Church? It was more likely reciprocal.

Sadly, most Catholics somehow still think that priests and religious offer all their sexuality to God, not because it is good but because it is "dirty." In their own lives they are still trying to operate on the Augustinian principle that married couples should economize their sexual activities, using intercourse only for reproduction and to still the passions. But priests and religious are better than the rest because they're not Getting Any.

For them the Church is made up of first-, second-, and third-class citizens, with priests and religious at the top. After them come the married laity, and, last of all, the bachelors and spinsters.

The several religious orders and congregations all have different attitudes toward the vows of poverty and obedience. The Jesuits, for instance, are rigid on obedience while the Franciscans emphasize poverty and detachment. But none of them sit loose toward chastity. Of course, like pregnancy, chastity is indivisible. It's either all or none.*

Those in vows are at the top of the heap. After them come the parish clergy, vowed to celibacy,** with an oath of obedience to the bishop, but able to possess and acquire money (by inheritance, gifts, royalties, honoraria, etc.). On a level with the diocesan clergy are the "pious widows"—"pious" presumably because they too are doing without.

Thus the great Christian commonwealth is divided according to sexual usage. The run-of-the-mill Catholic tries to "squeeze through" by keeping the Ten Commandments and Church law, while the elite keep not only the Decalogue but also the Gospel counsels of our Lord recommending detachment and moral castration.

But this turns sanctity into a profession that excludes the married laity. He who is serious in his pursuit of perfection will not marry, Conversely, they who marry are obviously not seriously in pursuit of perfection. And the Church seems to agree, for you could count the number of married saints on your fingers. Most of them are royal personages, canonized as much for reasons of expediency as for their life and miracles.

According to Garry Wills:

> Terrible misconceptions were bred by this set of norms:
> saintly Christian laymen feeling they could never practice the
> full Gospel—indeed, had no right to do so; lax religious
> priests and nuns, feeling superior "by virtue of their state"; the
> reversal of all the Gospel's reversals—the "first" making

*Hegel referred to the three vows as "The pernicious ecclesiastical institutions of celibacy, voluntary pauperism, and laziness."

**Summarizing the theology of St. Thomas, Lord Russell says, in part: Divine law "forbids birth control, as being against nature; it does not, however, on this account forbid lifelong celibacy."—*A History of Western Philosophy* (New York: 1965), p. 459.

themselves first; the idea of competitive virtue reintroduced after Christ had mocked it in his own rôles of slave and clown and criminal, and said "the kingdom" is saved as a whole, not splintered into individuals. [1]

Dr. Wills points out that this division of the Christian commonwealth left no place for the unmarried laity—the bachelor uncle, the maiden aunt. As he puts it, "They had not chosen, but only been rejected—nobody wanted them. A nun was the pride of an old-fashioned Catholic family; an old maid was its shame."

Now for a review of what our Catholic ancestors had to put up with from churchmen telling them how to operate with each other in bed. Remember now that all this stuff was binding under penalty of mortal sin. This was no trifle like Christian charity or justice. This involved matter of the greatest importance—nothing less than CHASTITY, the megavirtue!

We had brought the subject down to St. Augustine and his dismal view of sexuality, which prevailed substantially right on to our twentieth century. Later theologians would only apply his principles to current situations as they arose.

—Caesarius of Arles (470-543) taught that the woman who took a sterilizing potion was guilty of as many murders as babies could have been born. (Was this "sterilizing potion" the sixth-century equivalent of our present-day pill?) The only legitimate sterility for a woman was complete abstinence, with her husband's consent.

—St. Martin of Braga (d. 579) extended the condemnation of abortion after fornication to include contraception within marriage. The two crimes appeared similar to him. [2]

—We have already seen how Pope St. Gregory the Great went even farther than St. Augustine. Not only was pleasure an illicit motive but if pleasure was felt, the action was vitiated and the couple sinned at least venially.

—Up to 600, no pope had condemned contraception. Much, much later, Sixtus V (1521-1590) condemned it, but his action was revoked two years later by his successor, Gregory XIV. Thus, until the encyclical *"Casti connubii"* of Pius XI in 1930, there was no extant papal rejection of contraception.

—Our information on moral theology during the dark ages,

600-1100, is drawn largely from the "Penitentials," books advising confessors what penance to assign for the various sins. The handbooks compiled during this era refer to "potions" and withdrawal. All of them regard sterile intercourse as sinful, but coitus with one's pregnant wife is not as sinful as with a barren wife.

—During the thirteenth century the Church was troubled by the "Clean Ones," the Cathari, who slammed down the lid on all sex as "dirty." So the Church rephrased the reasoning of St. Augustine, especially in the works of Yves of Chartres and of Peter Lombard. It was during this century that Innocent III added his authority to Gregory the Great's mistaken idea that any pleasure in marriage is always a sin.

—From the fourth to the thirteenth century contraception was regarded as a kind of murder. St. Albert the Great (1193-1280) fought this idea, as did his saintly student Thomas Aquinas (1225?-1274), but the old superstition persisted right down to the time of the Roman Catechism in 1566. It was finally laid to rest once for all by the imposing authority of St. Alphonsus Liguori in the eighteenth century.

—Aquinas, ever the gentleman, thought that the pleasure of marital sex was only venial if the man treated his wife as a wife—with honor, respect, and fidelity; but such pleasure was mortally sinful if he dishonored his wife, for in that case he had lost control of both reason and nature.

—The female ovum was not discovered under the microscope until the early part of the nineteenth century. Until then, people had had the idea that the woman contributed hardly anything to the process of generation. She lay passive, the fertile field in which the man sowed his sperm, the active element. She was nothing more than a living incubator.

—From the time of St. Thomas until 1450, there was no Scripture text unanimously accepted as condemning contraception: no conciliar decrees; no explicit papal teaching. The only authorities that could be quoted were cannon law and St. Augustine. But all agreed that the pleasure of sex in marriage was sinful. Then come Martin Le Maistre (1432-1481) of Paris, teaching that a man might licitly have intercourse with his wife:

1. To father a child;
2. To quench the passion of lust;
3. To procure physical health and spiritual tranquility; and
4. In moderate quest of pleasure.

His ideas gradually took hold.

—In 1588 Sixtus V condemned abortion and contraception as homicide, imposing on the guilty an excommunication reserved to the Holy See. This was the first official condemnation of contraception, and it was formally rescinded by Gregory XIV two years later.

—The subject of birth control first became a popular issue with the publication of *An Essay on the Principle of Population* by Thomas R. Malthus (1766-1834) in 1798. He advanced the possibility that the population of the world might one day exceed the food supply. But his remedy was sexual abstinence rather than contraception. It was his followers who proposed artificial birth control: Jeremy Bentham, James Mill, Francis Place, Robert Dale Owen, and Charles Knowlton.

At this time, however, Rome was less interested in Protestant England than in Catholic France, where birth control seemed to be depopulating the country.

—The nineteenth century was a desert so far as theological speculation was concerned. There was not one writer of eminence —only a multitude of journeymen compiling textbooks for the instruction of seminarians, one author copying from another and all of them quoting St. Alphonsus.

—In 1880 Leo XIII (1810-1903) published his encyclical on marriage, *"Arcanum divinæ sapientiæ,"* with no mention at all of birth control.

—But by 1900 the use of mechanical and chemical methods of birth control was spreading rapidly. This was due to a change in the medical climate and to advancing research in science, sociology, and economics.

—If there was any one man apart from St. Augustine who was responsible however remotely for Paul VI's opposition to contraception, it was the charismatic Belgian Jesuit, Arthur Vermeersch. He literally made a career of fighting birth control. He made it his personal crusade and he was an able strategist. Alarmed at the falling birth rate in France and Belgium, he inspired the Belgian episcopate to issue a pastoral letter denouncing contraception on June 2, 1909. Other hierarchies followed:

Germany	August 20, 1913
Austria	January 23, 1919
France	May 7, 1919
United States	September 26, 1919

By underwriting Fr. Vermeersch's opinion in 1916, the Sacred Penitentiary had given it official status. By 1930 he was the leading moral theologian in Rome when, on August 14, the Church of England through its hierarchy meeting at Lambeth approved contraception. Pius XI found this development disturbing. Perhaps equally so was an article in the influential German monthly, *Hochland*, urging the revision of Church teaching on birth control. The Holy Father had also been told that parish priests were careless about enforcing the principles on contraception.

So he and Fr. Vermeersch put their heads together and produced the encyclical *"Casti connubii"* on Christian marriage, published December 30, 1930—"for thirty-eight years the most solemn and most complete presentation of the papal teachings concerning birth control. It was also the most authoritative teaching of the Church on the subject."[3]

(I had my years of undergraduate theology during this period, when our textbook declared—and the instructor agreed—that the wife whose husband approached her with a condom must resist "like a virgin under assault"—*"tamquam virgo oppressa."*—"Rush to the window and call for help, I suppose," was one comment heard by Frank Sheed.[4])

—The possibility of exploiting the wife's menstrual cycle as a means of birth control had been developed with some precision by Kysuaku Ogino (Japan, 1924) and Hermann Knaus (Austria, 1929). But apparently the Holy Father was not aware of this, nor was it widely known in Europe. There had been talk of it back in 1845 with the presentation of a study on the subject by Felix Archimedes Pouchet, but that was all. So, merely in passing, Pius XI approved rhythm—thereby not only standing St. Augustine on his head but at the same time necessitating a whole new line of argument by the antisex people.

Hitherto the ban on birth control had been based on the psychology of the agents: What was their intention while coupling? Did they sincerely want to make a baby, or were they at least resigned to accepting whatever the Lord might send? Essentially: *Did they have the right intention?*

But now the focus of morality shifted from the subjective to the objective, to "the integrity of the act." It must be clean, natural, wholesome intercourse, the way the animals do it. The seed must be able to flow freely into the womb without interruption by rubber, plastic, or metal contraption of any sort.—"You never saw a dog sit up and slip on a condom before mounting his bitch, did you? Well, then—!" (But then no one has ever seen a dog read a newspaper either.)

Vermeersch, at least, stuck to his guns, but the rest soon fell in line.

—Speaking to a group of Italian midwives, October 29, 1951, Pius XII frankly and explicitly approved the use of rhythm, and a month later, November 26, he expressed the wish that medical science would make the method more certain. As for pleasure, he said that one "may lawfully seek and accept it."

—The casual reader has likely missed the fact that so far none of the Church teachers has spoken of love in connection with sex. It has all been "procreation," "illicit pleasure," "release of tension." But nowadays romantic love and sexuality are practically inseparable. There is first "calf " love, then serious dating beneath a June moon with scent of honeysuckle, and finally courtship in full earnest, all building toward the consummation of love by copulation on the wedding night. Masturbation is derided as immature, and sex with prostitutes is disdained as bereft of love. Even the worldlings, even *Playboy*, share that attitude, an attitude now known among theologians as "personalism."

"Dietrich von Hildebrand in lectures given in Innsbruck in 1925 was the first great Catholic teacher of personalism," according to Fr. Sommer. "He stated that the marital act has only one function, namely procreation. But he held that it also possesses a special meaning for man as the expression and fulfillment of conjugal love and community of life in marriage. Moreover, he maintained that the marital act participates in a certain way in the sacramental meaning of marriage."[5]

For the first time in a pontifical document, the idea of copulation as an expression of love was mentioned when in his *"Casti connubii"* Pius XI listed among the several purposes of sex the development of mutual love.[6]

—Perhaps encouraged by this, in 1935 a German parish priest, Herbert Doms, published his book, *The Meaning and End of Marriage*, contending that the first purpose of sex in marriage is not procreation but sanctification. The pumping of sterile seed into a barren or a pregnant woman is futile from the aspect of making babies. Why, then, is it permissible? Because, said Fr. Doms, it helps the couple save their souls. It advances the work of their salvation.

But the Holy Office squelched Fr. Doms and quashed his proposition on April 1, 1944, with a condemnation of all those who deny that the first purpose of marriage is the procreation and education of children or who teach that the secondary purposes are not essentially subordinate to the primary purpose but are just as important as, and independent of, the primary purpose.

(Before Vatican II, the Holy Office was practically identified in the minds of churchmen with the Supreme Pontiff. Hence its decisions and decrees were final.)

It was self-evident that the newly discovered technique of artificial insemination could not possibly fit in with the integrity-of-the-act doctrine, but in condemning it as he did in 1949, 1951, and 1956, Pius XII gave warm support to the personalist rationale of Hildebrand and Doms. The family is not a mere biological laboratory, he said, but the marital act in its natural structure is a personal act, a simultaneous and immediate cooperation between the spouses.

Personalism was finally approved by Vatican II.

—Meanwhile, an antifertility pill, Hesperidine, had been synthesized in 1952. It was followed by a second type of pill in 1953 and they first appeared on the market in this country in 1960. For the first time in history, a happy society, based on power over nature, was within the grasp of men.

But Pius XII, September 12, 1958, said that the pill might be used only in therapy. Any use to prevent conception was "intrinsically evil." There remained related problems, however—problems not touched on by the Holy Father, and these were freely discussed among the theologians: e.g., use of the pill to regulate the menstrual cycle, before menopause, during lactation, after childbirth, for psychological sicknesses, in case of expected rape, even to cure sterility.[7]

—For five years Pius XII's ban on the pill stood unchallenged. Then in 1963 the American physician John Rock dropped a bomb with his book, *The Time Has Come*, defending the pill. He met the theologians on their own ground with cogent logic.:

My reasoning is based, in part, on the fact that the rhythm method, which is sanctioned by the Church, depends precisely on the secretion of progesterone from the ovaries, which action these compounds merely duplicate. It is progesterone, in the healthy woman, that prevents ovulation and establishes the pre- and post-menstrual "safe period." The physiology underlying the spontaneous "safe period" is identical to that initiated by the steroid compounds and is equally harmless to the individual. Indeed, the use of the compounds for fertility control may be characterized as a "pill-established safe period" and would seem to carry the same moral implications. [8]

Despite Pius XII's emphatic rejection of the pill in 1958, discussion continued as though the question were still open. Bishop W. M. Bekkers (d. 1966) of Den Bosch defended the pill on Netherlands television, March 21, 1963, thereby touching off wide-scale debate. On August 10, 1963, the Dutch hierarchy followed with an ambiguous statement. Two Dutch Dominicans, William van der Marck and Edouard Schillebeeckx spoke up for the pill, as did Fr. Louis Janssens, professor of moral theology at Louvain. As was to be expected, the liberal position was sharply controverted by conservative theologians here and abroad—in this country by men like the late Redemptorist Fr. Francis J. Connell of the Catholic University and the Jesuit Frs. Gerald Kelly and John C. Ford.

—Perhaps to damp down discussion, Paul VI announced in June 1964 that the Church was investigating and researching the problem of contraception. In the meantime, he said, the norms laid down by Pius XII were still in force. He repeated this statement in October 1966: The norms of Pius XII still held, but this time he added, "At least until we feel obliged in conscience to change them."

—During the years just before Vatican II, statements rejecting contraception were issued by the national hierarchies as follows:

India	November, 1957
United States	November 29, 1959
France	March 3, 1961
England (through Cardinal Heenan)	March 7, 1964
John XXIII, in *"Mater et magistra"*	1961
Paul VI, radio message	Christmas, 1963
Paul VI, to the UN	October 3, 1965

—At Vatican II Cardinals Alfrink, Léger, and Suenens, and Patriarch Maximos IV, all made speeches urging that love be made the equal of procreation as the first purpose of marriage.

—Pope John had appointed a commission to study the matter of the pill. In December, 1965, Paul VI enlarged this commission to a total of sixty-five members: clergy and laity (including women), experts in theology, medicine, economics, demography, sociology, and for practical advice, some married couples.

—December 7, 1965, Vatican II ratified the Pastoral Constitution on *The Church in the Modern World*, discussing at some length the relationship between sex and love in marriage and the wonderful power of creating and educating children. It speaks of illicit means of birth control such as abortion and infanticide, and then goes on to say that "sons of the Church may not undertake methods of procreation found blameworthy by the teaching authority of the Church in its unfolding of the divine law." A footnote states that questions requiring further investigation have by command of the Holy Father been handed over to the Commission on the Problems of the Family, Population, and Births. "With the doctrine of the magisterium in this state, this sacred Synod does not intend to propose concrete solutions immediately."

—The commission was in session from April 18 to June 9, 1966, when it presented a majority and a minority report to His Holiness.

The majority in turn submitted two papers: the one explaining their decision in favor of birth control, the other anticipating and refuting objections. They based their reasoning mainly on the right and duty of man to intervene in natural processes, including generation, to achieve proper human goals. They did not distinguish between mechanical and chemical means of intervention.

The minority held to the traditional teaching as *a priori* irreformable. Any change would only impair the confidence of the faithful in the Church's reliability as a guide in matters moral. It would also point the way to further "moral abuses."

The vote: 61 to 4 in favor of birth control.

—July 29, 1968. Pope Paul VI issued his encyclical *"Humanae vitae"* siding with the minority against any form of birth control except rhythm.

12

Pope vs. Church

The child looked up at us with tragic eyes—big blue eyes they were, beneath a crown of golden hair. But the sight of him there as he lay in the crib was breath-catching, for there did not seem to be a safe piece of skin on his body. There was a green and purple bruise beneath each eye and his right arm was in a cast taped across his chest.

"Roll over, Danny," said Sister Rita. As he lay on his stomach, Sister lifted his gown to show me his back. It was crisscrossed with welts and scars from his neck to his knees. Danny was between four and five years old.

"Perhaps you'd give him your blessing, Father," she said.

The visit to Danny's crib had been occasioned by my quotation of the pious fallacy that "There is no such thing as an 'unwanted child.' "

Sister Rita had registered emphatic disagreement. "The 'battered child' is the 'unwanted child,' " she had said, and she had made her point with Danny.

"What do people say when they hand you a child in that condition?" I asked. "How do they explain it?"

"Oh," she said, "they mumble something about how the boy fell down the cellar steps or maybe fell out of bed. It's usually a 'fall.' But I always get right to the point and ask them why in the name of God they have children at all if they don't want them, don't love them, and won't take care of them."

"And what do they say?"

"Well, take Danny's father. He said, 'My old lady don't hold for birth control. She's a strict Catholic. So if I want sex I gotta do it straight or I don't get none. We already had four kids and then Danny came and I guess we got to drinkin' too much. . . .' "

Yes, and Danny's mother could have quoted Pope Paul VI at her "old man" in support of her position, for in his encyclical *"Humanae vitae,"* published July 29, 1968, he threw the whole force of his authority as chief teacher and principal theologian of the Church against every form of mechanical and chemical birth prevention.

His tragically mistaken decision had awesome consequences, instantly shattering the good faith of millions upon millions of Catholics, producing in them a false conscience on birth control that will undoubtedly, according to their beliefs, cost them their eternal happiness. Such people will imagine they are giving grievous offense to God each time they yield to common sense urging them to use a sheath or get on the pill before intercourse. Objectively, of course, it will not be a sin.

Other results of *"Humanae vitae"* will be the lengthening procession of unwanted and battered children, increasing masses of Asians and Indians starving to death, and increasing shortages throughout the entire world.

A classic protest against birth control: "If you were to ask Danny whether he preferred living as a battered child to not living at all, he would certainly choose life." "Certainly"? I'm not so sure. Is existence inevitably preferable to nonexistence? Our Lord spoke of at least one instance where "it would have been better for that man if he had never been born,"[1] and I have a friend, a good and devout priest, who would rather not have been born at all than be faced as he is now with even the least possibility of everlasting damnation. Hell is so vividly real to the man of faith.*

In this matter of birth control, what Pope Paul did was to appoint a commission of sixty-five experts and then go against their

---

*In his *Eminent Victorians*, Lytton Strachey describes at length Cardinal Manning's lifelong fear of hell.

advice. Like the man who takes his car to the motor clinic—the mechanics check it over with their instruments, they test-drive it, they poke, pry, and prod here and there, and they finally come up with the verdict: it needs a new battery, a fan belt, and a valve job. The man listens, shrugs his shoulders, says, "I don't think so," and drives off. So why did he come around in the first place? And why did Pope Paul appoint a commission at all if he did not intend to pay them heed?

Indeed, why did he not heed their advice? Because, although they were absolutely right and he knew it, he was afraid that if he endorsed their judgment his predecessors might lose face—Pius XI, Pius XII, John XXIII—and so, to prop up a mistaken doctrine, he had to fall back on a tatterdemalion hypothesis that had been discredited at least a whole century before the Battle of Bunker Hill.

The official ban on artificial birth control was only thirty-eight years old, and yet Pope Paul was afraid to reverse it lest he further discredit the already badly frayed dogma of infallibility. By his timidity, however, he did even greater harm to the Church, for the reasons that favor contraception in most cases are self-evident and universally acknowledged, while his reasons against birth control have been knocked down, pushed over, and disproved times without number. We have already seen several disproofs and counter-arguments in Chapter X, "Why Sex?" But they throng the mind, there are so many of them. A few more:

—The genitalia: principally an organ of generation? Why not principally an instrument of love? Who knows? Our other organs are seldom meant for one purpose only. The mouth, for instance: is it principally for eating—or for speaking?

—The Holy Father says that, in general, we do not have unlimited dominion over our body—which body includes the generative faculty. But we do have unlimited right to dispose of our body and its organs for our own and the common good. A case can even be made for the *kamikaze* pilots of World War II. With reasonable cause, we are free to use our body and its organs as we think fit, even against their obvious material purpose, without sin, as by walking on our hands or standing on our head. The penis itself may be amputated for cause.

—For total birth control, marriage may deliberately be postponed until past the climacteric.

—We are told that it is a sin to eat or drink except for nourishment (in which case a box of chocolates has scarcely any right to existence in the Christian commonwealth). But compare excess in food and drink with sexual incontinence. It is practically impossible to commit a *grievous* sin of gluttony or intemperance, whereas we are told that objectively it is impossible to commit a *light* sin against the Megavirtue.[2]

In the encyclical, Pope Paul says he rejected the recommendation of his commission because it was not made unanimously. But on such a weighty and controversial issue, involving as it did so many prudential considerations, a vote of 61-4 must surely be adjudged morally unanimous. But the pope said that the majority were going against what the Church had taught "with constant firmness."

"With constant firmness" for only thirty-eight years! Before that, the question had never been proposed to the Holy See for resolution.

The basis of his decision against sex, the pope says, is not revelation but natural law—which he nevertheless accords the probative force of revelation, and which is presumably self-evident even to the uneducated, but which, strangely, was not at all evident to the sixty-one experts who voted in favor of sex. But the concession is there: the pope's ban on birth control is a theological conclusion rather than revealed doctrine.

The Holy Father thanks everyone for being so helpful but says that in the end he had to solve the problem all by himself: *L'église c'est moi*—the principle of Boniface VIII, revived by St. Pius X, used now by Paul VI. His was an "agonizing" decision. So why didn't he share it? Obviously, because no one else agreed with him. His was a singular opinion.

The perceptive reader will observe that in *"Humanæ vitæ"* as in practically all official Church documents, there is a constant and only thinly veiled bias against sex. In this case, for instance, science is odious and must be resisted whenever it extends the use of sex within marriage, but that same science is praised whenever it limits the use of sex.[3]

Here is Pope Paul's basic reasoning: "natural acts" have their unity from a singleness of aim to which all side effects or uses must be subordinated as secondary. Unless these secondary uses subserve the primary function, they are disordered and unnatural.

You see, we are back at casuistry, as I discussed it in connection with the fundamental option. Here we are, scrutinizing the physical, biological act of copulation without any reference to the mind of the lovers, trying to give it moral significance, and to hell with all other considerations! We are to judge the morality of intercourse merely from its animal aspects. In other words, we are to do it like the jackasses. They are to be our pattern, for—having no intelligence —they are bound to do it "according to nature."

In our Catholic theology, sex is the only area in which such theology with its compulsory subordination of side effects is strictly applied. We eat to live, true, but once a week Rotary and Kiwanis eat rather for fellowship. We eat to live, yes, but at mass we eat and drink to receive grace.

Nowhere is the antisex bias of the Holy See more evident than in its reaction to recent improvements in techniques of contraception. From the time of St. Augustine in the fourth century, although there were no normative statements made by the Sovereign Pontiffs, the criterion of morality was always subjective: did the married couple have reproductive intent?

Then when Pius XI, almost inadvertently, opened the door to rhythm just a little in 1930 and Pius XII later opened it all the way, saying that reproductive intent was no longer necessary, the antisex people cooked up their theory of the "integrity of the act," i.e., it has to be done "naturally," the way the rabbits and roosters do it.

One can only imagine the panic of the antisex people when they first heard about the pill, for the pill leaves the sex act intact: no condom, no withdrawal, no diaphragm—easy does it. "Christ Almighty! Now people will be able to have as much sex as they want and still go to communion every day. There won't be any sins to absolve. We'll be out of business. We can't have it! What'll we do? What can we say?"

Well, they certainly couldn't switch back to the doctrine of intent. Pius XI had dropped that overboard back in 1930. Still, some sort of rationale had to be worked out to keep the layman's fingers out of the jampot. We got that rationale with *"Humanæ vitæ."*

To read between the lines, Pope Paul wants husbands and wives to live within marriage like monks and nuns, like the Blessed Mother and St. Joseph. All his praise of marriage as a legitimate state in life with its own distinct dignity is only so much ritualistic cant. To Pope Paul VI marriage is no more than "a second-class form of monasticism."[4]

The present controversy over birth control is only one battle in the perpetual war between conservatives and liberals, the establishment and the outsiders, the have's and the have-nots. Those in power can see any change in the status quo only as a threat. Control of sexual mores is after all a lever of power and people do not easily renounce power. (Think of the perpetual Italian majority in the College of Cardinals.) Control of sexual and family mores and social attitudes toward sexuality is vital for general control of society, for its maintenance as now structured, and for the preservation of an economic system which favors those on top. And extending areas of sin also extends Church jurisdiction.

Nowadays, with the Church considered merely as an institution, there seems to be a certain degree of confusion between ends and means. An institution is founded for a certain purpose. But then there is always the danger that with the passing of time the original purpose will be forgotten and the institution itself turned into the purpose. The Russian revolution was meant to bring freedom to workers and peasants. But the institutionalists got busy, and means and ends were reversed, so that the USSR became the *end* with workers and peasants the *means.*

To harmonize with the popular image of the Church as immutable, eternal truth, all changes in creed and code must be introduced as "clarifications, elucidations of what has always been said." There must always be a precedent. That was the problem Pope Paul VI faced with his advisory commission on birth control. They were urging him to declare that what had almost universally been considered seriously sinful by the theologians had actually been quite virtuous.

And this he refused to do. He preferred the good of the institution to the good of souls. And—he was apparently amazed at this —the whole world jumped to its feet and denounced the fraud; it was too obvious. Transparent. By bulldozing the truth he had plainly stultified the Church.

Final causality, the basis of the Holy Father's reasoning, had been a museum piece in the world's house of philosophy since the time of Descartes, Newton, and Hume. His implication that the whole purpose of life is the continuation of life, and that that continuation, reproduction, is not just *a* good but *the supreme and absolute good* before which all else—personal, family, societal good—must yield: well, it was literally unbelieveable. Vatican II, by noting that its insistence on the procreative and educative good of marriage did not imply that it was "putting second the other ends of marriage," had only a few years earlier tacitly rejected that hierarchy of purposes in marriage now assumed by the pope in *"Humanæ vitæ."*

"The human race has passed from a rather static concept of reality to a more dynamic, evolutionary one," the council had declared,[5] and theology is not "a closed and completed canon of immutable knowledge."[6]

When we read our Holy Father's effort to derive a morality of sex from its animal aspects alone, we feel we must remind him—as if he did not know—that we are more than brutes and beasts and that our free moral acts are to be ruled therefore not merely by the laws of biology but as in everything else by right reason as well.

It is the old reality of mind over matter. Reason has enabled us to control practically all the functions of our body: we choose the foods we eat, varying them according to taste and needs; we physic ourselves and stop ourselves up; we use hypnotics for sleep and amphetamines to stay alert; there are anorectics to inhibit the appetite and anaphrodisiacs to cool the blood. And then, of course, there is the pill to suppress ovulation. If it is licit to use physics, paregoric, Seconal, Dexedrine, liquor, Preludin, all of which modify the organism in one way or another, why not the pill?

"Because it frustrates a possible goal of nature"? But "frustration of nature, far from being immoral, is man's vocation." "Is man bid to live only according to nature? Hardly, else he would go through life naked, eating uncooked hay, and sleeping in the forest. Live according to reason? Obviously, else why does man clothe himself with an artificial skin of wool, sit in a chair artificially carved from the forest, and eat cooked hay artificially fortified with vitamins?"[7]

The breakfast egg is the ovum of a verminous barnyard fowl. Is it not against nature to steal such things from under the hen and actually *eat* them?

"Because it frustrates a possible goal of nature"? In that case, "How can it be right to air-condition a room, plow a field, cut one's hair, transplant a kidney, give or take a blood transfusion, dam a river, or prolong life with chemicals and other devices?"[8]

Philosophically, at least, man's superiority to the other animals lies precisely in his unique ability to mold his environment instead of being molded by it. The power to reason and think is God's greatest gift, enabling us, alone of all God's creatures, consciously to direct our own destiny. We have the power to stop all procreation, individually by birth control, pandemically by radiation. And we have this power only because our nature includes rationality. In fact, it was God himself who gave man control over his own fertility, acting providentially at a time when birth control is practically an ethical imperative.*

The truth is that whatever progress we have made as a civilization has been at the expense of nature and by the use of so-called unnatural methods. If contraception is "unnatural" then so is TV, auto, phone, and every other device ever discovered to improve and raise the lot of man. In fact, all progress can be said to be a substitute of unnatural methods for nature's original ones. [9]

The Holy Father had admitted that he had had to make the decision against sex on his own and so now he was stuck with it—one man against the whole Church, for 600,000,000 Catholics immediately recognized "*Humanæ vitæ*" as a theological absurdity. He had said equivalently that white is black, and there was an instant, instinctive revulsion on the part of the Church. As we shall see, professional theologians protested by the hundreds, and when their superiors attempted reprisals, a declaration on the freedom of theology was addressed to the Roman authorities by first 40 and then by 1,360 professors of theology over the whole world. [10]

Now, when there is a contradiction between pope and Church, where is truth to be found? What happens when the whole Church rejects the judgment of the Holy Father in a serious matter? This is no longer a matter of speculation. The situation exists right now.

Newman had based his conversion on his conviction that "the whole world can't be wrong." ("*Securus judicat orbis terrarum.*") This is by no means mere poll taking or majority vote on vital truths. When theologians speak of "the mind of the faithful" (*sensus fidelium*) they intend to emphasize the presence of the Holy Spirit in the company of the believers.

Vatican II acknowledged this special charism, this instinct for truth, when the Fathers decreed: "Because they are anointed by the Holy One (cf. John 2:20-27), the faithful as a body cannot err in their belief. They manifest this special prerogative of theirs by means of a supernatural sense of faith that belongs to the people as a whole, when 'from the bishops down to the last believer,' they show universal agreement in matters of faith and morals." [11]

---

*The pill is a progesterone hormone medication. Whereas the condom and diaphragm (IUD, for Intra-Uterine Device) are anti-conceptive, the pill is a-conceptive. "Anti-conceptive" relates to the sex act itself, preventing implantation, while "a-conceptive" does not. It means that there is no interference with fertility as such, but rather a regulation of fertility, a matter of physiology.

"Humanæ vitæ" was released July 29, 1968. At ten o'clock next morning a Statement of Dissent was handed to the press in the name of eighty-seven leading American theologians, including seven full-time faculty members from Catholic University, as well as theologians representing St. Mary's Seminary, Baltimore, Fordham, Manhattan, Notre Dame, St. John's Collegeville, St. John's Jamaica, St. Bonaventure, Seton Hall, the Catholic Theological Union of Chicago, Pope John XXIII National Seminary, St. Meinrad School of Theology, and Christ the King Seminary.

It was repeatedly explained to the reporters that "the Statement of Dissent was not a rebellion or a revolution but a loyal act of theological interpretation by loyal Roman Catholics who accept the Petrine office in the Church."[12]

Eventually, a total of 700 American Catholic theologians associated themselves with the dissent. These gentlemen—indeed, the great majority of theologians—regard all encyclicals as open to mistake. They are not *ex cathedra* definitions. However, like decrees of the sacred congregations, they call for total compliance on the part of Catholics. Hence, one can be a loyal Catholic with true Catholic respect for the Holy Father and still hold that he is wrong on birth control. To quote Pope St. Gregory the Great: "The Church, instructed by the teaching of humility, does not command as though by authority, but persuades by reason."

How strict is the authority of an encyclical? What exactly is its power to bind? Well, the Holy Father is no ordinary teacher. His teaching authority comes from Christ and that authority can require assent even when his reasons are not convincing in themselves. Further, such assent must be internal and sincere. This is called "religious" assent. Merely external conformity or respectful silence is not enough.

But there is a still higher type: the assent of "divine faith." While religious assent rests on the authority of the Holy Father's teaching office, assent of divine faith is based on the unfailing authority of God revealing. While divine faith is supremely firm, internal religious assent is not absolutely certain, not supremely firm, not metaphysically but only "morally" certain, i.e., it rests on human reason judging data provided by human scholarship.*

And if the Holy Father should be mistaken? What then of

---

*Metaphysically certain: The whole is greater than any of its parts. Naturally certain: Water freezes at 32° Fahrenheit. Morally certain: Hitler was a bad man.

religious assent? First, presumption of right is on the side of the pope. But then, to the point, here are a few opinions of the professional theologians:

Assent is mandatory "unless by an equal or superior authority the Church should decree otherwise."—J. Salaverri.

". . . unless the Church should at some time decide otherwise or unless the contrary should become evident."—F. A. Sullivan.

". . . unless a grave suspicion should arise that the presumption is not verified."—L. Lercher.

". . . so long as it does not become positively clear that they are wrong . . . assent is prudently suspended when there first appear sufficient motives for doubting."—C. Pesch.

It is licit to dissent, to doubt or to continue to regard the opposite opinion as probable "if the decree should appear to someone to be certainly false or to be opposed to so solid a reason that the force of this reason cannot be shattered even by the weight of the sacred authority."—J. Straub.

"Religious assent is owed when there is nothing which could prudently persuade one to suspend his assent. The assent is morally certain; therefore, should motives appear, whether they be true or false (but from inculpable error), which persuade one to a different view, then in those circumstances the will would not act imprudently in suspending assent."—D. Palmieri.

Thus, while the Catholic "is expected to comply with papal teaching however it is communicated, his assent is, by definition, proportionate to the context and content of the pope's expression."[13]

In sum, the Catholic could have reason enough to justify withholding assent to a teaching of the ordinary magisterium of the pope.

The reaction of the American bishops to *"Humanæ vitæ"* was predictable. Our hierarchy is for the most part an alumni association of the North American College in Rome, which for that reason might better be called the College of the American Apostles. Our bishops form an exclusive gentlemen's club, practically all of whom wear the old school tie and associate on a first-name basis.

Actually, the North American College is not really a college at all; it is a boardinghouse with chapel attached. The chosen souls living there have their classes at the Gregorian University, where the lecture system is used and there is no attendance check. Lectures are given in a hall accommodating hundreds of students of every nation. They are given in Latin by specialists from France, Germany, Ireland, Spain, Italy—every country of the Christian world.

Now the average American boy finds fluency in Latin all but impossible and conversation in Latin metaphysically impossible. What then is he to make of Latin discourse spoken rapidly through a French nose or pushed through the thick vocal chords of a Bavarian? He gives up, of course, and spends his time in a back row catching up on *Time* and *Newsweek*.

But he need not fear failure, for there are no written examinations. These are conducted orally twice a year. And a few weeks in advance, coaches arrive at the college, armed with the questions to be asked. These same questions have been asked since the "Greg" was founded by the first Jesuits in the sixteenth century. The boys memorize the answers and pass. It's rather like the routine for passing the driver's test here in the United States. You get the little booklet ahead of time, read it over a few times, and then go out and let the examiner do his worst.*

There are no celebrated philosophers or theologians from the College. The students there seldom if ever think of the sacred sciences as a vocation, teaching and writing. I dare say there is not one of them who does not return fully expecting eventually to be made a bishop. And, pray, what need has a bishop of theology? They are good-living men, talented, cultured, generally good businessmen.

And, sure enough, while his stateside classmates are sent as curates to the boondocks, our Romano is appointed assistant chancellor in charge, perhaps, of youth work. Not much, to be sure, but never mind—he has his foot on the ladder and he has lunch every day with His Excellency.

Our Romano is ideal for the chancery: handsome, well-groomed, with a reflective face that looks as though it might be contemplating the Trinity when actually he is only wondering what tonight's dessert will be. With his superiors he is polite to the point of obsequiousness, always ready with a match for their cigar, a properly mortified chuckle at their witticisms.** Promotion is inevitable.

His first diocese is Frozen City, Alaska, with 11 priests and 23,000 Catholics. At this juncture an age-old principle of the Roman

---

*Hence the saying among churchmen: *"Doctor Romanus, asinus Germanus."*

**It has been said that bishops have no friends, but only courtiers. And they never hear the truth.

Church comes into play: If he ever expects to be promoted out of Frozen City, *he must remain noncontroversial.* Unfriendly publicity is fatal to the career of the aspiring bishop. To use computer talk, then, your usual bishop is programmed. He is extremely sensitive to pressure. If two conflicting petitions reach his desk, you may be sure that the one with more signatures will get the nod.

Why so? Because the hierarchy have a vested interest in the status quo. They have a good thing going for themselves. A bishopric is a fine, fat job. So "Let's not shake the plum tree, boys. Just relax and enjoy."

If the typical American hierarch, then, were to receive a directive from the Holy See ordering that as of the first of next year the Holy Sacrifice was to be confected with gingersnaps and lemonade rather than bread and wine, he would immediately begin inquiring about discounts on lemons purchased wholesale. He might direct his chancellor to inquire of the appropriate Roman congregation just how much sugar should be used and whether in case of necessity the use of other citrus fruits would impair validity.

Being American, probably of Irish descent, trained in Rome, and with a horror of controversy, it would not occur to him to ponder the substance of the document, to wonder if perhaps His Holiness had not gone round the twist. This, I say, would be the American, but not the French, Dutch, Belgian, nor even Cardinal Heenan's reaction. They are more philosophical over there, better trained in theology, accustomed to examine carefully whatever is set before them, and never to sign a thing without reading it. They have too often been tricked by their rulers. And then, convinced that something had gone very, very wrong, they would act.

In accordance with the first principle of Church politesse—don't rock the boat, don't "scandalize" the laity—there are wheels within wheels accessible to higher churchmen by which they can influence the Holy Father and even move the Church, all quite imperceptibly. And I am confident that those wheels are slowly turning even now, working toward the eventual reversal of Pope Paul's teaching in "*Humanæ vitæ*". It could happen overnight. More likely, it will take several years. It could be that this particular encyclical will simply become obsolete through lack of enforcement. It will just be forgotten.

In summer of 1968, however, it was still true, of the American Church at least, that "You can't fight City Hall." Following publication of the encyclical on July 29, a number of bishops made statements, of which that of the Archbishop of Washington was typical: "I call upon all priests in their capacity as confessors, teachers, and preachers of God's word to follow without equivocation, ambiguity, or simulation the teaching of the Church in this matter as enunciated clearly by Paul VI."

Sixty priests of the archdiocese balked, telling Cardinal O'Boyle that they could not in conscience accept the teaching of *"Humanæ vitæ,"* nor could they impose it on others. They appealed to Church doctrine on freedom of conscience. Whereupon, appealing to the same principle, His Eminence told the sixty that he, too, had a conscience, and that that conscience would no longer allow them to exercise the pastoral ministry within his jurisdiction.

It was a really tragic impasse. There you had sixty priests, each with achievements, ambitions, and a destiny. They must have been exceptionally devout, sensitive—and courageous, otherwise they would never have dared to take on "City Hall." Each had cost the Church at least $100,000 in education and formation. To blot out only one of them was, in material terms alone, like driving ten Cadillac limousines right off the dock and into the bay. But then, Cardinal O'Boyle was only doing his duty as he saw it. The fate of the conscientious objectors is still being negotiated, mainly through the agency of Cardinal Wright.

As for the dissenters at Catholic University, they too had their troubles. The university is a papal institution under the direction of the American hierarchy. The dissenters had to call in legal counsel and fight tooth and nail to hold their jobs. But they did succeed finally in establishing the right of Catholics to dissent from fallible papal teaching, however authoritative that teaching may be.

We Catholics belong to a Church that is ever learning. Christ promised that the Holy Spirit would lead us "into all truth."[14] So the Church not only continues to teach but continues to learn, becoming aware with the slow lapse of the years of fresh truths, or at least of fresh implications of the truth, so that the content of revelation does not remain static but expands as the years go on, promising an ever-increasing harvest of spiritual insight.

13

The Other Love

"Sweet youth,
Tell me why, sad and sighing, dost thou rove
These pleasant realms? I pray thee tell me sooth,
What is thy name?" He said, "My name is Love."
Then straight the first did turn himself to me,
And cried, "He lieth, for his name is Shame.
But I am Love, and I was wont to be
Alone in this fair garden, till he came
Unasked by night; I am true Love, I fill
The hearts of boy and girl with mutual flame."
Then sighing said the other, "Have thy will,
I am the Love that dare not speak its name."

—Lord Alfred Douglas, *Two Loves*, quoted
April 30, 1895, at the trial of Oscar Wilde

Since World War II, more especially since June 1969, that Other Love has pulled up its socks and now it is not just speaking but seems to be shouting its name. It is not the incidence but the visibility of gay sex that is increasing: Merle Miller, Gore Vidal, Truman Capote, the late W. H. Auden, Edward Albee, Tennessee Williams—all avowedly, unashamedly gay; the Loud Family on television with their gay son Lance; the parades, the picketing, the boycotts on behalf of Gay Liberation—all these developments are bringing homosexuality to public notice as never before.

The reasons for the predominance of males in Gay Lib are complex. Whereas girlishness is condemned in a boy, the parallel does not hold true for girls. The "tomboy" is tolerated. There is no suggestion of homosexuality in her case as there is with the sissified boy. Hence, girls grow up with less fear of it than boys. And hence, because the tomboy is accepted socially, girls are much slower to discover their homosexuality. The secretary of a lesbian sorority in New York has stated that quite a number of women are in their thirties when they first discover their sexual identity.[1] The boy who enjoys sewing at twelve is suspect, even though he is not gay; but what can a girl of that age possibly do to incur the same suspicion?

As a result of this delayed awakening, there are more wives than husbands—often with families—who are late in discovering their homosexuality. Such women are then faced with the difficulty of freeing themselves and completely rearranging their lives. So, many such married lesbians do nothing.

—The convention of the National Federation of Priests' Councils, March 1974 in San Francisco, was quite largely taken up with controversy over homosexuality.

—The National Conference of Catholic Bishops recently published a fifteen-page handbook, "Principles to Guide Confessors in Questions of Homosexuality."

—At a gay symposium held at Trinity College, Dublin in the spring of 1974, Fr. Enda McDonagh, professor of moral theology at St. Patrick's College, Maynooth, proposed changes in Irish law which would "decriminalize" homosexual practices between consenting adults in private.* More than 300 persons attended the conference. Senator Noel Browne estimated the gay population of Dublin at 8,000.

—Here in America headlines were made in the fall of 1973 when the late Dr. Howard Brown told 600 of his colleagues that he was gay. Dr. Brown was a professor at New York University School of Medicine and former health service administrator of the City of New

*Fr. McDonagh also signed a Statement of Dissent concerning *"Humanæ vitæ"*.

York. An interview later appeared on the front page of *The New York Times*, generating worldwide publicity. In the course of a speech delivered in June 1974 during Gay Pride Week at Stanford University, he made an impassioned plea urging gays to publicly proclaim their homosexuality.* "Coming out transcends any experience I've had in my life," he said.

—Even in Israel there are an estimated 150,000 gays. But in Spain there are no arrests made for sodomy because the Generalissimo stoutly insists that there is not one homosexual in all of his country. But there are an awful lot of arrests made for lewd loitering and for drunk and disorderly conduct.

Fifteen million American gays, all of them facing opprobrium and social rejection—at least 4,250,000 of them Catholics doomed in addition to theological odium! Speaking at Yale in December 1973, Dr. Brown estimated the number of gays at 10 percent of the general population. He figured 800 gay physicians in New York City alone. Police reckon the gay population of the city as 400,000.

These gays are specified as "actual and potential," which could mean that every sixth male and every eighth female is gay. But the weasel word there is "potential," meaning latent. The latent gay is sexually attracted by others of the same sex, but he refuses to admit it to himself and in fighting the tendency he often overreacts by lashing out at the overt gays and harassing them as best he can.** This is the man who marries a mother type and then wonders why he can't relate to her sexually. He buys *Playboy* each month just for the book reviews.

For reasons that are often obvious, sometimes puzzling, gays prefer and are skilled at certain kinds of employment over others: hairdressing, interior decorating, the ballet and the performing arts generally; composer Ned Rorem has said that "Today, organists in America are about 75 percent homosexual and a lot of them closets because they're in small towns"; the man interviewing Ned, himself a

---

*Until he "comes out," the homosexual is "in the closet" or a "closet case."

**If Ernest Hemingway saw a gay entering the restaurant where he was eating, he would smash his glass on the floor in outrage.—In his short story, "The Sharks," *(Assembly,* 1960), John O'Hara has Betty Denning say, "Let's just kill Mr. Simms." Why? Because he's gay and will probably have his gay friends visiting, and so he will "ruin" their stretch of beach at the resort. But Betty does not have to kill Mr. Simms. Someone else does it for her, and so the story has a happy ending. These examples of overt hostility are surely exaggerated reactions—suspiciously so?

priestly dropout, now editor of *Gay Sunshine*, estimates 40 percent of the Catholic clergy as gay.[2]

You just don't find many gays in small towns and villages. What happens is that when the small-town boy finds that he is gay, he cuts out just as fast as he can and locates in a big city where he can establish his sexual identity and find the social support of a gay community not to be had, say, in Shickshinny or Mahoningtown, Pennsylvania.

A survey taken in 1973 found that statistically there has been no significant change in the incidence of homosexuality since the Kinsey Report of 1948:

—20-25 percent of all males have tried it, every fifth single female, and every tenth married female. For most, the venture was early, transient, experimental.

—After the age of fifteen, only one in ten of today's men ever has a significant homosexual experience. (This confirms Dr. Brown's estimate.) After nineteen, only 10 to 12 percent of the single females and 3 percent of the married females ever have a lesbian experience.

—Nearly half the total sample feel that "homosexuality" should be legal. (By that they must mean the sexual expression of homosexuality.)

—Nearly half agree that "there is some homosexuality in all of us," and one in four agrees that "being homosexual is just as natural as being heterosexual." Every second woman expresses a definite tolerance of homosexuality in others.

A list of 160 gay achievers over the ages includes 94 litterateurs: poets, novelists, dramatists, critics; 16 composers and performing musicians; 13 actors and entertainers; 11 kings and emperors; 9 philosophers; 4 generals; 4 dancers; 3 painters; 2 popes; 2 diplomats; 2 athletes.

There are, as we all know, girlish gays. In fact, because as a freak he stands out from the crowd, the effeminate is accepted as the typical gay with his fluting voice, mincing gait, and flapping wrists. But in every large family there is at least one gay—generally "Mama's boy." And why don't we recognize him? Because outwardly he is just like us. Thus, gays are clerks, chemists, and students; salesmen, laboratory assistants, and truck drivers; bishops, priests, and nuns; busboys, waiters, and pants pressers.

In the *Saturday Review*, Faubion Bowers writes:

>   Today's homosexual can be open ("come out") or covert
> ("closet"), practicing or inhibited, voluntary or compulsive,
> conscious or unaware, acceptive or passive, manly ("stud") or
> womanly ("fem"). The difference between unconscious
> willingness and conscious unwillingness has thinned. Now the
> homosexual's variations are seen as such that he may act
> homosexually and not *be* homosexual, or be gay only off and
> on. He may be your next-door neighbor, the son or the father
> of a household, divorced, or a bachelor. He may wear a hard
> hat or a golfing cap. Conceivably, he is the boss who gives
> orders or the employee who takes them, the man who goes to
> parties and drinks too much and either babbles overflowingly
> or clams up and pouts in a corner. He might or might not
> belong to Alcoholics Anonymous or periodically lie on an
> analyst's couch. What he is *not* comes more quickly to mind
> these days: He is not a capon, a mental eunuch, an altered,
> failed, or lapsed man. Now, in his newfound self-recognition,
> he is not even hetero-imitative. He is simply turned on
> sexually by men.[3]

Nevertheless, most Americans still regard homosexuality as a
sickness, which yet should be punished by law. The one who is
shocked into self-recognition by a gay experience, his parents, or
religious superior, thinks immediately of psychiatry. But psychiatry
cannot change a person's sexual orientation. It can only help him gain
control and adjust to society.

Psychoanalysis, psychiatry, and psychology do not lead public
opinion; they follow it. In another day, public opinion was outraged
at masturbation. Psychologists and physicians considered it depraved
and injurious. Then Kinsey changed the climate and the head doctors
fell right in line. One supposes that in the Middle East and the Orient
psychiatrists try to build a yen for boy-love into their patients.

In view of the hundreds of thousands of men and women not
distressed by their homosexuality, not rejecting themselves as moral
failures, the American Psychiatric Association has stricken homosexuality from the list of illnesses in its diagnostic manual.[4]

Here are a few more or less disconnected observations on the
subject:

—One must always distinguish between the pædophile—a person whose main erotic pleasure comes from sex with children—and
what might be called the "normal" homosexual. The pædophile is
more commonly known as a child molester. He is sick.

—Sexuality does not change one's basic character. Like the heteros, homosexuals are divided into givers and takers, reliable and unreliable, the truthful and the liars, and so on.

—Most gays believe that homosexuality is beyond one's control: about 55 percent here in America, 80 percent in Amsterdam, 88 percent in Copenhagen.[5] The gay seems to have a much stronger libido than the hetero, and because of his more numerous opportunities, he exercises it twice or three times as often. The statisticians invariably express amazement in a footnote that, whereas the average hetero has intercourse twice a week, the gay can make it three times a night and oftener, because when he fellates another or is pathic in anal intercourse, he is not spending any seed. Some gays go to the bar night after night, and they nearly always make out. The same chap will often absent himself from the bar for fifteen or twenty minutes, each time with a different partner.

—It is a mistake to think that the gay prefers a youth who resembles a girl. The gay wants a Man—a "butch," an athlete, a Marine, a cowboy.

—Gay Lib argues not that homosexuality is preferable but only that it is permissible. Homosexuality is neither infectious nor contagious. It cannot be spread by word or action. All that that can do is bring the latent gay to self-recognition and perhaps spare him an impossible marriage or give him pause before he pronounces the vows of religion. Homosexuality is a biological condition like having curly hair or being left-handed.

Comes now a brilliant sixteen-year-old to consult his priest about a personal problem.* Jim has discovered his sexual orientation and found himself unmistakably gay. He likes nice things, books, clean clothes and hands, and he detests contact sports. He dreams with climax about the bigger boys and fantasizes himself as their slave. Girlie magazines leave him cold, but hard-core gay porn drives him into sexual delirium. What is right and what is wrong? For Jim is a good Catholic boy and wants to be a faithful servant of God.

The priest tells him, and Jim is appalled.

"You mean I can never enjoy sex, either with myself or with anyone else? I can never again for the rest of my life have an orgasm

*But, sadly, they seldom do. Either they see the Father as an angel of purity above all sordid sex—especially gay sex!—or they have been insulted, humiliated, bullied by some ignorant lout in the confessional. So most of them somehow settle their conscience and just don't confess it.

without grievously displeasing our Lord? Why, you might as well tell me it's a sin to go to the bathroom!

"If priests can scarcely keep chaste even with the grace of holy orders, and if married people have trouble keeping chaste even with the grace of matrimony, what chance have I? Don't you think, Father, that Christ should have instituted an eighth sacrament for people like me?"

That's a good question. But if Jim's priest hands him Fr. John F. Harvey's advice from the bishops' booklet, Jim is going to find it sublimely unreal:

> [The priest] should show the person that he can live chastely in the world by means of a plan of life, which will include personal meditative prayer, spiritual reading, reception of the sacraments, and some specific work of charity in the world. Two other elements which should be stressed are regular access to spiritual direction and the formation of a stable friendship with at least one person.

May I ask any of my priest readers, including Fr. Harvey, when he last made a formal meditation, did any systematic spiritual reading, or presented himself to his director for a spiritual conference? Why, not even a mature, professional religious can maintain so extensive a program of spirituality, as we priests well know. What then of the poor gay with a living to earn and, as is so often the case, a mother to support?

Left to himself, the gay will inevitably drift downhill into frequent moods of depression, self-hatred, and despair, which can too often end in suicide—perhaps the gay's greatest temptation after sex, not so much because he does not find satisfaction in gay sex, but because of the social pressures, the hysterical fear, the ostracism brought to bear on him by a society formed and encouraged by a Church founded by a God of love and forgiveness.* The gay can't go it alone. That way lies suicide. He must seek out other gays, not so much for sex as for social support, for reassurance. It is only in the homosexual community that the gay is not an outcast.

---

*"At a certain state of development, antihomosexual laws constitute a choice weapon in the hands of skillful arbiters of power who intend, on moral pretexts, to dispose of burdensome adversaries or seize on coveted riches."—R. De Becker, *The Other Face of Love* (New York: Grove, 1969), p. 101. The Templars and Sir Roger Casement come to mind.

(To judge by the parable of the Pharisee and the publican, homophobia* is as hateful to our Lord as it is to the gays. It is naked pride.)

Getting back to Jim: as he matures and notes the sharp conflict between Church teaching and his own God-given instincts and appetites, being an intelligent youth and sensitive to this dichotomy, like my young Chicano friend, he gives up his religion.

But, as Sartre once remarked, "It is impossible to liquidate one's Catholicism. If one succeeds in tearing oneself away from it, one escapes half-dead and marked for life. "John O'Hara said substantially the same thing: "One does not easily part from the Catholic Church."

Sodomy seems to be in moral theology what the Trinity is in dogma: the great incontrovertible. But why? Why does the great majority simply accept gay sex as the ultimate in moral degradation? Members of our generation at least have been conditioned to react with horror at the very mention of the word "sodomy." The occasional individual can perhaps learn tolerance in a notional way, just as the Mississippi redneck after a spell at a Northern university can simulate respect for and concede at least a philosophical equality to the black. Deep down under, though, his flesh crawls at the very thought of any "nice Southern girl" waltzing around the dance floor in the arms of a "big black buck." And that is how most people feel about the homosexual, no matter how sophisticated they appear. That is why they react with loathing, and beneath their crust of perfunctory courtesy, they want nothing at all to do with anyone or anything gay.

But why this unquestioned horror, the social and theological odium directed at the homosexual? The theme is evidently so distasteful that few of us have taken the trouble to think it through for ourselves. I am convinced that the overriding objection is aesthetic rather than theological.

There is also the morality of the innumerable herd, whose only reason for not doing a thing is that it just isn't done.

Then, too, it is so convenient when one can pack all morality into the Sixth and Ninth Commandments according to the formula: immoral = unchaste = disreputable. The upper classes can generally hide their violations of the sex code and, in accordance with the equation just stated, white-collar crime is exempt from social censure. Petty larceny is theft, but grand larceny is "business acumen."

*"Homophobia"—an etymological monstrosity: "fear of the same"—meaning what? But it is gaining currency with the meaning "hatred of gays."

The moral status of sodomy is not incontrovertible. In fact, I can think of no human act that can be universally condemned just out of hand. And such controversy is wholesome. There are many positions once seriously taught that have since been abandoned chiefly because of vigorous and sustained protest. The minority has since become the majority opinion.

"Everything that the Council has taught about the nature of this 'new age' further exphasizes the need to keep debate open in complex issues. It means further that respectful dialogue is to be preferred to premature anathemas."[6]

With regard to the possible adjustment of doctrine to recent findings on the number of homosexuals, their physiology, psychology, and human exigencies, Vatican II left us clear guidelines:

> Recent studies and findings of science, history, and philosophy raise new questions which influence life and demand new theological investigations. . . .
>
> In pastoral care, appropriate use must be made not only of theological principles, but also of the findings of the secular sciences, especially of psychology and sociology. . . .
>
> May the faithful, therefore, live in very close union with the men of their time. Let them strive to understand perfectly their way of thinking and feeling, as expressed in their culture. Let them blend modern science and its theories and the understanding of the most recent discoveries with Christian morality and doctrine. Thus their religious practice and morality can keep pace with their scientific knowledge and with an ever advancing technology. . . .
>
> Theological inquiry should seek a profound understanding of revealed truth without neglecting close contact with its own times.[7]

Now, getting down to specifics, the usual condemnation and the event from which the act is named derive from God's destruction of the city of Sodom, presumably because of the inhabitants' fondness for homosexual practices.

According to Fr. Charles E. Curran, "D. S. Bailey has revived and revised an interpretation which maintains that the Sodom story does not refer to homosexuality or to homosexual acts. The word 'to know' does not necessarily involve a sexual connotation, but rather could be interpreted as a violation of hospitality."[8] Bailey says that the first explicit reference to buggery as the reason for Sodom's destruction appeared in Palestine only in the second century before Christ. Six Old Testament references speak of sin as the cause of Sodom's punishment, but they do not identify the sin as buggery.[9]

One must not forget either that homosexuality was not recognized and differentiated until the latter part of the nineteenth century. Until then sodomy was regarded as no more than an affectation of the depraved. Apparently it never occurred to anyone that it could be the answer to a biological need of people with no other sexual outlet.

As for St. Paul's stern denunciation of sodomy in the first chapter of his epistle to the Romans, Christian scholarship always has to adjust the Bible to the intellectual, moral, and social condition of ages for which it was never written. There must always be a kind of equation or perpetual correspondence between the interpretation of revealed truths and the intellectual progress of humanity. After all, St. Paul was only a man, a mere human being, formulating the revealed perception in accordance with his intelligence and in the language available to him, i.e., in accordance with the *un*revealed history and culture in which he happened to find himself.

We find that certain absolute statements of our Lord require copious and complex qualification: for instance "If you ask the Father anything in my name, he will give it to you."[10] "Ask and you shall receive, seek and you shall find, knock and it shall be opened unto you."[11] For over forty years the whole Church prayed daily for the conversion of Russia, and it didn't happen. Obviously, then, our Lord's promise must be understood as modified by several ifs, ands, or buts. The trouble is that we don't know just what they are. So, obviously, St. Paul's blacklisting of sodomy must be similarly qualified.

According to the Dutch Catechism, "The very sharp strictures of Scripture on homosexual practices (Gen. 19; Rom. 1) must be read in their context. Their aim is not to pillory the fact that some people experience this perversion inculpably. They denounce a homosexuality which had become the prevalent fashion and had spread to many who were really quite capable of normal sexual sentiments."[12] That catechism was commissioned by the hierarchy of the Netherlands and was given an imprimatur by Cardinal Alfrink.

As I said in an earlier chapter, an act of sex is to be judged natural or unnatural not from the quality of the act but from the nature of the agent.

> Frustration of nature is morally evil only when man acts contrary to *his* nature as a rational being—when he behaves unreasonably. . . . The frustration which is morally evil is the frustration of the whole and not merely of the part . . . . In the matter of sexual morality it is not enough to condemn an action as wrong simply because it frustrates the natural purposes of the sexual faculty; an action is proved to be wrong only if it frustrates the nature of man.[13]

It is apparent from the bishops' booklet that Fr. Harvey is uninformed on the complete or "absolute" homosexual, of whom the Dutch Catechism speaks. As was St. Paul. "Complete," "absolute"—terms used to separate the true homosexual from the bisexual, who is capable of perverting his native appetite and substituting a member of the same sex for one of the opposite sex. To continue: the absolute gay is intrinsically incapable of sexual interest in the female. This characteristic is intrinsic or absolute rather than extrinsic or relative. It is not merely that he doesn't like blonds, or fats, or any particular type of woman, much less any particular woman. His lack of sexual interest extends to all women, however beautiful and charming. He might wish that he could marry and bed down a billionairess or a duchess, but he can't—not for a billion dollars, not for the grandest title in the *Almanach de Gotha*.

How did he get that way? Did he choose his parents? His place of birth? Was it he who decided that he should grow as tall as he did? Did he elect to be gay? Certainly not. And he could no more acquire a taste for girls than swim to Ireland. In other words, it's not his "fault," if that's what society wants to call it.

This boy-love is not against his nature. On the contrary, he finds it not only right and natural but beautiful, too. It is the fulfillment of his desires, the completion of his personality.

Since there never was a "natural" usage for the true gay to pervert, to deviate from, then he is not a pervert. He is not a deviate. And he is not included in St. Paul's condemnation of men who have "given up natural intercourse with women," for this person is a virgin, never defiled with the opposite sex. Remember? He gets to follow the Lamb all over heaven. He couldn't have relations with a woman to save his soul. He would find it physically impossible.

In more dramatic form, the gay faces the same problem as the married man who has been morally separated from his wife by

"Humanae vitae." Right here in the United States there are 15,000,000 gays unable to satisfy their second most powerful drive without sin. These people eat and drink, they sleep, but when they get horny they can relax their tensions only by masturbating or by perpetrating "that abominable and unnatural crime which cries to heaven, which is not even to be named among Christians." The gays fall in love with one another and their instincts lead them to effect sexual union as best they can. They did not choose their condition. It was handed to them by their Creator.

Again the dilemma: a natural appetite that can't be satisfied except by what is, objectively at least, a dreadful sin—or so say the theologians.

Is God at fault? Impossible. So it must be the theologians who are mistaken, who should review their data, check out the latest research in Scripture, biology, and psychology, and then reconstruct their syllogisms.

But if the theologians are mistaken, then the gays can appease their sexual drive not only without sin, but even virtuously.

Let's try it another way: Here is Jim, our talented gay teen-ager, now starting college. As he looks into his own being, into his biological drives and instincts, he finds that here at least the claims of religion do not correspond with his internal experience. To illustrate:

Jim is cold. He shivers and stamps his feet and blows on his hands. Finally he calls the building custodian and asks for more heat. "But you can't be cold," the custodian says. "The outside thermometer reads eighty-four and last night's paper predicted another heat wave." Now which is Jim to believe—the janitor, or his own intuition? Is he cold or is he not?

Even so, as 15,000,000 Americans have relations with members of their own sex, both Church and State are united in assuring them that they must be deluded, for homosexual acts are "against nature"—again, whose nature?—and therefore both a mortal sin and a felony.

The gays have to do it or go berserk, and so they do it. When they find that Church teaching on sex does not make sense for them, they form their own principles and square their conscience accordingly, as is happening right now with married couples on birth control. So husbands and wives have stopped confessing birth control because they no longer think it's a sin. But most gays stopped confessing sex years and years ago, and for the same reason. Nor does their reticence invalidate the sacrament so long as they are in good faith, both gays and married couples.

Oh, the occasional gay may confess it as a sin but he doesn't really believe it. He is moved to confess it by a kind of atavistic guilt feeling, a hangover from his boyhood "inoculation," but intellectually he cannot see how his actions have hurt God, himself, or his fellow men.

The more thoughtful gay will grant that objectively it may be wrong, but for him it's not a mortal sin. In partial support he can quote Fr. Adolph Tanquerey, S. S., whose textbooks, in my day at least, were used in Sulpician seminaries all over the world:

> If there is discussion of the imputability of acts committed under the influence of these tendencies [sadism, masochism, fetishism, homosexuality], it can be said that responsibility is generally reduced, though not entirely eliminated. For because of their vehemence, these tendencies, if they are to be repelled, require greater efforts of the will, but they are not insuperable unless, in certain extraordinary cases, they so upset the mind as to prevent mature reflection.*

The more thoughtful gay will also recall that mortal sin results from a confluence of grievous matter, sufficient reflection, and *full consent* of the will. What Fr. Tanquerey is saying, then, is that acts of sadism, masochism, and homosexuality, are usually venial for lack of consent—in which case they are not necessary but free matter for confession, i.e., the gay does not have to include them in his confession.

An objection to the gay apologia may accuse them of pride, of reasoning that "Because I do it, it can't be a sin." To which the gay responds by modifying the subordinate verb: "Because I am compelled by my nature and biological structure to do it, it can't be a sin."

Another objection: Hitler said, "It's so because I want it to be so."

Response: It's so because the gay finds it so. It is a fact. He did not choose homosexuality over heterosexuality.

*Si de imputabilitate agitur actuum qui sub influxu istarum propensionum fiunt, statui potest generatim responsibilitatem minui sed non tolli. Istæ enim tendentiæ, propter suam vehementiam, majores quidem conatus voluntatis exigunt ut repellantur, sed non sunt insuperabiles, nisi in quibusdam extraordinariis casibus mentem ita perturbent ut maturæ deliberationi obstent.—Synopsis Theologiæ Moralis, (Paris, 1931), Vol. II, p. 23 in the Supplement.

There are those who say that homosexuality is Nature's own answer to overpopulation. For "Nature" read "God." In which case sodomy becomes licit?

Necessity knows no law.* *In extremis*, private ownership disappears and it's everyone for himself with no question of theft. The first human beings had to commit incest and take a plurality of wives. God permitted divorce. He adjusts his law to existing needs. Does not the same reasoning favor the gays? Just as Cain and Abel had to use their mother and their sisters for sex, so the gays also must use their own kind. May they not be equally confident of a divine dispensation?

Let us now compare sodomy with intercourse between a man and his wife past her climacteric. Or perhaps the husband is sterile as the result of an injury. Or the woman has had her ovaries tied off. My stipulation is that there be no possibility of pregnancy. Call them Elmer and Bertha.

Now a husband may have relations with his wife:

1. To make a baby;
2. To release sexual tension;
3. To fortify the marriage bond.

When Elmer and Bertha make love, then, they are only doing it for fun—because they love each other. It amounts to mutual masturbation. But the theologians warn us that even in this case, where nature has already foreclosed all possibility of pregnancy, if Elmer uses a condom during intercourse the action is spoiled, gravely sinful, and Bertha is bound to resist her husband "like a virgin under assault."

In fact, since it is only mechanical and chemical birth control that is sinful, it is licit for the married couple, far from intending conception, to take advantage of the wife's sterile periods, hoping to God that she does *not* get pregnant.

Well, then, since Bertha is incapable of conception, would Elmer be allowed to sodomize her for the sake of a little variety? Front or back, both are holes, both are sterile. And they *are* married. But "Strictly forbidden!" cry the theologians. And this I confess I must take on faith, for I can see no good reason for their judgment.

What redeems Elmer's and Bertha's vaginal masturbation is that they are man and wife. From this some Catholic theologians have

---

*"*Ad impossibile nemo tenetur.*"

tried to rationalize gay sex by analogy with marriage. That is, if two fellows can hit it off together, learn to love each other, and find themselves sexually compatible, then they may live together permanently with all the obligations and sexual privileges, other things being equal, of man and wife. Their exchange of sex is no sin.

But the analogy with matrimony is all wrong. For one thing, it reeks of sacrilege, blasphemy, and bad taste. "Let holy things be treated with reverence."* Already some of the preachers are using the marriage ritual to bless such partnerships, the "bride" arriving in high drag with a veil and a white satin gown for what is nothing more than a parody of the sacrament: two roommates playing sex together on a long-term but inevitably limited basis—"inevitably," because such agreements rarely last longer than a few years. The bond is compatibility rather than love: there are no children, no property or inheritance rights to be considered. It is not a marriage; it is not a sacrament.

It also raises problems that sound plain silly when put in words: Is each bound in conscience to render the conjugal debt? Is it a lifetime contract, subject to annulment? What about duties of state, such as washing clothes and dishes, making the bed, cooking the meals? Would infidelity be sinful? What if one of them procures a sex change?

If a man is lucky enough once in his lifetime to find the chap he would have married under other circumstances, then let them work out an agreement, shake hands over it, and pitch in together as roommates and forget all this rubbish about being "married" and living as "man and wife."

It undoubtedly has advantages over promiscuity. But apart from that, what exactly is wrong with promiscuity? Since relatively few gays are provided with a congenial mate on a permanent basis, promiscuity is the usual thing. There are drawbacks, to be sure—the possibility of disease, lice, internal rupture, anal fistulas, and the like, but these are extrinsic to the moral situation.

The crucial question: is sex between gays a sin? That's the pivot. Once we settle that, the gays will know where they stand. If it's okay, then any question of promiscuity is irrelevant, for the quality of the relationship has nothing to do with it. The gay may do it with whomever he pleases and as often as he wants, and we advise our gay

* *"Sancta sancte."*

friend not to overdo it just as we might tell him that he is drinking too much or smoking too heavily.

One thing at least is certain: if sex is wrong for the gays, it is no more heinous or "abominable" than the sexual sins of the heteros. As to the liceity of gay sex, Fr. Curran agrees with H. Kimball Jones. "If the homosexual relationship contributes to the humanization of man, then such a relationship, even though it is not the ideal, can be accepted and even encouraged by the Church." Fr. Curran agrees "almost totally" with Jones's conclusion:

> Thus, we suggest that the Church must be willing to make the difficult but necessary step of recognizing the validity of mature homosexual relationships, encouraging the absolute invert to maintain a fidelity to one partner when his only other choice would be to lead a promiscuous life with guilt and fear.[14]

Fr. John J. McNeil, S. J. also prefers gay "partnerships" to promiscuity, but only as the lesser evil, presumably for those who cannot abstain entirely. Fr. Curran is more liberal. In carefully guarded language, after thirty-seven closely reasoned pages of print, he concludes that gay sex is wrong. It is a disorder resulting from original sin. But since the gay did not choose his condition, although it is wrong, for the gay it is not always a sin. He would prefer to see the gays paired off in stable, loving relationships, and through his much distinguishing and subdistinguishing, one senses his feeling that the homosexuals should not overdo it.

Separating essentials from trimmings, then, here is what we get: The act of sodomy is central, and that includes all the foreplay. "Partnerships," "stable, loving relationships," considerations of promiscuity and its disadvantages—all these things are marginal, extrinsic to the sex act itself. Now how can it be all right for Bob to have sex with Al but wrong for him to do it with Vince? And what possible difference can it make that Bob and Al have been roommates for three weeks, three years, or three days? That doesn't affect the sexual act. There is the same degree of jollification no matter with whom it is done. I would suggest that you go back and reread Fr. Curran's reasoning in the light of these considerations.

All gays will be interested in Dr. Valente's conclusion that if birth control be licit, the consequences extend farther than we dream.

Sterile intercourse remains the same, whether vaginal or anal. The law of nature is supposed to require the seed to be deposited in the vagina. Once that requirement is knocked out, the seed can be deposited anywhere or nowhere, by withdrawal, use of a prophylactic, masturbation, homosexual sodomy, fellatio, and even bestiality.[16]

The gay distinguishes three kinds of associates. There is the one he meets for sexual relief. Usually there is little affection, no community of interests, no parity of education and culture. They merely help each other out, after which they shake hands and don't meet until the next time. Nevertheless, each is necessary to the other.

It is sometimes objected that such a useful transaction is both "depersonalizing" and "dehumanizing." But the nurse's aide gives his patient an injection or inserts a catheter. Does this "depersonalize" or "dehumanize" either of them? I don't see it.

The second type of association exists between lovers.

The third kind of associate is just a friend—nothing romantic, in fact the idea of sex never occurs to either of them.

It is California—especially San Francisco, Los Angeles, and San Diego—that leads the rest of the country in the war for Gay Liberation. With its benign climate, its restless minority that is singularly immune from human respect and susceptible to bizarre cults and causes, and its army of police who find it easier to harass the gays than to fight the hoods and muggers, the whole state has become a veritable training ground of gay leadership for the rest of the country.

The Battle of Stonewall was fought in Manhattan, true, but it was only the spark that exploded the ferment seething for thirty years—beneath the surface in New York but above ground on the West Coast. It was there that the Mattachine Society had its beginning. And One, Inc., publishing the first gay periodical with national distribution. And the first segregated sect. And the first gay synagogue. And the gay version of AA: Alcoholics Together. And Help, Inc., the first attempt at legal self-insurance. And *The Advocate*, with its nationwide circulation of 39,000—the first gay newspaper. And the first gay settlement house.

And in 1968, looking out over the Catholic gays scattered like sheep without a shepherd, there was an Augustinian friar who decided to do what he could for them, so he founded "Dignity."[16] This was in San Diego. Now there are chapters in all the principal cities from coast to coast.

From their statement of purpose:

> Dignity is a national organization of gay Catholics and other persons who wish to see Christ's love expressed to and among all men and women regardless of sexual preference. Our membership consists primarily of Catholic gay people, but also of many concerned people, gay and otherwise, clergy and laity, who seek a more constructive interrelation between the Church and gay people. . . .
>
> We believe that gay people are indeed members of the Catholic Church and responsible followers of Christ. We are working within the Church to help both gay people and the Church understand that gays express their sexuality in a manner consistent with Christ's teaching, ethically responsible, unselfish, and uplifting. . . .
>
> Our goal is to help the gay Catholic achieve a sense of dignity .˙. . and to change the Catholic conscience from its puritanical fear and ignorance to one of true Christlike love and acceptance. Dignity does have a message: God loves all men and women.This is the good news Christ came to teach us.*

There were two hundred members including several priests at their first national convention in Hollywood. There they were addressed by Fr. John J. McNeil, S.J., dean of studies at Woodstock College, New York.

I shall write now as a priest seriously advising his gay readers. Should the gay try to change himself by psychiatry? Well, try it this way: Should the black bleach his skin and try to pass for white? Should the Jew have the surgeon rebuild his foreskin? And what about the Chicano? The Indian? Should they try for acceptance as Anglo or paleface?

I wonder if Alexander or Frederick the Great ever felt the need of psychiatry, or Leonardo Da Vinci, Cole Porter, Sir Isaac Newton, St. John the Apostle, Sophocles, or Ludwig Wittgenstein—all of them gay. How would the treatment have affected them and their work?

Why should the gay try to change himself by psychiatry? The question is not so much *should* he as *can* he. I don't think he can. But if he could, why should he? "Because it's easier living as a hetero." Perhaps. But isn't it rather cowardly, yielding to social pressures that are infamously unjust? Running from the battle for Gay Lib at a time

*Or, as the Reverend Troy Perry puts it, "The Lord is my shepherd, and He knows I'm gay."

when your brothers and sisters are most in need of your support and with best chance of success?

If someone hurts you because you're gay, hurt him right back; not from hatred, but rather as the good father must occasionally discipline an erring son: to teach him a lesson.

If a law injures you, help change that law. If public officials are unfair to the gays, get rid of them! Vote them out! And, finally, if society is hostile, change society! That's what Gay Liberation is all about.

What about marriage? Wouldn't that turn the homo into a hetero? No, no, and again no! It would only make two people miserable. Why lead some poor girl down the garden path only to disappoint her on her wedding night? If you are not stirred by a girl right now, what makes you think the sacrament of matrimony will make a difference?

Career people have been known to arrange a marriage of convenience, both bride and groom being gay and both having an understanding about sex before entering into the contract. The Germans call this sort of thing a "Joseph marriage" for obvious reasons; it is not uncommon in Hollywood. One occasionally sees an ad in *The Advocate* appealing for such a partner. But it is a tricky business, and the gay should give it long thought and get competent advice before coming to a decision.

The Church does not hate gays. The Church hates sodomy. We are trying to change that opposition, to show that it is a mistaken hostility, that sodomy is licit, at least for gays. The gay may be tempted to protest, to "get square" by quitting the Church. But where would he go? Where else can he find the mass and the sacraments, solid and sincere belief in the Apostles' Creed—so satisfying to the intellect, and all the devotional accessories that so satisfy the emotions?

If gay sodomy is evil, then it must be evil for everyone regardless of his religion. God does not give us a choice in moral codes or life-styles. We do not pick and choose the way we thumb from one television channel to another. If gay sodomy is evil, joining another church will not make it right.

But, on the other hand, if the homosexuals are sincerely persuaded that gay sodomy is permissible, then they have no need to build their own private little chapel within the Mother Church, to form an esoteric sect within the Christian commonwealth. Separatism, segregation, is not the answer. The answer is assimilation.

The Catholic has an instinct for unity. It is the duty of every Catholic, no matter what his sexual nature, to help stop disintegration of the Church wherever he sees it. Now surely this book, especially this present chapter, has given the gay arguments and princples enough to form his conscience on gay sex and still receive the sacraments—so, Mr. or Ms. Gay, spread the word: Gays can be just as good Catholics as the rest and still have their sex. Don't let them quit the Church, for their own and good and ours—because, you see, we need their help in forming a consensus. We need them on the team.

14

The Judge

Conscience is an implacable tyrant: it can't be bribed or killed; it is the only one of our intellectual faculties that stands aloof, independent, beyond our control.

Conscience is that part of a person that feels bad when everything else feels good.

Hamlet: "Thus conscience doth make cowards of us all."

Richard III: "My conscience hath a thousand several tongues,

"And every tongue brings in a several tale,

"And every tale condemns me for a villain."*

It has been said that the neurotic has too much conscience, the psychopath too little. When conscience is sick it is a scourge; in the

*A few other choice comments.—Karl Barth: "Conscience is the perfect interpreter of life."—Oliver Cromwell: "As to freedom of conscience, I meddle with no man's conscience; but if you mean by that, liberty to celebrate the mass, I would have you understand that in no place where the power of the Parliament of England prevails shall that be permitted."—James Joyce: "The agenbite of inwit."—Anonymous child: "My mind will hurt."—Mark Twain: "It is by the goodness of God that in our country we have those three unspeakably precious things: freedom of speech, freedom of conscience, and the prudence never to practice either of them."

end it may drive its subject to a psychiatrist. One thinks of adolescent scrupulosity over sex when young people first begin to stagger under the load with which the theologians have burdened humanity.

Because it has trained us into good habits, and also because its influence inevitably overflows into the emotions (where it has no right to be), a false conscience is sometimes hard to correct. For example, for a lifetime our conscience has trained us to Friday abstinence; then one day the Church repeals that law. But just the same we may still have to fight our conscience whenever we want to eat meat on Friday.

As the Church gradually empties out the last traces of Manichaeism and Jansenism from her moral theology, letting in the clear sunlight of right reason, the veil of superstition and bogus asceticism will disappear from the Church's view of sexuality—but not for us. We have been trained in the old rigor, and even though reason tells us that "this" is no longer condemned as sinful, our emotions, guided by a conscience that is now misbehaving, will likely still give us hell if we do it.

Conscience is the judgment of the practical reason about the moral goodness of an act. It sizes up a given situation, measures it against the moral law, and then gives us either a green or a red light.

It is each man's point of contact with the moral law, the Code of Decent Behavior: subject meeting object. As interpreted by conscience, this Code is not instinct, for it often opposes instinct, as when it urges a soldier forward in battle or forbids a father to molest his daughter.

Instincts are sometimes in conflict. On a sinking ship, self-preservation tells a man to grab a life jacket. But then the herd instinct—or is it race preservation?—bids him give it to this pregnant woman. Which instinct shall he follow? Conscience will decide.

The strange thing is that conscience, the Code, often favors the weaker instinct: the soldier does not want to die; the passenger does not want to drown; that father's instincts may be crying for incest. Then conscience does not just intervene, but it sets to work and consciously beefs up the weaker instinct, trying to make it prevail, suggesting motives for doing the right thing.

But conscience: Isn't it perhaps just something we've learned? A matter of training, education, indoctrination?

"I try to be decent because that's the way I was brought up."

But here I spot a fallacy. Try it this way: "The earth moves around the sun because that's the way I was taught." That gets things backward, doesn't it?

In the same way, conscience and the Code do not bind because we were taught that they do. The child is not talented because he is taking piano lessons; he is taking piano lessons because he is talented. Our parents and teachers explained the Code to us in growing detail as our physical and mental powers expanded and we were able to take it in. From Mother's Darling to schoolboy, through puberty and adolescence, our problems in behavior became increasingly complex, and we had to learn how to resolve them according to the Code as interpreted by conscience or end in psychiatry, jail, or a mental institution of some sort.* For kick and struggle as we may, every one of us is bound by the Code from the onset of reason and we have to live with ourselves.

So, as we mature, we find ourselves under a Code of Behavior which we did not make, which we can never quite shake off no matter how we try, and which we know we ought to keep but sometimes don't.

This law could only have been imposed on us by some outside power. I say that not only because it sometimes makes the most outrageous demands on us, but also because of the strange phenomenon known as guilt that follows on violations of the Code.

Guilt is more than the cold recognition that we have done a rotten thing. It flows over into the emotions and makes us miserable. It fills us with feelings of shame, inadequacy, dishonor. We feel somehow dirty and smaller than those around us. At the same time, there is an urge not just to reform our behavior, but in some way to make restitution to the Code, to make good our misdeed, even to undergo punishment. Haven't you ever muttered to yourself, "I ought to be kicked"?

This sense of shame and inadequacy is different from what follows on failings that don't involve the Code. You go through the whole day with egg on your chin. Or someone whispers that your fly is open. There is a moment of embarrassment, but that's it. No harm done. You don't hate yourself. It's all over.

But lose your temper at your child and maybe give him a good belt across the face, and what happens? You hate yourself all the way to work. You have broken the Code. You could crawl through the

*"I am liberating man from the degrading chimera known as conscience."—Hitler.

keyhole. Not only will you never do it again, but you will somehow make it up to the kid: You will take him out next Saturday for a big afternoon at the circus.

Peering more deeply into ourselves, we find that guilt can follow not just on bad actions involving another person, but also on the things we do when we are alone and unobserved. The man who kicks a cat or tortures a puppy. The one who slakes a tantrum of anger and hatred in the privacy of his own apartment.

Guilt always involves a sense of having let someone down. Not just self. Nor the partner in our misconduct. Nor the family. Nor society. Then whom?

Who else but the Lawgiver? The Code fills us with a sense of responsibility, and responsibility necessarily involves someone above us.

You and I find ourselves subject to a Code; we are not our own. There is someone or something giving us directions to behave in a certain way and those directions must be coming at us from the outside, like a beam or a radio wave broadcast by Almighty God with each man's conscience as his receiving set.

Now in explaining the Code I was choosing examples in which good and evil were sharply defined. For instance, to kick your mother down the cellar steps is unmistakably bad. But most human acts are not that obvious; there are problems in morality. That is why we have theologians arguing among themselves, and law courts, with courts of appeal, and a Supreme Court.

A "true" conscience is one that has all the facts right. I know that this is Good Friday and I also know that meat is forbidden on Good Friday. The false or "erroneous" conscience has the facts wrong. I know about the law requiring abstinence on Good Friday, but I only imagine that today is Good Friday when actually it is not. More usually, though, the false conscience is mistaken about the law.

The "vincibly" ignorant conscience is wrong through the agent's own fault. He doesn't know whether or not meat is forbidden on Good Friday, and he doesn't give a hoot. He's not trying to find out either. He's going to have his steak no matter what. Other instances of vincible ignorance:

"I don't care to know who is responsible. Just see that it never happens again."

"Don't tell me. I'm not supposed to know that."

The sincere conscience must always be followed. Perhaps it is mistaken, but the agent is in good faith and does not know that. He does not sin.

Much rhetoric has been expended on freedom of conscience. This is a concept that developed when Europe settled down after the wars of religion that followed the Reformation. Until then we Catholics believed that we had a monopoly on truth, and since presumably everyone could count on the grace of God, no one could contradict Church teaching in good faith. If he did, he was a menace to the Christian commonwealth and had to be put out of business. But then up came the Lutherans with the same idea, then the Calvinists, and the Baptists, until the slaughter of Protestants by Catholics, of Catholics by Protestants, and of Protestants by still other Protestants, threatened to depopulate the continent.

So freedom of conscience was dearly bought, a practical compromise, and within the Church it is still a touchy subject. We are still the "copyright owners" of Christianity. For reasons of expediency we have had to make concessions, but always only in fact and never in principle; and while Vatican II made considerable advances toward a more liberal view, especially in the matter of ecumenism, the expression "freedom of conscience" was studiously avoided. Although our Code of Canon Law, No. 1351, states that "No one is to be forced against his will to embrace the Catholic faith," people on both sides of the fence are still forced to practice a creed alien to their deepest convictions or prevented from exercising their differing beliefs openly. The Baptists are still given a hard time in Spain, the Waldensians in Italy. Switzerland still bans the Jesuits.

Churchmen have been given to declaring, "Error has no rights." But in a public address delivered in Rome during the Council, Cardinal Bea pointed out that this is sheer nonsense, "for error is an abstract concept incapable of either rights or obligations. It is persons who have rights, and even when they are in error, their right to freedom of conscience is absolute."[1]

Where freedom of conscience became controversial here in America, it involved the right to object conscientiously to, and refuse participation in, what the objectors considered an unjust war. But many of those fighting in Vietnam and those supporting them at home thought that such a position was just too convenient and was motivated by cowardice rather than by honest conviction.

It comes down to this: Of prime importance in the objective

moral order is the law of God.* It is clear in its broadest aspects—"Do good, avoid evil"—but obscurities develop in its application to particular cases. The experts, the theologians, work over the various problems and try to reach a consensus on solutions. Where controversy develops on vital issues, the Supreme Pontiff intervenes as *ex officio* teacher and first theologian of the whole Church.

But all of this machinery, its working and its product, is subject to final review by conscience, yours and mine—the ultimate judge. And if we sincerely and in good faith decide that a mistake has been made, then before God we must follow our own conscience—indeed, in such a case, however rare, we actually sin if we go against conscience by adopting our Holy Father's opinion. This is what is meant by supremacy of conscience.

Cardinal Newman described it to the Duke of Norfolk in his usual sonorous rhetoric:

> The rule and measure of duty are not utility, nor expedience, nor the happiness of the greatest number, nor state convenience, nor fitness, order, and the *pulchrum*. Conscience is not a long-sighted selfishness, nor a desire to be consistent with oneself; but it is a messenger from Him who, both in nature and in grace, speaks to us behind a veil, and teaches and rules us by His representatives. Conscience is the aboriginal Vicar of Christ, a prophet in its informations, a monarch in its peremptoriness, a priest in its blessings and anathemas, and, even though the eternal priesthood throughout the Church could cease to be, in it the sacerdotal principle would remain and would have a sway.[2]

The Church teaches that the sacrament of penance is the ordinary means of flushing sin and guilt from the conscience. It is beyond all doubt that Jesus gave his priests power over sin, although as far as we know he did not explicitly command "confession by ear." He himself forgave sins right and left without ever hearing a confession—but then He could read hearts. However, the apostles, too, forgave sins right and left without ever hearing a confession—and they could not read hearts. Just so, in case of necessity, a chaplain can have a whole regiment simply say the Confiteor, after which he can absolve them all together.

But if confession as we know it is the *ordinary* means of obtaining

*Divine law, divine-positive law, natural law, and the law of nature: all gathered under the general heading "Eternal Law."

forgiveness, then any other method has to be extraordinary. This is quite something when one reflects on the fact that we Catholics and the Orthodox are almost the only people in the whole world who believe in confession. So far as we know, then, everyone else must get by on perfect contrition.

Before going farther into the sacrament of penance, let me speak of perfect and imperfect contrition. Perfect contrition looks to the love of God for motivation; imperfect, to love of self. Perfect: "Most of all because I have offended thee, my God, who art all-good and deserving of all my love." Imperfect: "Because I dread the loss of heaven and the pains of hell."

Venial sin gets its very name from the fact that it is easily forgiven (*venia* = favor): imperfect contrition suffices, or a sincere little prayer, kissing the crucifix.

Outside of confession, mortal sin is forgiven by perfect contrition. Now, my generation and those before us were afraid that this doctrine somehow impaired the dignity, the usefulness of the sacrament, that it could even one day make confession obsolete. So the pardon of mortal sin without the sacrament was not just soft-pedaled, but was made extremely difficult by reason of the fact that, we were told, it is just about morally impossible to make an act of perfect contrition.

"Morally impossible"? When it's the only means of forgiveness available to Protestants, Jews, and everybody else—to Catholics as well when we are in a jam with no priest available, as in an accident or in time of war.

Perfect contrition comes easily to the normally devout Catholic. He just pulls the rosary out of his pocket and studies the crucifix for a few moments. He recalls one or other of the stations of the cross, a mystery of the rosary, some particular kindness God has wrought for him. If he can join it with a sincere resolution of amendment, his sins are wiped out.

It was Lateran IV, only seven hundred years ago, that said we must go to confession at least once a year. But the one who observes that minimum is by no means to be despised as a slack Catholic. Orthodox usage is very sparing with confession—three or four times at most in a lifetime: first communion, marriage, and the deathbed. That's about it. It was like that with us too in the first ages of the Church, when the idea was to stay away from confession through not committing serious sin. Of course the "great sin" in those days was not sex, but rather backsliding from Christianity to paganism.

It is Church law that before receiving holy communion we must first clear all our mortal sins by confession. It is "Church law," not natural, or divine-positive law, so therefore it can be dispensed with when necessary. If Greg is in mortal sin, unable to get to confession, but must now choose between receiving holy communion or losing his reputation (one thinks of a wedding), what is he to do? Well, we used to be able to plead a broken fast, but that excuse has become awfully thin in just the last decade or so. No, Greg just makes an act of perfect contrition and receives without a second thought. No sweat, no sacrilege.

In the sacrament we are bound to confess only mortal sins (not those doubtfully mortal, much less the venial sins) but we must confess all of them, together with any circumstances that may change their nature. This is known as the Law of Integrity—also a Church law allowing of dispensation.

Now most Catholics are careful about integrity almost to the point of scrupulosity—and far too many priests with them!* I suppose it's a good thing. It somehow appeals to our American feeling for honesty and fairness to "come clean" with our dear Lord. "No sense telling anything if you can't tell it all." But, as Church law, it admits of judgment. To suppress mention of a sin for a reasonable cause is not just permissible, but a matter of common sense. And, actually, when you think of it, can one possibly have anything but a reasonable cause for skipping a sin? The only such causes I can think of are fear and shame, which have obviously made it impossible for this penitent to confess *this* particular sin to *this* confessor, and of course moral impossibility is a reasonable cause.

In sum, we do our best. But, for the record, willful and senseless violation of integrity is a sacrilege that invalidates the sacrament.

Violations of the seal by the priest? As to the direct violation, linking a name with a sin—"John Smith once confessed idolatry to me": in the billions of confessions heard since 1215, it is bound to have happened. But no one need worry on that score. It is the indirect violation, perpetrated unknowingly by the confessor, that happens all

---

*I knew a hospital chaplain who was a "nut" on integrity. When he was hearing a dying man's confession, the nuns would gather in the hall outside praying for the two of them as they "listened without hearing" to the struggle being waged inside: "You told 'three or four small lies'? Think, man. Was it three or was it four? In a few minutes you'll be facing Almighty God in judgment. Now try again. It might help if you could remember just when and where you told each of those lies. What? Only 'white' lies? Man, there is no such thing as a 'white' lie. All lies are black. . . ."

too often and can do quite as much harm. There is the priest who sobs, groans, or exclaims over certain sins in such a way that he can be heard outside. Or the confessor in a boys' school who always assigned the stations as penance for masturbation, until someone wised him up. In a case like that, the students could have considered themselves excused from mentioning that particular sin.

For some years, in a two-man parish, I had to hear all the confessions because no one would go to the pastor. Hour after hour he would sit idle in his box, until some stranger might happen to wander in on him. Then the fun would begin. You could hear him all over the church.

"*How* long? . . . You *what!*? . . . God, *no!*—not *that!* Whatever made you do a thing like that? . . . How often? . . . *Seventeen times!* Man, you must have thought you were a stud *bull!* Did you get a disease? . . . Well, now, thank God for that. For your penance, for your *holy* penance, I want you to say . . ."

The poor penitent would slink out of the box with flaming face and practically crawl out of the church on his belly with embarrassment.

Any danger of such an indirect violation of the seal dispenses the penitent from integrity. It happens most often with the "loud" confessor. This principle would apply more especially to the gays, because their sins are socially so repugnant. But one must have at least imperfect sorrow for any sins not mentioned.

Why confession, then, if all sins, however grave, can be forgiven without the sacrament? Well, apart from Church law requiring confession at least once a year, and sacramental absolution of all grave sins before communion, there is the towering truth too often forgotten that it *is* a sacrament and as such an *opus operatum*.* It not only wipes out

---

*"A sacrament is called this because its validity and efficacy depend on God, not on the subjective dispositions of men (even those produced by divine grace) as such (*opus operantis*). This does not mean that the grace of the sacrament will in fact have its wholesome effect in the recipient if he frustrates it by unbelief or obstinacy in sin. But this subjective disposition which is necessary to fruitful reception of the sacrament, the genuine readiness to accept God's forgiveness and sanctification, does not cause the efficacy of the sacrament, it is required as a condition before the grace of God proffered in the sacrament can become operative. The same is true of the attitude of the person administering the sacrament: be he saint or sinner, as long as he intends to administer the sacrament and uses the appropriate ceremonies, it signifies, even when administered by a sinner, the objectively valid pledge of God's grace, the historical tangibility of his salvific will in Christ for the life of the individual and of the Church."—Rahner and Vorgrimmler, *Theological Dictionary.*

sins, mortal and venial, but it confers a pledge of grace for the future. There is then a double effect: therapeutic and prophylactic. It is both physic and tonic. Don may confess that he has this dreadful hatred of his boss, that since his last confession he yielded at least four times to thoughts of hatred and revenge, but that now he is sorry and fully intends to get along with the boss if he can. The sacrament remits the guilt of Don's hatred and at the same time helps him keep his good resolution.

Strengthening the spirit is, of course, the big reason for frequent confession, the "confession of devotion" as it is called. Some nuns and other saintly types don't commit one mortal sin in fifty years, and yet they confess every week. In their case it is the tonic rather than the purgative that they are after. In fact, the regular checkup of frequent confession is a virtual necessity for any Catholic in earnest about making spiritual headway.

One really can't expect his confessor to be a psychiatrist. Every priest has had a few courses in psychology, it's true, but it was "rational" rather than "applied" psychology. And, by force of circumstances, only few of us priests are intellectuals. Most priests leaving the seminary mean well, but frequent changes from parish to parish require that their personal effects be few and easily mobile. Hence they can scarcely accumulate a library.

With a routine that keeps him constantly on the jump answering calls at the door and in the office, and with parish chores, the priest finds it fairly impossible to immerse himself in personality problems and their remedies. He literally has not the leisure needed for concentration and study. At most he can only try to keep up with current developments in his field by glancing each week through the diocesan paper and subscribing to a few clergy reviews.

What the confessor does offer, besides the sacrament, is a shoulder to cry on, an objective view of one's spiritual situation, and the kind of practical advice one would get from a business or professional man. In counseling his penitent, the confessor does have the help of the Holy Spirit. Best of all: if rightly received, the sacrament always brings peace of mind and heart.

It only remains to say that whenever you have sins of sex to confess, make it a point to hide your identity. If, in the course of a dull evening hearing elderly ladies and gentlemen with a sprinkling of teen-agers, the priest is unexpectedly brought wide awake by a penitent confessing everything from bank robbery to embracing a heifer, he is naturally going to be curious and will turn himself inside out trying to see who it is—easy enough, usually, for the door of the confessional is pierced for ventilation. Hence my advice:

Confess sex only to a strange priest, and never, never let him see your face or know your name. Get to church only after you know he is safely stowed away in the box, and then carefully keep out of his range of vision. Remember that the priest can see an awful lot right from where he sits, so don't cross in front of him. Get in line on the side nearest the exit and then, after your confession, slip right out of the church. You can say your penance next morning at mass.

At what point on the road from infancy to maturity does one become capable of mortal sin? To answer that, we must examine the formation of the typical born Catholic from the cradle until he reaches his majority. I use the word "formation," because although indoctrination of the Catholic through formal instruction is a great part, it is by no means the whole of it. The catechism—dear God!—as children in grammer school we were taken though it once a year from cover to cover, if not in the parish school, then in special classes after the children's mass on Sunday. We often learned without understanding, but we learned, and to this day I can recite the whole of the Baltimore catechism word for word.

More subtly, the system worked on the emotions: holy pictures at home and in school; the holy water font at the door of each classroom; the May altar to the Blessed Mother in each classroom, with all the pupils encouraged to bring in bunches of daisies and violets, lilacs and daffodils; opening and closing prayers, and the Angelus, recited in chorus as we knelt upright on the benches; the Sisters, dressed as we imagined our Lady must have looked; the crucifix up front; a holy card for the child who did well; and every Monday morning, the checkup on attendance at yesterday's mass.

When you begin inoculating a child of six with all this training in such an ambience, keeping it up through eight years of grammar and four of high school, perhaps sending him on to the diocesan college, you have built the Roman Catholic religion into the young person's mind, heart, and will. He will never be comfortable—at home—outside the household of the Faith.* His reaction to any situation touching on belief or morals will usually be predictable. With such intensive basic training, lasting through sixteen years, he

*I know, I know. There were Hitler and Stalin and any number of apostate founders of new sects with their followers. But my statement is at least generally if not universally true.

is practically assured of salvation. I mean it; by the time he gets out of college, his character is set in the right mold and it would take a moral miracle to break that mold.

(You must understand that, except for certain reservations which I am about to express, I am not knocking this system. I consider it part of the Church's success in holding her communicants, divinely inspired, and I am sorry to see it breaking up.)

According to the usage established by Pope St. Pius X in the first decade of this century, if the child in grade school is to develop a healthy spiritual life, he must be taught the habit of regularity at the sacraments. So once he has made his first holy communion, by means of stick or carrot as needed, he is driven to the confessional and the communion rail on the first Friday of every month.*

The day before, Thursday, from third through eighth grade, all the pupils are lined up and marched over to the church, room after room, for confession. Depending on the number of children and the supply of confessors available, some pastors get the program going right after the morning masses; others start after their siesta. It is all done on school time, for that is when the nuns have the children under control and it keeps the kids from being underfoot when the grown-ups want to confess later in the day.

There may be from two hundred to a thousand children eight to fourteen years old. I used to dread it, sitting for hours in a closet the size of a coffin, on a warm afternoon in the fall or late spring. You would finish up one classroom of thirty-five or forty children, hoping that it was the last, but no, a fresh troop of juvenile criminals would come trooping down the aisle to stand and wait for Sister's cricket, the signal to genuflect. You tried to average out the time used in one confession, then multiplied it by forty. "Late for lunch? Well, I don't care. I'm walking out whether they're all heard or not. Let them come back this afternoon." And so it went.

In most instances, Sister would hold a little warm-up with her class beforehand, reviewing the formalities, giving the children motives for sorrow, suggesting points for their examination of conscience; and this was good. But for the most part it made the kids' confessions tediously monotonous. The brighter kids would flesh out Sister's hints with "sins" and little inventions of their own. But the

---

*But this usage is gradually disappearing, as you will gather from the following pages.

dullards would merely recite the nun's list in a singsong voice and you would get it dozens of times in one afternoon:

"I disobeyed my mother, I disobeyed my father, I disobeyed my uncle, I disobeyed—"

"All right now, child. You were disobedient. So what else?"

"Aw! Now you made me forget what I wanted to say. Now I have to start all over again. I disobeyed my mother, I disobeyed my father. . . ."

Besides disobeying, the brighter youngsters might tell fibs, forget to feed the cat, talk in church, wet their pants, fart during prayer, talk back, and commit other such abominations against the Lord. The priest sits there for three or four hours hearing the whole school, and at the end of it all he can be fairly positive that not one sin, mortal or venial, has been confessed that day, and that just about every one of his abolutions has been invalid for lack of matter.

To commit a serious sin one must have grave matter, sufficient reflection, and full consent of the will.

But when does a person become capable of "sufficient reflection"—indeed, of any reflection at all?

In the year 529, Justinian set the age of reason at seven; canon law accepted his decision. Accordingly, in England, up until the eighteenth century, children of ten were hanged for theft. But the State considers that a youth does not have sense enough to vote intelligently until he is eighteen. In the eyes of the Church, a man under twenty-four is not mature enough for ordination, and until he is thirty-five he has not judgment enough to function as a bishop. The State stipulates corresponding requirements of maturity for various civil offices. The President must be at least thirty-five.

How, then, can anyone possibly think that a seven-year-old child could acquire intelligent comprehension of the supernatural realities required for the responsible renunciation of his right to ever-lasting happiness?

He can do objectively grave harm—Clorox in the soup, sugar in the gas tank—but subjectively, no.

Current research in developmental psychology has discovered these data:

> 1. The "age of reason," defined in terms of cognitive development sufficient to enable the child to comprehend concepts, grasp relationships, and understand distinctions,

occurs at the onset of adolescence, that is, between eleven and thirteen years of age in almost all children.

2. Autonomy of judgment sufficient to make responsible moral decisions manifests itself somewhat later, probably between twelve and fourteen years of age.[3]

Mortal sin is the religious analogue of a felony, venial sin of a misdemeanor. Yet in the Church we have been regarding our fourth-grader as capable of a felony—a capital crime—for which he is to be wiped out by Almighty God. What court in civil society would even indict a child of ten? See how far our pastoral practice has lagged behind modern jurisprudence and contemporary psychology, how badly it stands in need of updating, of *aggiornamento*.

The child lives in a state of subjection. If he runs away, he is brought back. He is answerable not to God but to his parents; it is his parents who are answerable to God for him. Would anyone think of letting a child follow his own conscience? He may not even choose his courses in school; he cannot contract debt nor be punished for a felony. How, then, can he have sufficient judgment to swear away his own soul?

It is only the exceptional schoolboy, perhaps one in a thousand, who is able competently to manage the abstract, relational, and evaluative concepts required if he is to renounce his Savior and deliberately choose everlasting damnation.[4]

The reason a child can't renounce his Fundamental Option is that he has never actually had judgment enough to make a Fundamental Option; how can he abdicate what he has never had?

If the child has not yet been able to take in the idea of God as the final purpose of his existence, then he cannot renounce Him by mortal sin. But if as yet there be no subjectively recognized and accepted final end, then there can be no question of means to this nonexistent end, no deviation, no partial turning from it.

According to St. Thomas, "Before a man comes to the age of discretion, the lack of years hinders the use of reason and excuses him from mortal sin, wherefore, much more does it excuse him from venial sin, if he does anything which is such generically."

Commenting on this in the English translation, Fr. Bernard McCabe writes: "Before one arrives at the age of discernment, when he can see the distinction between good and evil, or what is called the use of reason, he cannot commit a sin of any kind, and cannot have venial sin in his soul."[5]

The child is *non sui compos*, and hence he is impeccable.

The corollary is that although God will reward the good child, since the preadolescent is also premoral, not only is he incapable of sin but also of virtue or merit: "It does not distort the concept of God to say that he would reward striving to do good and ignore the lapse from good at this age."[6]

Naturally, reason does not dawn in a flash. The person does not go to bed a child one night and come awake next morning an adult. No, it is between the ages of nine and thirteen that he transfers his responsibility from his parents to God. He is beginning to think in abstractions, acquiring the power to apprehend and embrace God as his final end, the ultimate purpose of his existence. By degrees he establishes a direct personal relationship with the Deity, one not mediated by his parents. At first these insights with their accompanying sense of responsibility are inconsistent. He is only in the process of becoming a completely moral individual. That process is usually completed by the time he enters adolescence.[7]

The compulsory first Friday routine (compulsory through moral pressure) has been dropped in most parishes. But still if a preteener turned up in the confessional, the priest could only give the child his blessing, for an attempted absolution would certainly be invalid for lack of matter.

I am so happy about all this. It means that there are no children in purgatory, much less in hell. And heaven will be aglow with them, ringing with their laughter and their shouts of joy.

15

The Secret Service

Masturbation has been called America's "dirty little secret." Just about everybody does it, but nobody talks about it. In an expansive mood, maybe after a few drinks with "the boys," a man may concede that he worked at it now and then as a kid, that once at camp there was a "circle jerk," but there he stops.

The very sound of the word is unpleasant. I find myself writing around it, preferring the expression "self-sex." Others call it "manual orgasm," even "ipsation." Of course, "self-abuse" went out fifty years ago as being judgmental. "Onanism" used to be the clinical term but that too is just about passé, since the Scripture scholars have concluded that poor Onan was punished not for spilling his seed, but for disobedience. The German is *"Selbstbefriedigung,"* "satisfaction of self by self."

Researchers are surprised to find that for Americans masturbation is the most shameful and guilt-producing of all sex acts—which is quite something in view of anal and oral sex. Sexual surveyors find that almost no adults can bring themselves to tell others, even mates, that they still occasionally masturbate. And yet the classifed ads for "j.o. partners" are numerous in the columns of the subcultural press. Strangely, most of us are neither ashamed nor secretive about other kinds of self-pleasure (eating, lying in a hot bath, staying in bed late). Why, then, are we ashamed and secretive about self-sex?

The reason can most likely be found in the typical parental reaction to a child's first exploration of his genitals. Preverbal signs of embarrassment and/or disapproval make such a deep impression that later liberating concepts fail to fully remove the effects.

Nevertheless, only one in six of today's younger men considers masturbation wrong, as against one in three of the older men.

By the age of thirteen, three out of four boys and every second girl have masturbated to climax. By age twenty, over 90 percent of all males and 40 percent of all females have done it.

Of grown men, 94 percent masturbate; of women, 63 percent. From the ages of eighteen to twenty-four, the average incidence is once weekly for men, 37 times a year for women. After the age of thirty, men masturbate more often—on an average of 60 times a year.

The ancients certainly were not embarrassed by the subject. Martial called masturbation his "left-handed floozy" and referred to it again and again in his usual half-sneering way. But he did not hesitate to use self-help in a pinch: "Another Ganymede, my fist, helped me out." Elsewhere, "Often my left hand comes to my help in your place."

Ramusius of Rimini wrote to a friend:

"I suffer, dear Donatus, from so frightful an erection, I am fearful for my penis. Being wounded, my right hand can do nothing; I have no money; Hylas is not here; no vulva opens for me—no chance for sex; appease my desire that I may live—and you can do it cheaply."

Juvenal, Diogenes Lærtius, Ovid, the *Priapeia*, Scioppius, Petronius, Lampridius, Pliny, Aristophanes, and others, all speak openly and unashamedly of masturbation. The fact that (I suspect) the monks of the Dark Ages suppressed most of the classical references to buggery but passed so much comment on masturbation along to us, would indicate that if shame over the practice is a Christian development, it must be relatively recent.

If masturbation were not available society would have to invent it for its own protection. In masturbation, "anything goes." Physical wishes and emotional promptings which are censored in everyday living can be "let out of the bag" in the isolation of masturbation.

By discharging* hostile and aggressive fantasies, masturbation protects children and women against rape. It keeps husbands faithful to frigid wives and wives faithful to distant husbands. It guards the unmarried against pregnancy and premature paternity. It helps bishops and priests keep celibacy: for them it is "occult compensation." It keeps schoolboys out of brothels. It is Social Security in a very special sense. If masturbation were abruptly to become universally impossible, I dare say that within a week the whole world would be frantic.

This self-service is especially helpful to those who have no easily available partners. Dr. Albert Ellis distinguishes seven groups:[1]

1. Males, mostly young, where there is a strong local taboo against necking, petting, and intercourse among the unmarried. A kid may be frantic with desire for a "girl friend" who won't even let him kiss her.

2. Girls in the same situation. If they surrender, they may lose their reputation.

3. Segregated prisoners.

4. Men in the Service.

5. Men in isolated jobs, e.g., forest rangers, weather forecasters in remote outposts, sailors, explorers, spacemen, etc.

6. Long-term hospital patients.

7. Students of either sex in boarding schools.

The advantages of masturbation as we all know and as Dr. Ellis tabulates them:[2]

—It is always easily available;

—does not injure anyone;

—is free of all risk;

—relieves tension;

—costs nothing;

—is quick and easy;

—requires neither the ritual nor the ceremonial of sex with a partner;

*The term is Freud's.

—can be accomplished at home, school, or office, by a simple trip to the lavatory;

—requires no chemical or mechanical precautions against disease or pregnancy;

—can be done in bed while sick or merely restless.

In this same vein, Kinsey writes:

> For the boys (in this study) who have not been too disturbed psychically, masturbation has, however, provided a regular sexual outlet which has alleviated nervous tensions; and the record is clear in many cases that these boys have on the whole lived more balanced lives than the boys who have been more restrained in their sexual activities.[3]

And still, despite the compelling need for masturbation for the protection of society by providing the individual with a safety valve, it has been stigmatized as "shameful" and condemned first by the Church and then by the society formed by that Church—the very society which masturbation protects. But one would expect that stance as consistent with the Church's inveterate opposition to all sexual pleasure and also as part of her program for controlling society. Where you or I would say, "Sex is good, except—," the Church always begins, "Sex is bad, except—."

Now, according to official Catholic teaching, lust, booze, and avarice are all deadly sins, equally wicked, interchangeably vicious. But, in practice, lust is singled out for special denunciation as the Supersin. Clearly there is disorder here. Why?

Because, when it comes to sex, the Church always thinks in terms of babies—more customers—and never, never of pleasure: The population has to keep expanding at whatever cost, and the resultant babies have to be cared for during their term of helplessness. Hence, the sexual drive of the entire population must be funneled entirely toward the manufacture of more children, but only within the framework of a family. And that is how our Western society came so strongly to disapprove of any sex not directed toward reproduction —anything, that is, except intercourse in marriage with no protection against pregnancy. That lets out sodomy, even between man and wife, fellatio, cunnilingus, and masturbation.

With this in mind, one begins to understand the reasons behind social disapproval of prostitution, bastardy, homosexual practices, and other "sins." All such recreation, while releasing tension, diverts sexuality from the presumed need of society for still another baby, and the care of that baby. In other words, the Church has manipulated the pressures of society on a man, "respectability," such that whenever he gets horny, the only socially approved course of action open to him is sex with the possibility of impregnating his wife. Any sex exclusively for pleasure is literally damnable.

Although they are completely rejected by society, we have the prostitutes always with us, "as in the beginning, so now, and forever." Sex with a hooker serves much the same function as masturbation. It is quick release, impersonal, and no threat to the family. And a man can do things with a "pro," and ask services from her, that he would never think even of mentioning to his wife.

Pornography offers much the same release. The most timid-looking men come into the porno shops and buy paperbacks dealing with bondage, whips and high heels, spanking—every imaginable kind of kinky sex. But one can be sure that at home their sex does not go beyond the conventional.

As it tolerates prostitution and pornography, our antisexual society ought also to tolerate masturbation as an outlet for the overflow of sexual vitality in a safe and transitory way, especially for the adolescent, for whom society is not yet able and willing to provide a spouse. Why, then, the stern social disapproval of masturbation?

It springs from the need for official antagonism toward all extramarital and "futile" sex. To keep sex within the family it is necessary to condemn every other kind of sex, no matter what. If the sexual activity is not aimed at producing a child, if it is merely for fun, for relaxation of tension, it has to be evil.

The ideal for Catholics would be a kind of indult or privilege allowing youth to relax themselves by masturbation or by the use of condom, diaphragm, or the pill, with girls. Such a concession would be limited to young people, and perhaps prisoners and other hardship cases, within certain age limits or other considerations, on the expiration of which, the full rigor of the law would obtain. It would be awkward, but it could be worked out.

But even one exception, however useful the reason, would crack the rigid code that has governed sex for two millennia; it would be a foot in the door. And don't forget that Pope Paul VI, against all reason and common sense, just recently refused to crack that code, even though the whole world starve to death. He would not concede a play function to sex. He would not grant that sex is good. "Sex is bad," he intoned, "except—." So masturbation is out—even for prisoners,* farm boys, and astronauts.

This unrealistic and unnatural attitude toward sexuality goes far toward explaining

—why religion is considered a "very important value" by only 42 percent of today's noncollege youth, as against 65 percent only five years ago;[4]

—why, among college students during the same five years, the percentage making the same value judgment dropped from 38 to 28;[5]

—why religion ranks only thirteenth among the "very important values" of noncollege youth, fourteenth among college students;[6]

—and why Pope Paul VI recently told a group of pilgrims that "The Church seems doomed to die."[7]

However, once the Establishment takes a stand, there is a recognized procedure for propagandizing it. The priests in Sales & Promotion and the Public Relations experts take over and come up with a dozen or so verses from the Bible, statements by the hundreds from the Fathers and Doctors of the Church, impressive endorsements of the current line from renowned philosophers and jurists. Thus the position becomes entrenched. I know how it works. For thirty years I was on the team myself, selling infallibility, apostolic succession, talking down birth control, and such.

If tomorrow the pope decided that everyone should be strangled on his sixty-fifth birthday, the S&P and PR boys could put it across within eighteen months. They could do the same if the Holy Father changed his mind on masturbation. But as I shall explain in a moment, he will never make an explicit statement on that subject; he will let popular disapproval continue in force because otherwise the principle of denial of sex for pleasure, without the intention of repro-

---

*"'Can you guess what it's like in chokey . . . hundreds of men . . . strong men in their prime . . . cut off from women. Not nice to think about, eh? Sex is dirty when it's to do with convicts. The prison visiting committee . . . sanctimonious bastards . . . don't even give it a thought. But they would all right, by God, if they were in there. Day and night, week after week, month after month, it works on you till you think you're going crazy. You can't help human nature. You lie there in your cell at night and think . . . imagine a woman waiting for you outside . . . beautiful, young, wanting you . . . waiting . . . until you're ready to smash the walls down with your bare fists in an effort to get out.'"—A.J. Cronin, *Beyond This Place* (Garden City, N.Y.: Doubleday, 1957), p. 227.

ducing, would be tainted. The seed must not fall on the ground—not where anyone can see it, anyway.

And that is just why the Holy Father is never likely to speak out explicitly on masturbation. It is because *although it is officially condemned, it is unofficially condoned*. It is a practice that is never detected. It is never reported to an ecclesiastical superior, much less to the police. It is the "secret service." No partner, no witnesses, no Polaroids. No one is ever going to report a cardinal of the Holy Roman Church for playing his organ, because no one will ever know. So, you see, there is no problem, for masturbation simply does not exist.

And thus, "it is possible to fulfill the needs of the society by having strong condemnation, and at the same time provide a mechanism whereby the functional value of masturbation as a release for adolescents and others is not lost, becuase it becomes an act so widely accomplished that the condemnation is almost universally trangressed."[8]

This kind of duplicity on the part of the Church is not unknown among the "many societies in which the adult attitudes towards sex play in children or towards premarital affairs in adolescence are characterized by prohibitions that are apparently not very serious and in fact are not enforced. In such cases sexual experimentation may take place in secrecy without incurring punishment, even though the parents know perfectly well what is going on."[9]

The Church is careful not to make her condemnation of masturbation explicit. It is not mentioned by name in papal documents. But reprobation is implied in her generally negative attitude toward all sex and her frequent explicit prohibition of nonreproductive sex. Thus the implied condemnation covers the reality of its universal nonobservance, which is concealed. They exist side by side, the facade and the reality, "as a mutually complementary and mutually reinforcing system; and the activity could become so widespread as to be useful, without incurring punishment, so long as it was not openly acknowledged."[10]

Sadly, it was just such expediential ambiguity that led Fr. Charles Davis to quit the Church. He was fatally scandalized by what he saw at Vatican II as a consultant to Cardinal Heenan. One of England's ranking theologians, professor of theology at Heythrop College, editor of the *Clergy Review*, and an internationally celebrated author, he "disaffiliated" publicly on December 21, 1966. He said that he expects the true Church to be "a zone of truth," and this, he says, the "Institutional Church" is not. In his bill of particulars he cited, among other items, the calculated mistranslation of encyclicals, the deliberate use of ambiguous language in Roman documents, and the Church's being forever ready to compromise her mission to mankind when institutional advantage seems to demand this.[11]

So here we have it all over again with this doublethink on masturbation. The problem is the harm done to souls. The conscientious Catholic who takes his training seriously is convinced that he is committing a mortal sin every time he "plays with himself." He accepts the word of his teachers in religious education but feels that he is too weak to resist.

Theologically there is no case at all for the prohibition of masturbation. It is not once mentioned in the Bible—not in Leviticus or Deuteronomy; not by our Lord, not even by the stern St. Paul; none of the Fathers, Doctors, and relatively few of the theologians speak of it. Apparently it was a commonplace of daily life taken for granted like voiding, expectorating, or passing wind. It was morally vacant until the Jesuits arrived on the scene at the time of the Counter-Reformation in the sixteenth century—and of all Church personnel, the Jesuits take the darkest and most negative view of sex.

—By decree of St. Ignatius, a Jesuit will not even touch another person beyond the conventional handshake lest the contact make him horny.[12] (The Basques must be even more inflammable than the rest of us ever imagined.)

—It was an early Jesuit general who committed the entire society in perpetuity to teach and defend the bizarre opinion that every sexual offense, however slight, is objectively grave.

—A Jesuit youth, St. Aloysius Gonzaga, is held up as the model of sexual repression.

—It was the Jesuit theologian Arthur Vermeersch who led the battle for overpopulation and world starvation in the early decades of this century.

—And some fifteen hundred years after the founding of the Church, it was the Jesuits who first fingered masturbation as a chink in the Church's barricade against nonreproductive sex.

Once they had trumpeted their disapproval of self-sex, they were mindlessly copied by the other theologians right down to this present. To this day, the Holy See has been silent on the subject and in practice there is a consensus, not only of confessors but also of the faithful, agreeing on the permissibility of masturbation.

As a rule, priests hearing confessions don't give anyone a hard time over masturbation; they scarcely comment. Nor does this attitude mean that they are laxists. Rather, they are guided by intuition shaded by experience. They know, or at least they sense, that masturbation is no more "dirty," no more "evil," than nail biting, nose boring, or thumb sucking, and the teener should feel no more guilt over his actions than over copying an assignment or drag racing—if that much.

Sadly, during their young years the state of grace for most males—subjectively, at least—depends on their refraining from masturbation. They see this as the first real test of their Christian convictions. It is sad because masturbation is not a sin. They only think it is and, as I quoted Dr. Kinsey, boys who masturbate are usually better off than those who don't. They are not so tense—"uptight," as they call it nowadays.

There are 27,000,000 American adolescents, of whom statistically about one in four is Catholic, for a total of 6,750,000.[13] Of these anguished souls, Bishop Francis Simons writes:

> For one who believes in God it is intolerable to have to think that God made the observance of his law so difficult that such a large proportion of young people find it impossible not to fall into gravely immoral acts. For many priests this makes it all but certain that there must be a flaw in the traditional Catholic view. . . . The misery and moral harm inflicted on such youth, the warping of their notion of God, the breaking of their spiritual order, are incalculable.[14]

As we have seen, the "flaw in the traditional Catholic view" is the notion of sex as exclusively reproductive. Since, for seven years, the adolescent has the physical power of sexuality without the social capability of marriage, his only outlet is masturbation.

Sexual tension accumulates; it keeps building up until it is discharged, and the teener has release literally within reach. For all of us, but especially for a kid who is without money, car, and know-how, masturbation is the simplest and quickest means of gratification: pleasure without responsibility, psychophysiological release for self-love, sustained by endless fantasy.

Adolescent girls, too, are capable of orgasm, and current surveys document that they also masturbate. "The diffuse 'funny feeling' attendant upon romantic daydreams in a thirteen-year-old girl is in no way morally different from the phallic urgency accompanying the frankly erotic fantasies of the pubescent young boy."[15]

> One fifteen-year-old girl reported that [while masturbating] she thought not only of "things my boyfriend does to me and good-looking men I've seen someplace before or that I've talked to," but also of other "more useful" things as well:" And I could find out a lot of my fears that way because I've tried masturbating to some thoughts that I didn't dig. Such as oral sex, you know. That was a long time ago, and I've finally come to that thought. Anal sex I tried masturbating to, but I couldn't come to that. I'm not really free about that. I have had that [anal sex] with my boyfriend before, but I didn't really dig it, you know."
>
> Another seventeen-year-old feared that she might be a lesbian because of her lack of interest in men, so she masturbated while picturing naked women and girls in her mind to see whether or not she could have a climax. "I couldn't ever come while I thought about them," she told us, "so I was sure that that wasn't my hangup. I was glad for that!"[16]

But continence is much harder for boys than for girls. Entertainer George Carlin, a Catholic, does a skit on confession:

> In my diocese in New York, when Puerto Ricans started moving in, they make a rare display of tokenism for the fifties—they brought in Father Rivera. All the Irish guys heavily into puberty went to him to confession because he didn't seem to take the sins personally. It was three Hail Marys and back on the street with Father Rivera—he was known as a light penance. But he wasn't ready for the way Irish boys confessed. "Bless me, Fodder, for I have sinned. I have touched myself in an impure manner. I was impure, impurity, impureness. Thought, word and deed, body, touch, impure; sex, dirty, impure legs, impureness, touch, impure, dirty, bodies, sex, rub. And covet, Fodder, heavy on the covet."[17]

(I wonder if girls still treasure their virginity or what, in fact, they understand by the term. After several years of frantic necking, petting, and masturbating, with orgasm following orgasm at five-minute intervals night after night, is a girl still a virgin merely because technically she still has her hymen intact? The statues guarding the Town Hall in Copenhagen are said to blow their trumpets every time a virgin passes. Many years ago, when I asked my tutor in German the word for "virgin," she was honestly puzzled—and she was a Heidelberg Ph.D. At first she said it was an archaic word, "certainly obsolete." Then, as she glanced at my Roman collar, "Oh, yes," she said, "it's still current as a religious term—'*die heilige Jungfrau Maria*'—but it's never used outside of church circles." Perhaps the Danes and the Germans are more realistic than we.)

You will remember from the last chapter that until their thirteenth birthday boys and girls are morally impeccable. At that point they begin to acquire responsibility. But until they are seventeen or eighteen they are still lacking somewhat in maturity. Their decisions and judgments are subject to abrupt reversals. They are impulsive, influenced by violent mood swings. Can you remember yourself at fifteen and sixteen—the vows of eternal friendship, oaths of perpetual enmity—so easily made and as lightly abandoned? During early and middle adolescence, through seventeen to eighteen, moral decisions are neither free nor mature in a consistent and sustained manner.[18]

From the onset of adolescence to about eighteen, occasional masturbation—with some periods of more frequency and intensity caused by anxiety—is statistically, psychologically, and morally normal. Finally, at seventeen or eighteen, just about when he picks up his high-school diploma, comes the passage into moral maturity. Now he is on his own; he has finally reached the age of reason.

Among the absurdities of moral theology: the boy who chooses to masturbate at home rather than risk getting his girl pregnant is actually making the worse choice, for he is choosing an "unnatural" rather than a "natural" sin. But even that outmoded theology would have to give him points for prudence.

> Ten percent of all American female adolescents report that they have been pregnant at least once. Eleven percent of all younger nonvirgin girls and 28 percent of all older nonvirgin girls report having been pregnant. Twenty-eight percent of all nonvirgin girls with intercourse experience during the preceding month report they have been pregnant, compared with 7 percent of all nonvirgin girls who did not have intercourse during the preceding month.[19]

"If two people are going to have a baby that neither person really wants, is it all right for the girl to have an abortion?" In response to this question, 56 percent of all Catholic adolescents favor abortion. "Girls whose personal religious preference is Catholic, however, are less inclined to favor abortion; only 31 percent of Catholic girls agree with the statement."[20]

Our Catholic morality of sex still includes great, awkward anachronisms that hold the believer captive and impede him in the free exercise of his faculties—prohibitions and condemnations that once may have had meaning and function but which are now useless, left stranded high and dry on the shores of this nuclear age, where they can only generate resentment and alienate the Christian.

Within just the past few decades, the structure of society has changed, as has industrial technology, and these changes make those moral anachronisms doubly hurtful: not only have they become meaningless but they are tormenting a new class of people—the teen-agers. We used to call them adolescents, but our teen-ager matures physically two years before his parents did. He leaves home earlier—for college or for his stint in the Service. These are the people who are hurt by a moral anachronism which says they must not use their sexual powers, i.e., they must not be what they are. We nourish them with milk and fresh orange juice and keep them blooming with health and vitality, while at the same time we block them off from the waist down.

Nevertheless, 71 percent of the boys and 56 percent of the girls have had intercourse by age fifteen.[21] As their immediate reaction to their first experience of intercourse, they felt, by descending percentages, excited, afraid, happy, satisfied, thrilled, curious, joyful, mature, fulfilled, worried. Only 17 percent felt guilty.[22]

Because the adolescent has a stricter idea of marriage, he engages in premarital intercourse, for the strange thing is that sex before marriage tends to be followed by good marriages and more of them.

> Most young people want to be married and have children—eventually. But their concept of marriage turns out to be a stricter and longer-range one than most young people feel has been demonstrated by their parents, many of whom *with* marriage have been serial monogamists in pursuit of the one "ideal marriage" among many that would satisfy them.[23]

Kinsey found that a chaste courtship without intercourse leads to little and poor sexual relations within marriage; and both the boy and the girl are permanently stuck with each other. Many a man has

married after a chaste courtship only to find that his wife is frigid and
has a pathological fear and hatred of sex; he can't even touch her. I
have known several cases like that. There is wisdom in the saying,
"Never buy a horse until you've ridden her."

A certain amount of sex before marriage leads to more and better
sex within marriage: Practice makes perfect. Once married, the
Catholic must abruptly and completely reverse all his past mental and
physical attitudes, training, and habits toward sex. It is much to be
feared then that the boy who has exchanged a few chaste kisses with
the girl he later marries will be a spiritless drudge imprisoned in a
flabby domesticity, fated to be bored silly for the rest of his life. And
that goes for her, too.

> If we urge young people to place themselves at the
> extreme point of total continence before marriage, we shall
> presumably base our arguments either on the reward to be
> reaped in an after life, or the satisfaction to be reaped in this
> life from conformity to a moral injunction. The danger is that
> they may identify this reasoning for what it is, namely an
> appeal to rewards and satisfactions which have many things in
> their favor, but are not related to those of love. To regulate
> one's sex life by reference to extraneous matters is something
> we sharply blame in other contexts, as for instance when a
> prostitute regulates her sex life by reference to money.[24]*

What the Catholic must work and pray for is an adult conscience
that is forever rid of the casuistic approach to life with its constant
fussing over sin and guilt and taboos of every kind. St. John says,
"Perfect love casts out fear." St. Augustine advises us to "Love God,
and do as you please." In other words, the one who sincerely loves
God need not worry about commands and prohibitions, for he is
above the law. So make up your own mind; then don't worry!

When it comes to sex, "Think positive!" Not "Sex is bad,
except—" but, "Sex is good!" Sex is good except when it is cruel,
diseased, violent, commercialized, and so on. Sexual intercourse is a
joy, a good which can be spoiled. It is not, as the Church would have
it, a dirty and dangerous thing that can be redeemed only by matrimony, for love is larger than matrimony, and love is achieved
through coupling. Love is not the condition for intimacy. It is the
other way around. Intimacy begets love. Without orgasm in inter-

*Reprinted by permission of the Harold Matson Company, Inc., © 1964 by Way-
land Young.

course, there is only the tension of romantic passion—which may or may not turn into love.

If a boy and a girl, each a virgin, can be said to possess love, what shall we call that bond between the man and wife who live together, make love together, climax together, and have children? If the lesser be love, then there can be no name for the greater. But the lesser may lead to the greater, and that is God's finest gift to mankind.

Before going on to the subject of "bad" thoughts and desires, now known perhaps more familiarly as "fantasies," let me give you a few gruesome examples of sexual morality as worked out by two theologians: Piscetta and Gennaro. Their book, *Elementa Theologiae Moralis*, Vol. VII, Turin, 1940, has been used by many priests during their seminary years.

First, there is a pejorative evaluation of just about anything that can be done in bed except a short quick deal with the man on top. From that they go on to argue that if a man with syphilis wants to couple with his healthy wife, she has no right to turn him down, because there is a possibility, however remote, that the disease may not be passed on to the child, in which case there would be one more client for Holy Mother Church (paragraph 280). It is understood, of course, that the syphilitic may not use a condom, for that would violate the integrity of the act and thus turn it against nature.

Again, if her physician has warned her that her next sexual encounter may be her last, she still may not refuse her husband, for the physician just might be mistaken (paragraph 277). The authors also recommend cauterizing or amputating the clitoris to "remedy" lesbianism (paragraph 167).

Now whom are we to follow? Our Lord? Or clowns like Piscetta and Gennaro? It is no wonder that so many of our contemporaries are first disgusted and then bored—not with Christ but with the Institutional Church which claims to teach with His full authority through the writings of such as Piscetta and Gennaro.

So, in this matter of "bad" thoughts and desires, let us bypass the theologians and search out what our Lord himself had to say on the subject, for it is he after all who is our Master.

As already seen, in the Gospels Jesus touches only twice and then only incidentally on sex. There is the woman taken in adultery. But adultery here is only the occasion of an object lesson on hypocrisy. Concerning adultery, he does not commit himself as either opposed or lenient toward it. Whether it had been adultery, theft, or blasphemy that she was taken in, the lesson would have been the same: "Let him among you who is without sin cast the first stone."

There is also the saying that he who desires a woman has already committed adultery with her in his heart. Again, this is not a judgment on adultery. This is a saying about the relation between desire and act, as when He said, "He who hateth his brother" murders him. Both examples make the same point. Religion must be internal, a disposition of mind and heart, rather than a set of merely external observances.

By now it should be dawning on the reader that the Church practices a kind of double-entry bookkeeping in her moral theology. There is the official teaching as set forth in the textbooks, taught to the seminarians, and relayed to the laity in catechisms, Sunday sermons, missions, retreats, and pamphlets. And this teaching is really uptight. But then, alongside, there is the unofficial theology as counseled in the confessional by implication or by silence, and practiced by the faithful.

Accordingly, we have seen that sodomy is an abomination, the worst of the worst; but then, as Tanquerey informs us in the finest of fine print, for gays it is generally a venial sin.

Birth control: Our Holy Father explicitly forbids it as seriously evil, but the people are not convinced, still practice it, don't confess it. No priest is likely to be so imprudent as to recommend the practice or even try to straighten out an erroneous conscience. Rather, when he hears it confessed, he will pass over it in silence, and thus *"Humanae vitae"* will become a dead letter, if it has not already fallen to that state.

Masturbation: officially condemned at least by implication, unofficially condoned.

As between the official theology and its actual practice by the laity, right is with the morally unanimous judgment of the faithful in either accepting or rejecting what they are told, for they, too, have the Holy Spirit.

Besides, as we have had it so painfully brought to our notice only recently with *"Humanæ vitæ,"* official theology is apt to be institutional theology, favoring the structure and the interests of the higher clergy, at the expense of the poor struggling pilgrim in the pew.

Bad thoughts? Yes, there are such things: thoughts of hatred, the planning of murder, vengeance, blackmail, rape, robbery. Such thoughts are sinful according to their duration and intensity.

But sexual fantasies of the kind needed to accomplish masturbation—such daydreams are not sinful. The boy pictures himself treading "acres and acres of breasts, and they're all mine." He ejaculates, his fantasy collapses, and who has suffered in any way at all? Or he has *Playboy* at his side as he sprawls across the bed, pants and briefs at half-mast, blissfully pulsing under the jackhammer of orgasm. He doesn't know the girls, has never met them, and never will meet them. *Cui damno?*

The one case explicitly forbidden in both Old and New Testament concerns the other fellow's wife. Our Lord says that if you desire her, you are already guilty of adultery. It follows, then, that since thought must lead to desire, one should not even think about her.

In this matter of fantasy, as in so many areas, we leave school all keyed up to the point of scrupulosity. We try to confess not only the number but even the quality of our fantasies—"natural" or "unnatural." But then we gradually loosen up until one day we notice that we are no longer confessing "bad thoughts and desires," either because they are no longer entering into our mind and will, or because if they are we no longer count them sinful.

There are three different levels of sexual morality, in each of which, even if it were wrong, fantasy would be permissible: the single life, engagement, and marriage.

The unmarried person has a right to relax his tensions by masturbation, which he can hardly do without some help from his imagination. This can be assisted by pictures, magazines, or movies in a theater, in a bar, or at home.

Engagement offers a kind of "learner's permit." If a boy and a girl on a date may have sex fantasies, an engaged couple have even more right to fantasize.

Marriage actually demands fantasy, and the facility should be there. Husband and wife should have unlearned the habit of automatic rejection during their courtship. Now they should work at encouraging fantasies.

In general, when a person suppresses or rejects fantasies the moment they appear, he is only compounding his problem by damming up his sexual tension—which, as we have seen, is cumulative. It keeps piling up. There is also the possibility that by suppressing fantasy, one may impair imaginative power capable of constructive use in the arts.

In fine, "It is the task of parents, teachers, confessors, and counselors to prevent the formation of an attitude that sex fantasies are impure or dirty and should be avoided at all costs."[25]

16

Theme and Variations

The Church still bases its morality on conformity with or deviation from a supposed absolute standard, thought to run like a straight line through human sexuality. Those who waver or break over in any way are called "deviates," "perverts," and—in more Christian times—they were generally cremated alive. So people kept their mouths shut about the quality of their sex fantasies and actions.

Then about a hundred years ago, the Germans began rooting around in the human psyche: Sigmund Freud, Albert Moll, Richard Krafft-Ebing, and the English Havelock Ellis. They discovered numerous syndromes in sexuality, related characteristics, typical of whole groups of people, people in the hundreds of thousands. These syndromes were variations of the conventional heterosexual relationship between man and wife. Under the increasing influence of psychiatry and especially with the publication of the Kinsey Report in 1948, the world was finally rid of concepts in sexuality such as natural, unnatural, deviate, and perverted.

But in her morality of sex the Church is still back in the dark ages. She acts as if she has not yet heard of Freud, Moll, Krafft-Ebing, or Kinsey; her physiology and psychology are still that of Aristotle, Plato, SS. Paul, Augustine, and Thomas. But as civilization no longer follows the physiology and psychology of the ancients, so it rejects a morality of sex based on their antiquated notions. Unless the Church catches up with reality and assimilates the findings of contemporary research in the behavioral sciences, our religion will sink to the status of phrenology, alchemy, and astrology; a superstition practiced here and there by little groups of bright-eyed fanatics impervious to all reason.

The rest of this chapter accepts as amply demonstrated that a principal purpose of sex is reproduction, but equally principal is relief of tension by satisfaction of the sexual appetite. Both mind and conscience boggle at the idea that God created 15,000,000 American gays, 27,000,000 adolescents, and untold other millions of sexually disadvantaged persons, to live as involuntary priests and nuns, reluctant psychological eunuchs, kicking and struggling in constant rebellion against their condition.

Would God make a person with a short leg and then bid him walk straight under penalty of damnation? Those millions of sexual variants abhor the thought—as do we. And yet that is exactly Church teaching regarding the variants. Now, no one is going to stand by and see himself virtually condemned to hell. So such people either adjust their conscience along the lines I have been suggesting, or they stop going to church, or perhaps, as in the case of the gays, they affiliate with a segregated sect advocating a morality which to them at least seems more compassionate, more realistic, more Christlike. Now let's get on with the discussion.

Our sexual needs and preferences form a pattern that, like ears and fingerprints, is unique. We can group various sexual expressions into general classifications as physiologists anatomize the human body, but beyond that we cannot go. Psychologically, no one is ever an exact sexual duplicate of anyone else.

Why? Because, apart from the physical differences among people—color, height, weight, glandular pressures—your sexuality began shaping up even while you were still inside your mother. Were you nursed or bottle-fed? By your mother or a nurse? Did your nurse perhaps masturbate you as an infant to help you unwind for sleep? It all makes a difference. Perhaps one day there was a fleck of grit on the diaper that kept rubbing your perineum, alternately tickling and irritating it for the better part of an afternoon. Maybe when you were three or four, some older kids took down your pants and played with your privates. It all added up and made you what you are today in the way of sex.

—In *The Joy of Sex*, Dr. Alex Comfort speaks of a man who could only climax by getting into a tub of cooked spaghetti.

—The poet Swinburne—and many of his compatriots—used to hire a madam to thrash his bare bottom.*

—In London the going rate is "one quid for one," i.e., $2.50 for each stroke of the cane—a wooden rod about as thick as your little finger. To inflict a stroke, it is raised high over the shoulders and then brought crashing down with all possible strength across the buttocks. Three such strokes would be an ample dose. The pathic often provides costumes so that the beating can be dramatized. For instance, he gets himself into a schoolboy outfit and pretends that she is his mother, governess, or teacher; or the whole thing may be carried off in drag.

—Another man—and this is not infrequent—may have the girl dress as a nurse, powder and diaper him, and then tuck him in with a bottle.

—There is no limit to fantasy where sex is involved. One prostitute tells of a patron who keeps a coffin on hand. He garbs her in a white gown, crowns her with roses, puts a Bible in her one hand and a rosary in the other. Then she climbs into the coffin. You can imagine the rest.[1]

Well, it's every man to his own taste. I love eel and snails, but can't stomach oysters. Some men like a lot of hair on their face; others prefer it on their head; and then there are girls who like the ape-man, with hair all over him, and for all I know he may like the same hirsute arrangement in his women. We all differ in our tastes on practically everything, but especially on sex.

With a difference: We do not choose our sexual variations like ordering *à la carte*; our sexuality is not a matter of taste. Rather, it is

*"The English vice." In the English public schools such as Winchester, Eton, and Harrow, the boys are disciplined in this way. A Winchester "old boy" once told me that the boys frame these canings in a sexual context. Lying in bed nights after lights out, as they listen to the swish and thwack of the cane rising and falling, the suppressed sobs and cries of the delinquent being punished in the prefect's apartment, just about all of them are masturbating. The association often carries over into adult life, as in the case of Swinburne. Where the graffiti in American lavatories will solicit or offer fellatio, those in the English lavatories very often concern caning, either as agent or victim.

more a *table d' hôte*, a fixed preference, implanted somewhere along the line from conception to the present moment. This preference is limited and determined by capability. Outside his proper métier, the male is physically unable to effect penetration and climax, and the female is overcome with disgust, nausea, and she sometimes suffers bodily pain.

But we must not look down on anyone just because his chromosomes and genes may have endowed him with a sexuality different from our own.* Certainly I'm not condemning people who eat those slimy things known as oysters—ugh! do you chew them or just let them slither down the gullet by themselves?—and in return I expect them to mind their own business about my eel and snails. Likewise, how other people have to get their jollies is no affair of mine, nor are my sex ways any business of theirs. One way is neither better nor worse than another, always with the provision that there must be mutual consent. Violence, physical or moral, is out.

"What is normal in sex?" asks Dr. Comfort. It is whatever sex ought to be, he replies: "It ought to be a wholly satisfying link between two affectionate people, from which both emerge unanxious, rewarded, and ready for more."

"Abnormal" accordingly means:

> 1. Unusual for the time and place—e.g., intercourse ten times a day as a regular thing; or intercourse on the corner of Hollywood and Vine.
> 2. Unusual and disapproved: "It's abnormal in Papua to bury dead relatives, and abnormal in California to eat them."
> 3. Unusual and handicapping—e.g., a really worrisome sexual obsession, such as a compulsion to dig up cadavers. (It is this sort of thing that gives heterosexuality a bad name.)

Of the "spaghetti man" Dr. Comfort says merely that his behavior is "odd."

So if you must talk about "normality," any sex behavior is normal which:

> 1. You both enjoy,
> 2. Hurts nobody,
> 3. Isn't associated with anxiety, and
> 4. Doesn't cut down your scope—e.g., insistence on operating only in the dark.[2]

---

*Each of us has a private madness—if not sexual, then something else, and blessed is the man who can afford his own asylum.

In everything concerning sex, our attitude, as opposed to that of the Church, should be positive. Where the Church is restrictive, we favor freedom. According to our view, sex is "in possession." You are master of your own sexuality and can do with it what you will, and anyone who tries to stop or restrict you had better come up with a pretty powerful argument. This goes against the current Catholic idea that the Church is keeper of the human phallus and vulva, and that whenever we want the use of them we have to apply to her and prove our case.

Everyone has a God-given right to sex. If the priest wants to live without it, that's his privilege. But he makes a free choice.

The gays have their own built-in prescription, calling for sodomy. As for the oddballs enacting their little psychodramas with the London prostitutes—the cross-dressing, symbolic whipping, the coffin—they are harmless but seemingly necessary for these people to induce orgasm. Is there any reason then why they should be stopped from doing what they must? Their fetishes and obsessions are to their sexuality as insulin to the diabetic. Neither can function without his specific.

Sexual activity should be an expression of mutual love; that is the ideal. But the man and wife, no longer joined by love but rather by convention, concern for home and children, or mere expediency—she a useful cook and housekeeper, he a dependable wage earner—such people need not feel guilty when they couple just because at the moment they feel horny. Sexual activity is rarely altogether meaningless. The fast-stepping bachelor sizes up every woman he meets as a possible wife. The gay, cruising parks and bars, is in constant search for a meaningful relationship. Even the prostitute may see every client as a possible husband and a means of finally achieving "respectability."

But let us imagine a contact that is absolutely meaningless. Even so, it would be harmless rather than evil, a morally indifferent act.

St. Thomas's argument against fornication is surprisingly frail. He pleads the injustice done to the potential bastard, for every child coming into the world has a right to be met by loving parents and reared in a decent home. A further injustice is done to the society which must bear the burden of supporting the child in the absence of the parents. But apart from considerations of contraception and the pill, which can definitely preclude pregnancy, what of the woman who is barren or the man who is sterile?[3]

Fr. Vermeersch defines chastity as "that virtue which orders the sexual appetite according to right reason illuminated by faith." The operative phrase there is "right reason," of which the individual conscience must be the final judge.

Modern researchers, journalists and sociologists seem to agree that in spite of more frequent usage of manual, oral and anal forms of sex stimulation and gratification, vaginal intercourse has not decreased significantly. The prevalence of more liberal sexual attitudes has not dissuaded the great majority of Americans from the conviction that sex is deeply related to the ideals of love, marriage and loyalty. Though more openly sensual and pleasure-seeking in their sex activities than past generations, modern Americans are also more other-conscious in their relationships than ever before.

The uninformed think of sadomasochism (S/M) in terms of the mayhem and murder described in the works of the Marquis, but its serious devotees actually form a sort of subculture of their own halfway between the heteros and the homosexuals. The cult is most conspicuous among the motorcycle gangs. It is usually a set of ritualistic sex games involving special costumes—leather pants and jackets, tricked out with all kinds of zippered pockets, chain epaulets, and the like—and played out with stylized gestures in stereotyped proceedings. There is only a pretense of pain given and accepted; any actual pain is merely symbolic.

> The sadists who make themselves and other people miserable or ill or dead, are simply the thwarted, stupid or exhibitionist minority of that particular craft, and for every one of these there are ten or a hundred well-adjusted people, filling what they call responsible jobs and never raising an eyebrow, who are perfectly happy beating each other up in private. It is a way of life and, like homosexuality, goes on a sliding scale: there's some of it in many people who don't swear by it.[4]

It has been remarked that the American male is either a "breast man" or a "leg man." To judge from current magazines, the mammary enthusiasts are in the majority for the obvious reason that the man can see all the legs and backsides he wants in any locker room. He even has them himself. But breasts—only girls have them, and so breasts have come to symbolize the physical differences between the sexes.

Now when a man confronts his beloved, both of them splendidly naked as God made them, he sees her almost as a vision from heaven. She is a worthy temple of the Holy Spirit, made by the Almighty to help continue his work of creation on earth, and by God she looks it!—"How wonderful is God in all his saints, and holy in all his works!"—"Dear God," the man thinks, "if this be sin, it is Thyself who hast seduced me."

But see now how his instincts take over and drive him. He feels he must unite with this splendid vision and somehow go into her, with all her radiant beauty, so that they two may become one body. If it were possible he would like to chew her up and literally eat her alive. But that would only destroy what he so urgently loves.

Watch now how he seeks out the "frontier" regions, the apertures of the body where inside meets outside (and happily they are all erogenous in various measure): the eyes, the ears, the nostrils, lips and mouth, the nipples, the naval, vulva, and anus. What he is doing, I think, is trying to get inside the beloved, trying in some blindly atavistic way to make actual contact with her soul.

Although—as one can judge from the statues of classical antiquity, all of which have a solid and well-rounded foundation—the buttocks had always been well regarded as much for their beauty as for their erogenous potential, under Christian influence they were shrouded in modesty and came to be disdained as one of the "dirty" areas of the body, suggesting the privy and the disagreeable processes of elimination. Of course in earlier Christian centuries, if they were fastidious, people took a sponge bath once a week and a tub bath maybe two or three times a year. So they must have reeked.

However, as the years pass by in this post-Christian and obsessively clean century of ours, stimulation of the buttocks and even the anus are becoming more acceptable in sexual activity. More Americans are admitting that they have engaged in such stimulation in the way of fingering, kissing, and tonguing (known as "rimming") of the anus.

There is a variation on this theme known as partialism. Paul, a young friend of mine, answered the doorbell of his apartment in Paris one evening, and there stood his next-door neighbor. Paul happened to be wearing open-toed sandals without socks. The neighbor, a man perhaps ten years older, collapsed at Paul's feet and began licking and slobbering over his toes. Paul happened to be quite rich and perhaps in consequence highly sophisticated. He was interested rather than shocked, so he invited the neighbor inside and let him play with his feet until the neighbor came to climax.

For some unknown reason, a person's whole sexuality will sometimes be focused on one particular and often irrelevant part of the other person's body. It may be the breasts. As soon as the girl pulls off her shirt, such a man will zoom in on her bosom and get to work. He won't care if she never takes her skirt off. He won't kiss her lips or even look at her face—just her breasts, chewing, sucking, and munching on them, possibly ending by pressing both breasts over his organ and getting himself off in that rather clumsy fashion.

Others will make for the bottom cheeks in the same way.

On the other hand, a schoolmate of mine was stimulated sexually through his scalp. He would sit in the barber chair the whole time with an erection, hoping and praying that he would not disgrace himself before it was all over. About one in ten, I am told, is similarly sensitive in his buttocks. His wife excites him not so much by fondling his genitals as by stroking and kneading his bottom. The least unexpected touch in that area (the "goose") is enough to send him over the chandelier.

Fetishism, on the other hand, refers to material objects. The police are all too familiar with the nuisance who plucks women's panties from neighborhood clotheslines so that he can try them on, preen himself before a mirror, and then masturbate. The underground press is loaded every week with classified ads inserted by people with the most various and bizarre fetishes, looking for partners to share the fun.

Transvestism or cross-dressing would be grouped under fetishism. Says Dr. Comfort: "A transvestite is a person who, while staying fully in his or her own sex role, feels an intense compulsion at times to dress the opposite sex role, and an intense release of anxiety (not so much a kick) when they do so. They are not 'homosexual,' and a bisexual person who dresses the opposite sex to please a partner isn't a transvestite."[5]

"They are not 'homosexual.'" But most of them are, and the one place in any big city where you are most likely to meet a bevy of "drag queens" or catch a drag show featuring female impersonators is a gay bar. You are not going to find them in a riverfront saloon or a businessman's bar.

Incest can produce offspring who are mental deficients, albinos, deaf-mutes, dwarfs, schizophrenics. It can result in such extreme psychological distrubance as frigidity, nymphomania, alcoholism, and homicidal tendencies. It is much more frequent than meets the eye.

—In 1940, the incidence of incest was estimated at one in a million.

—In 1950, Kinsey found it to be one in 100.

—In 1970, Dr. John Woodbury found it was one in 20.[6]

(Our source does not tell us whether these acts were between parent and child or between siblings.)

Abraham's wife, Sarah, was also his half-sister. And to retain dynastic control, Cleopatra was born of six generations of brother-sister unions. Such marriages were also permitted, even encouraged, among the Incas and certain other preliterate societies; and in a few warlike tribes, sex between brothers and sisters was and still is encouraged before battle with the idea that it makes the soldiers braver. Among the ancient Greeks, half-brothers and half-sisters by the same father were allowed to marry, but never those having the same mother. There was occasional Amerindian tolerance of incest. But otherwise it seems to be generally taboo.

Until 1918 our canon law forbade intermarriage up to sixth cousins—in other words, as far as, and perhaps sometimes farther than, the family records could reach. But the new code relaxed restrictions quite a bit. Second cousins may marry now, but not first cousins. (The same degree of kindred exists between uncle and niece.) For a good solid reason, a dispensation is granted in the case of first cousins. A typical reason for such a dispensation would be that the cousins, living next door to each other, had been engaging in sex play from early childhood.

The theological objection to incest holds that it offends the virtue of piety, which enjoins respect for members of the family according to the various degrees of kindred. (This again assumes that to have intercourse with the consenting relative is nevertheless to be disrespectful or abusive toward that person—a restatement of the old bias: "Sex is bad, unless . . .") But the chief reasons are those of prudence. There is first the genetic truth that children of closely related parents are likely to be defective. And then the fact that unless the members of a household are made sexually inviolate, their very accessibility invites intercourse. It becomes just too easy.

I knew of one family, lower-middle-class but fervently Catholic, in which three daughters and four sons ranging in age from thirteen to twenty, all slept in the attic of their little house—one big room like a dormitory. Somehow or other a Saturday morning orgy developed into a regular thing. This was after the oldest boy had returned from

CCC camp with an encyclopedic knowledge of sexuality—straight, gay, and every other way—which he proceeded to demonstrate with and for his younger siblings.

Their mother went to market every Saturday morning, and as soon as they heard the front door close, they were at one another to the point of exhaustion and never mind the combinations. It was first come, first served.

Their incest continued into adult life, for once reserve is broken down among people, it is seldom restored. Now that they are all married, if sex with his wife is cut off for one of the boys by reason of pregnancy or illness, he still calls on a sister for relief—which she is only too happy to provide as a matter of familial piety, affection, and loyalty.

People used to hang for incest and they can still go to jail, but nowadays they are usually sent to a psychiatrist.

I shudder at the cases I have known. In one parish, most of a particular group had immigrated from the same small town. Only God knows how much intermarriage had occurred in previous generations, but when I arrived on the scene, there were two sets of first cousins married, and in both cases all the children were defective, their intelligence ranging from "slightly dippy" to outright imbecile and halfwit.

Elsewhere, a father had impregnated his own daughter and the offspring was pathetic. One could hardly tell whether it was man or beast—a slobbering, inarticulate creature, shambling through life with gross animal features.

Current studies seem to indicate that within the nuclear family incest is almost nonexistent except for minimal contact between brothers and sisters. Including relatives outside the nuclear family, and petting as well as intercourse, over 10 percent of the males and slightly less of the females have done it. This is a substantial increase (25 to 50 percent) in the last twenty-five years.

But then, again, are such sample studies truly representative? I am thinking of my own little Jukes Family, Catholic, lower-middle-class. Do the surveys consider any of the thousands crowding the tenements of Manhattan or other major urban communities?

Since the Kinsey Report of 1948, the incidence of sex with animals is down by 3 percent for males, 1.5 percent for females. Nowadays human sex is easier to get.

Forty or fifty years ago, male folklore singled out the ewe as the sexual companion of the lonesome farmboy or sheepherder. He would don a pair of hipboots, into each of which he would tuck a hind leg, steady the brute with his hands, and then set to.

Current studies seem to indicate that in our time bestiality is limited to isolated and infrequent incidents. Cases of repeated sexual contacts with animals by adults are negligible.

Apparently, a certain few women rely on household pets for sex by cunnilingus. Coupling of a woman with a beast—the celebrated "donkey show" of Tijuana and Juarez—is scarcely heard of anymore.

Seminarians in the old days had lots of time to gossip and confabulate. Among the non-facts solemnly passed from one deacon class to the next was the idea that a titular bishop would *ipso facto* be suspended if he ever set foot in his see city. There was also the story of the archbishop who only toward the end of his life discovered that he had never been baptized; the midwife had merely dipped him into a tub of water with the words "God bless you!"—which meant that his cathedral was illuminated all through the night for a week or so as he tried to catch up, first with his own ordination and episcopal consecration, and then with all the people he had invalidly confirmed and ordained over the previous ten years.

Another such story tells of the undertaker who discovered that the pastor, lately deceased, had been a woman. Or had he? He had had a beard, but instead of a penis, he/she had been equipped with a vulva. But why should a trifle like one's personal plumbing equipment be enough to determine one's gender? I have an idea that if the pastor's temperament and mentality had been masculine, if he had felt enough like a man to act the role convincingly for all of a lifetime, then he had in fact been a man and his priestly ordination had been valid.

(It is more social usage than anything else that has restricted the priesthood to men. Our Lord chose men to be his apostles, first bishops, and the teachers of his Church, because the society of his day would have scoffed at women acting in that capacity. As recently as a century ago, one could have said that no woman could be a doctor or a lawyer and it would have been for the same reason that women are not ordained—not because of any intrinsic inadequacy, but merely because it was unaccustomed and therefore the public would not accept them in those professions and in that vocation. But times change and the day of the priestess is bound to come. It has been predicted that at Vatican III the bishops will bring their wives; and at Vatican IV they will bring their husbands.)

Every month an estimated ten persons—transsexuals—have their sex altered by surgery.[7] They had been born with the wrong sexual apparatus. It is increasingly common now and increasingly accurate as well to distinguish between gender and "genital sexuality." The attendant physician—anyone, in fact—can determine the genital sexuality of the newborn infant at a glance. If it has a tassle, we call it a boy—if not, it's a girl.

But we have learned only recently that gender is sometimes independent of genitalia. Gender is a state of mind, whereas sex is merely a state of the body. Usually they harmonize: both are either male or female. But occasionally they clash, much to the distress of the girl who finds herself a prisoner in a boy's body, or the boy imprisoned in a girl's body. Until 1951, such people could only try to fit soul to body; but there was a young veteran in New Jersey who thought there must be a better way: why not rather make body fit soul? As George Jorgensen wrote to friends in 1950: "The answer to the problem must not lie in sleeping pills and suicides that look like accidents, or in jail sentences, but rather in life and the freedom to live it."[8]

> Sometimes, a child is born and, to all outward appearances, seems to be of a certain sex. During childhood, nothing is noticed, but at the time of puberty, when the sex hormones come into action, the chemistry of the body seems to take an opposite turn and, chemically, the child is not of the supposed sex, but the opposite one.[9]*

Describing the physical tests prior to his operation, George—the future Christine Jorgensen—wrote to his father:

> All glands seemed completely normal, with the exception of the sex gland. My male hormone output was reduced to a point just higher than the normal female output, and the female output was higher than is found in the normal male patient. The male and female hormones act against each other; therefore, I had a bit of a chemical war going on within me, one trying to outdo the other. In the normal male person, the predominance of the one hormone keeps this imbalance at a minimum. After one year of daily examination, it was shown that the male glands were doing me much more harm than good. Consequently, the operation removing them, known as "surgical demasculinization."[10]*

*Reprinted by permission of the publisher, Paul S. Eriksson, Inc.

As a result of the worldwide publicity following Miss Jorgensen's operation, the surgeon began receiving an average of a hundred letters a month requesting a change.

According to Jan Morris, another intelligent and articulate transsexual, "No one has ever been able to convince a real transsexual that his convictions about his true nature were wrong. No doctor or scientist can say where the conviction comes from, and for me it is a spiritual question, a matter of my soul, much deeper and broader than sexual preference or mode."[11]

All the transsexuals I know are gay, although Morris says that this is not always the case. My transsexual acquaintances support themselves as go-go dancers in gay bars or—those with more talent—as female impersonators in gay revues. As one would expect, they are extremely sissified, vying with one another in their effeminacy. They are all on testosterone, proud of their budding breasts, ready to rip open their shirts and show them off at the least sign of interest—and even otherwise. (The breasts that I have inspected would hardly make a good handful; they were scarcely more than mosquito bites.) These boys devote themselves to passive sex with gays. They all carry cards signed by their physician testifying to the fact that they are in transit from sex to sex and hence required on occasion to go about publicly in drag. This is for immunity from arrest.

But, as Jan Morris observes, as soon as the gay male is made female, his erstwhile lovers reject him, for they have no interest in the female; they want a man. And transvestites, once changed, lose all satisfaction in dressing like what they have now become, for theirs was a paradoxical sort of pleasure that came precisely from dressing opposite to their genital sex.

"I was three or perhaps four years old," says Morris, "when I realized that I had been born into the wrong body, and should really be a girl." Before her sex change she had sired three sons and a daughter, who now regard her as their aunt.

Dr. Donald Hastings of the University of Minnesota Hospital turned twenty-five men into women during 1968 and 1969, removing the male genitalia and installing artificial vaginas. Nine of the twenty-five have since married.

The problems created by transsexuality in the morality of sex and marriage are nothing less than shattering. Does such surgery actually accomplish a transition from one sex to the other? Are the norms of sexuality for the individual to be governed by gender or genital sexuality?

When James became Jan Morris, could she have continued cohabiting with her wife Elizabeth after the fashion of the lesbians, or did the transition *ipso facto* nullify the union? (In actual fact, Jan is now divorced from Elizabeth and lives apart from the family. There would otherwise have been too many civil complications. He had confided his gender problem to her before their marriage.) If so, may Jan now contract a second marriage, this time with a man?

Morris has said that "To a male transsexual, the idea of a male being attracted to another male is not only rather unnerving, but unnatural."

Miss Jorgensen's operation lasted seven hours.—"With skin grafts from the upper thighs, plastic surgery constructed a vaginal canal and external genitalia. It was a completely successful operation."[12] But of course in all such cases there is no possibility of reproductive sex. In the reverse operation the surgeon constructs a rudimentary penis from the clitoris. Prevenient impotence is an invalidating impediment to marriage and a clitoris/penis is obviously incapable of insemination. According to present legislation, then, no transsexual male can contract a valid marriage. But what about the female?

Suppose it is a bishop or priest who crosses the line. Does the change invalidate his sacred orders?

Basically, we are all *voyeurs*. Sex is fascinating, physically exciting, and we all wonder about the other fellow's performance. The "peeping Tom" is wrong not because he wants to watch people operate but because in violating their privacy he becomes an unjust aggressor. His activity is an extreme form of reading other people's mail or tapping their phone.

Like trimming one's toenails, sex is an intensely personal activity. If a couple choose to invite others in to watch, to perform on a stage, or before a camera, that is their affair. But no one may force himself on them.

From my observation the voyeur is usually an older person. He has no longer the physical charm necessary to attract suitable partners, and anyway it's just too much trouble to make a pickup or get a call girl and then negotiate a motel room, plus the snack, and the booze, and the chitchat, and all the rest of it. It's so much easier just to pay five dollars for a two-hour showing of uninterrupted sexuality. The talent may not be beautiful, but at least they have youth and vitality.

The unsophisticated teen-ager loves to fantasize over dozens of girls thronging him with their naked bodies. He naturally supposes that if one woman is fun, two must be twice as much fun. But experience teaches that while one woman is indeed fun, two women are only half as much fun, for the second is no more than a distraction from the first; and three women are no fun at all.

What about watching other people go at it? Well, I am a sexual liberal myself, but it annoys me to read other such liberals putting sexual activity on a level with other human activities such as eating, drinking, or playing baseball. If people may eat, drink, and play or watch baseball with others, why—they ask—why cannot sex play be similarly unrestricted? But surely they must see that by comparison with the other functions, sex is dynamite. It is inflammatory. A man can watch others play a game of baseball without feeling the least urge to get out there and swat a ball; he can sit with his cronies while they get high on liquor, and he need not get the least bit thirsty. But he can hardly watch sex play without wanting somehow to get into the act. That is why the responsible storekeeper will display his girlie books on the highest shelf of his rack, with the comic books on the lower shelves.

Wife swapping is adultery, against the Sixth Commandment of the Decalogue and the plain teaching of our Lord. A man's exclusive right to his wife's body, and hers to his, is inalienable. Before God, he has not the right to forswear that right. He may not hand her over to another for sex, nor may she consent to his adultery. In the practical order, wife swapping begets jealousy and if anything goes wrong there is always the question, "Whose baby is it?"

The orgy is vulgar. It is something rather like pulling down the partitions in public baths and restrooms.

In fine, sex is good but it is not the whole of life; it must be used in moderation. For there is also religion, music, literature, sport, scenic beauty, and so much else that is enjoyable in life. It is especially the youngsters in their early and middle teens who require direction and supervision. Their first encounter with sex is for them like being ushered into a candy store, free to help themselves. They will be tempted to overindulge and perhaps do themselves harm. At that age they will have trouble enough controlling their natural instincts without giving them access to movies and magazines which can only tend to excite them sexually beyond all reason.

17

The Family: Group Insurance

The very name sounds grim: "wedlock." The cage. A man spends the first half of his life trying to get inside and the rest of his life trying to get out of it. Indeed, without marriage, what would our television and nightclub comedians have to joke about? And where would we be without our mother-in-law and traveling salesman jokes?

But nobody joked about Adolf Hitler and the Party in the days of the Third Reich, nor do they joke about the Comintern and the Politburo under the commissars—not openly, at least. The difference is that marriage is a secure institution, firmly rooted in the nature of man. It is unshakable, whereas the totalitarian state, if ridiculed and derided, could be badly hurt.

For as long as history can remember, the boy growing up has had two principal objectives: to get a job and then get married. Founding a family gives point to his existence. It adds to his dignity and gives him status in the community. Through his children, his achievements and ideals are projected into the future. It is the normal framework in which human life unfolds. Marriage offers a life dedicated to chastity.

The family is the nuclear unit in society, the basic unit in the community. Through its solidarity—"All for one, one for all!"—it affords mutual insurance.

It has been said that while the final nuclear blasts are still mushrooming over the earth, somewhere a man will drag himself out from under the debris and then set forth in search of wife and children.

"Marriage is a contract by which man and woman become irrevocably united for the procreation and education of children. It has its origin in the natural law. God gave it in the beginning a sacred character; and Christ raised it to the dignity of a sacrament of the New Law."[1]

The exchange of consent is the contract and the contract between two Christians is itself the sacrament. The bride and groom confer it on each other, with the priest standing by merely as the canonically required witness. According to current legislation in the Western Church, the contract is dissolved only by death. If procreation were excluded by either party, the contract would be null. (But try to prove it!) Its origin in natural law is self-evident. Getting married is just about the most "natural" thing a boy or a girl can do. The first bride and groom were Adam and Eve, whose marriage was blessed by the Creator in person. Its sacramental dignity has been maintained by the Church from the first.*

In consequence, the Church claims full, independent, and executive power over the marriage of all the baptized—Catholics, heretics, schismatics—because there can be only one Church, one baptism, so that whoever is validly baptized enters that one Church, whose head, of course, is the Bishop of Rome. That power belongs to the Church alone. It includes legislative, judicial, and coercive power: that is, power to prescribe the necessary form, to establish impediments affecting both liceity and validity, and to decide all matrimonial causes. The State, however, has power over the merely civil effects of the sacrament.

(Marriage is the most natural, the most human, and the best, but not the only and not necessarily the most efficient means of perpetuating the race. The basic problems are the care of the mother during her term of pregnancy and confinement, and the care of the child

---

*It is sometimes said that our Lord instituted the sacrament by his presence at Cana. But he said nothing to indicate such intent and similar logic would suggest that his mere presence at any social occasion turned the function into a sacrament.

during his infancy—neither very difficult. Christian society has always taken care of its foundlings and orphans. That program would simply be extended. Many such schemes were dreamed up during the nineteenth century. The USSR in its efforts to dissolve "bourgeois morality" at first tried to implement some of them, but utopia remained an impracticable dream, "free love" was again shackled, and in 1937 Russia reverted to its age-old "bourgeois morality.")

Love can be merely physical. It is how the typical male reacts to a picture of Marilyn Monroe: "Wow!" Actually, it is more "passion"—animal attraction—than love. It is that magnetism in mankind and animals that induces mating.

Sentimental love may or may not be compounded with physical attraction, but it certainly involves the feelings and the affections. It is "puppy love," the adolescent "crush."

But neither physical attraction nor sentimental love is a strong enough basis for the lifelong contract of marriage. There must be above all a spiritual love, a unitive impulse of mind and soul that is peculiar to mankind and that alone is a bond strong enough to hold a couple together for the long pull.

Attraction of some sort is the one note common to all love: physical, sentimental, and spiritual. Affection and fondness may also be based on attraction. But conjugal love must ordinarily be founded on reverence as well. In merely romantic love, you want the other person; in real love, you want the other person's good, as well.

Having chosen each other for lifelong companionship of the closest possible intimacy, bride and groom ratify their contract before the Church represented by the bride's pastor, and before the community in the person of their witnesses and guests, after which they set about the delightful business of making a baby. They have a right to all the necessary ritual.

Since the marriage contract gives both parties title, each to the other's body with the right to whatever is entailed in reproduction, there is no reason why they should not increase in virtue and gain merit by maximizing the pleasure of sexual congress, in view of the fact that the goal of insemination takes in the entire process and not just the climax. There is a strong connection between sex pleasure and marital success.

Current studies of sexual behavior in America are widely publicized and the marketplace is rife with manuals of technique and other stimulating materials, literary and otherwise. Over the past twenty-five years there has been a reported increase in the average incidence of sexual intercourse in all age groups. Obviously the dissemination of sexual information has contributed to this increase.

National magazines and popular journals are frequently reporting on the growing usage of oral-genital sex, digital and oral-anal foreplay and a great variety of other partial and total body contact techniques. Shame and self-consciousness about these sexual activities are lessening among partners of all ages. Medical science is even offering hormone help to older persons and encouraging them to engage in a more active sex life.

Which is all to the good so far as the Church is concerned. Anything that forestalls divorce by fortifying the marriage bond is to be encouraged, so let's have marital sex ever more abundantly! In fact, as an inducement, I would suggest a substantial partial indulgence —at least 500 days—for each act of sexual congress, with a plenary indulgence for both parties in the event of pregnancy.

The new permissiveness resulting from the so-called sexual revolution has not produced any catastrophic dissolution of existing social standards. Alarmists may think otherwise, but as we enter the latter half of this decade the institution of marriage and the family seem to be adapting to the changes that have taken place.

New attitudes and consequent behavior have modified our culture from within, bringing much that is vitalizing, pleasurable and beneficial to our American way of life. This has been accomplished without destroying existing values. The process has been one of social enlightenment and adaptation, not of annihilation.

As a general principle, ideally, and by everything that's right and good, marriage should bind in conscience until death:* "I, Thomas, take you, Annamarie, for my lawful wife, to have and to hold, from this day forward, for better, for worse, for richer, for poorer, in sickness and in health, until death do us part."

(They so often gaze cow-eyed into each other's face while repeating the formula after the priest. I am just as often certain that they talked this over right after she jockeyed him into proposing.)

What are they thinking? Do they really mean it—or do they

*The death of the husband, that is, for he usually goes first and she collects the insurance; the only way a man can survive his wife is by blowing her head off. After women pass a certain age they achieve a kind of natural immortality; they just keep living on and on. My beloved aunt died last October at the age of ninety-seven, praying for strength to persevere in holy virginity and lamenting that she was being cut off in her prime.

have their fingers crossed? Are they making a mental reservation—"So long as it works out," "So long as we both shall love," "Until something better comes along"?

But no, our two lovers are sincere. They really do love each other and mean to make a go of it in a lifetime partnership; and they should have that option. It was certainly our Lord's counsel and he is helping them now with one of his sacred seven sacraments.

But it doesn't always work out that way. Contemplating the middle-aged Englishwoman, Nathaniel Hawthorne wondered whether "a middle-aged husband ought to be considered as legally married to all the accretions that have overgrown the slenderness of his bride. . . . Is it not a sounder view of the case, that the matrimonial bond cannot be held to include that three-fourths of the wife that had no existence when the ceremony was performed?"

In practice, however, the ideal of the unbreakable marriage seems to be an exclusively Catholic property. Moreover, it is a value that is solidly rooted in the mind and the emotions, especially of the women, as many a non-Catholic husband has discovered to his distress. So far, to every Catholic, divorce is the very sacrament of adultery. The Catholic's relief from an unhappy marriage can come only from doubling his daily intake of rye.

But reality falls far short of the ideal. When I entered the parish ministry, every sixth marriage in America was ending in the divorce courts; now it is better than one in three. Msgr. Victor J. Pospishil estimates the number of Catholic couples who terminate their marriage by divorce every year at around 70,000.

> If we say, then, that they have thirty years of married life still before them, we would say also that there are approximately 2,100,000 Catholic couples or 4,200,000 individual Catholics living either in invalid marriages or in obligatory isolation. Of course, nobody has ever had the experience that 10 percent of the congregation or parish to which he belongs in a Catholic town or city are divorced. However, let us not forget that most of the Catholics living in marital unions considered invalid by the Church have left the Catholic community, either to join non-Catholic religious denominations, or to live without any religious practice.[2]

But the Latin Church's total rejection of divorce has prevailed only for the past nine hundred years—and even since then there have been exceptions. The pope dissolved the marriage of the French King Henry IV and Marguerite de Valois so that he could marry the zealous Catholic Catherine de' Medici, and all that Henry VIII of England wanted was what Rodrigo Borgia (Alexander VI) had just recently granted in favor of his sacrilegious bastard Lucrezia.

Msgr. Pospishil writes that until the eleventh century "there was no difference between the Eastern and Western Churches on the question of divorce. It was conceded on many grounds."[3] For example; adultery, chronic insanity (three years for the husband, five for the wife), disappearance of a partner for five years, implacable hatred on both sides and, since the sixteenth century, serious incompatibility of temperament.

The theologians reasoned that our Lord allowed divorce in the case of adultery. The Gospels are full of counsels and precepts. "What God hath joined together let no man put asunder"[4] is not a commandment but rather advice on a par with "Lend, expecting nothing in return."[5] It is an evangelical counsel rather than a legal norm.* No man may "put asunder": hence, private authority is insufficient. A marriage cannot be ended merely by mutual agreement. God must act through the Church—specifically, through the pope.

St. Paul allowed divorce and remarriage for a proportionate cause and was well aware that he had no support in the oral tradition of our Lord's teaching: "The rest is from me and not from the Lord," he says,[6] and then he goes on to expound what we have since come to call the Pauline Privilege.

According to the Eastern canonists, when Sacred Scripture teaches that the marriage bond is broken only through death or adultery, it is not to be taken too literally, but rather as offering a few guidelines, which may be extended to analogous cases. Thus, the moral equivalent of physical death is civil death incurred through condemnation to a degrading punishment, and religious death through apostasy. Prolonged absence and willful desertion are analogous to natural death. Besides adultery properly so called, there is presumptive adultery, which can assume various forms.

Consensual divorce with the right of remarriage was accepted in both East and West if the other spouse entered religious life.[7]

Msgr. Pospishil has lined up a host of Fathers, Doctors, and

_____

*Similar Gospel imperatives which are advice rather than commands: "Take no thought for tomorrow," "Turn the other cheek," "Never take an oath." There must be at least six others.

theologians, who assume the permissibility of divorce and remarriage—men such as Origen, Basil, Gregory Nazianzen, Ambrosiaster, Epiphanius, Theodore of Tarsus (Archbishop of Canterbury), Cajetan, and Catharinus. He says that "In the three centuries following the Council of Trent, around thirty books were published by Catholics denying that the indissolubility of marriage was an infallible doctrine of the Church."[8]

The Romanian Uniates granted divorce until 1858.

". . . All civilizations, nations, and religions have permitted divorce and remarriage, except the Western Catholic or Roman Church in the last millennium. . . . During all these centuries, all the Eastern Churches, anti-Chalcedonian no less than Orthodox, permitted and permit divorce and remarriage in respect to all marriages."[9]

Why did the magisterium change—and why must we be different from the rest of the Church—an underprivileged majority, so to speak?

Bishop Simons holds with the belief that Christ only recommended rather than commanded marriage until death in every case. Thus:

> If we do not claim that the Church imposed a positive divine law in this matter which goes further than the natural law, we must either suppose that He gave a spiritually more advanced view of marriage, as required by natural law, than mankind possessed then and possesses even now, but which He wished His followers to accept and to which mankind would be expected gradually to grope its way; or we must suppose that He called in strong terms for a more perfect observance of the spirit of the law without raising the minimum that might be expected in certain cases. We do have other sayings of Christ which seem to impose as a matter of grave moral obligation a higher standard of conduct than is strictly imposed by natural law, in which also the Church has stood for a milder interpretation.[18]

For the last two centuries, there have been two major schools of thought in Judaism: Orthodox and Reform, with views on divorce that range from relatively rigorous to permissive.* Nevertheless, although

*Comment of one Jewish editor: "Divorce is fairly easy—though certainly not encouraged—among Orthodox Jews."

they may permit divorce, Jewish and Eastern Orthodox families have remained among the most stable in present-day society.

Before the Communist takeover, the Chinese used to allow divorce in favor of the man, not for a bagatelle like infidelity but for really important reasons, such as, for instance, the excessive loquacity of the wife. Now one could understandably tolerate a wife who slipped out for an occasional spot of fun with her boyfriend, but not a wife who never shut up: and still divorce remained uncommon.

When we ask a Catholic canonist why the Church refuses a divorce in even the most agonizing cases, he begins burbling about "the wedge" and "the foot in the door."

"Once you open the door even the least bit, people soon force it wide open. (This is bad? If so, why?) Look at the Orthodox! Admitting even one reason justifying divorce would only be the thin edge of the wedge. Next you would have an analogous reason, which would make two reasons. A softhearted pontiff would make an exception for some nabob, and there you would have three reasons. So it's best to keep the door locked and bolted shut with no divorce allowed for any reason under the sun."

Now this assumes that using his power of the keys the Holy Father can dissolve the sacramental bond of matrimony. Practically all theologians concede that he can do this. The pope could grant a divorce, then, but he won't. And his refusal seems to be based not so much on a mistaken interpretation of Christ's word as on considerations of expediency.

I tell our canonist about a friend of mine, Patrick, in his middle twenties. Patrick grew up tall, straight, and chaste, under strict Catholic parents—an Eagle Scout, Catholic grammar and high school. Ivy League college. Although he was an athlete on several varsity teams in high school and college, was popular and belonged to a good fraternity, he had never had a voluntary orgasm—he told me this and, knowing him, I believe it—he had never had a deliberate waking orgasm until he met Dorcas. Then, after several dates, one night Dorcas spread her legs for him. He told me that it was as though the gates of paradise had just swung open. He had never dreamed that such sensations, such pleasure, were possible on this earth. But in his innocence he also thought that his Dorcas was the only creature this side of heaven who could offer such delight. He must have her. She was only vaguely Protestant.

Well, he got her, and all very properly. She took the instructions and signed the promises, the necessary dispensation was granted, and they were married by the priest. But that night she told Patrick for the first time that she was diabetic and must never have a child. Patrick plowed right on into her. After all, she hadn't minded handing it out before marriage. So she got pregnant. The baby was normal and both survived beautifully. Over her protests, Patrick took the baby to his pastor and had him baptized. Dorcas immediately divorced him for mental cruelty, alleging that he had impregnated her at the risk of her life and had then, against her express will, had the child baptized in a religion of which she did not approve.

So here is Patrick at twenty-six—big, handsome, well-to-do, and stranded. Could not the Church dissolve the bond between him and Dorcas so that he could have a second go at marriage? After all, it really was not his fault.

Our canonist follows Patrick's history with compassionate interest, but at the end he shrugs rather helplessly: "Ah, yes," he says, "there are always a few victim cases (to be precise, 4,200,000 at this moment in the United States alone) who must suffer for the common good, because, you see, if we let even only one such case slip through, it would end in a torrent." And those 4,200,000 souls just might slip into heaven. What a calamity!

Now one can appreciate the illustrative power of "the wedge" and "the foot in the door," but they refer not to fact, nor even to probability, but only to a future possibility. It *might* happen. It *could* happen. But not necessarily "It *will* happen." So why penalize anyone at all for the sake of a mere possibility? Penalize? No. They have only one life on this earth and it is being wrecked through no fault of their own.

"If we let divorce get a foot in the door—" granted that more than that "foot" would be an abuse. But it is still only a possibility. We are discussing it in the subjunctive, the conditional mood. And since when has abuse abrogated proper usage?* That was the fallacy of Prohibition. Because some people abused liquor, it was forbidden to everyone. So with divorce: because some—perhaps even many—may try to take advantage of the Church, no one at all is to be given a hearing.

What is a "victim case" anyway? Why should there be even one? "Why should I be a victim? Why should I be the patsy? Why me?" A "victim" of what? To be sacrificed for what? Just to save principle? For the sake of the law? But doesn't that get the priorities backward?

---

*"*Abusus non tollit usum.*"

It was our Lord himself who said that the law was made for man and not man for the law. To make a human being suffer needlessly if not unjustly merely to preserve intact the principle of a universal nonexceptionable obligation smacks of pharisaism, the very thing our Lord came into this world to destroy.

Bishop Simons points out that the welfare of mankind is the basis of all natural law. Hence, a general rule meant to safeguard the greater good of mankind does not apply when it becomes an obstacle to it. Bishop Simons applies his reasoning to several controversial issues of our day, e.g., abortion, tyrannicide, suicide, birth control, and divorce with right of remarriage.[11]

This concept of the victim case is the root mistake of every totalitarian society: the community is all; the individual counts for little or nothing. He can in fact be liquidated when the common good requires it—in which event he becomes one of those much-to-be-regretted victim cases.

The moralists and canonists constantly argue that if divorce and free love were legalized, marriage would disappear. Is marriage then such a delicate institution that it can't take care of itself? On the one hand, we are told that it is a divine institution, based on human nature and reinforced by the sacramental grace of the Lord Christ. But, on the other hand, we are told that it can't survive competition. Is a divine endowment so feeble, and faith so weak? Is human nature so shallow? If marriage is good, it will survive. Otherwise it will sink. Deservedly.

So the Holy Father has forbidden artificial birth prevention as a sin, if not against chastity, at least against obedience. "Well," as one man remarked, "let's be fair about it. The pope is entitled to his opinion, too."

But it's not all that simple. As the vicar of Christ and visible head of the Church, the Holy Father is also our chief shepherd, lawgiver, teacher, and theologian. He has the constant help of the Holy Spirit, and when he wills it he is infallible. Nevertheless, he cannot turn good into evil, nor evil into good. He can neither convert falsehood into truth, nor subvert truth and turn it into error. If there is a conflict between our judgment and his, his gets the benefit of the doubt, but still the final decision rests with each man's conscience.

It has been said facetiously that you should never commit a sin unless you absolutely have to. But the kernel of truth there is that if you absolutely have to do a thing, it's likely not a sin and certainly not a mortal sin.

So, after your tenth or twelfth child has been born, you may feel that you have done quite enough for the propagation of the species, and yet you are only thirty-five and still endowed with quite a terrific potential. So you may be tempted to disobey Pope Paul's injunction and practice a little birth control now and then.

If the Holy Father forbade birth control from fear of race suicide, he might well have considered the following estimates and statistics:

> If we take a human couple of the time of Cheops, that is, 3000 years B.C., and suppose their descendants to be doubled every 30 or 35 years, and to be only subject to the ordinary causes of death—famine, war, and contagious diseases excepted—what number would such descendants have reached at the present time? To express it no less than 26 figures would be required. We wished to discover how the crowd would find room, and calculated that it would not only cover the face of the globe, but that on the top of it there would be other layers of humanity as far as the star Sirius!

—His Holiness might also have pondered St. Augustine urging the wider practice of celibacy and higher esteem for virginity, since, as he said, "The means of filling up the number of the elect abound in all nations."[13]

—Finally, our Christian era is but one breath in the lifetime of all humanity, and there are still plenty of people around despite approximately 1,750,000 years without the sacrament of matrimony and divinely inspired guidance on birth control.

Although adultery is a sin of frailty, very human and understandable, it is still a heartbreaker, expressly forbidden by divine positive law: a condemnation reaffirmed by our divine Master as reported in all three of the synoptic Gospels and underscored by St. Paul in two of his epistles. The evil of adultery is beyond debate.

It is a sin against both purity and justice, a violation of the married person's contract with his partner. In every marriage there is inequality of love. The one loves more than the other. One loves, the other permits himself to be loved. Hence, no marriage is ever broken up by an unfeigned, equal, and simultaneous consent of both partners. One of them always gets hurt, is always betrayed. Whether one makes love with a new person before or outside marriage, or even after the divorce, he always has the discarded mate breathing down his neck.

What does the young husband—call him Paul—think when he first meets a girl he would like to have in bed?—"First, it would be a sin against God. Second, it would be a sin against my wife Patricia." The first consideration is abiding. It was absorbed in childhood and then nurtured his whole life long. It will be there before, during, and after his adultery, when he is pulling on his socks next morning.

But the second consideration can gradually be rationalized and finally altogether suppressed. Paul knows that if he keeps on with his new playmate and comes to love her, he will care less and less whether or not Patricia is hurt. He also knows, or thinks, that in time Patricia will stop being hurt, will adjust, and in the end may even find herself some other man. The fate of the children will be pondered and a decision will be reached. But the sense of sin and the guilt will remain.

Alternatively, Paul may start from the other end: "Although it would be a sin to go ahead, it would also hurt my newfound mistress (and myself) if I did not."

And within two years all will be the same. Few lives are wrecked by switching wives, husbands, or lovers. Would that it were as true of their souls!

St. Augustine wrote sixteen hundred years ago that "If you do away with harlots, the world will be convulsed with lust," and St. Thomas Aquinas noted that statement with approval eight hundred years later. Current studies indicate that the majority of people today disapprove of adultery. It figures; we don't generally approve of our sins.

As for the new alternatives about which there is so much talk —open marriage, mate swapping, group sex, group marriage, etc.—the data suggest that they are mostly just talk.

Owing largely to sexual liberation, divorced and separated persons are sexually more active now than a generation ago. Much of the onus has since been lifted from such formerly scandalous carryings-on. Their sex lives correspond roughly with those of married people under twenty-five.

By manipulating the concept of "respectability" ("What'll the neighbors think!"), the Church has always appealed to pharisaism as a means of enforcing "public decency." At the behest of St. Paul, she invites all of us to anticipate Christ in separating the sheep from the goats. We are all admittedly sinners, but my sins are such warm, friendly things, you know, whereas yours are downright disgusting.

The innocent victim of such hypocrisy is the poor little child born "*ex patre ignoto*," as pastors note it in the baptismal registry: "Father unknown." Most non-Christian peoples make little or no distinction between the legitimate and the illegitimate baby. There are evidently two sorts of culture: the pagan who finds a baby on his doorstep and thinks as by reflex, "What a darling child! Let's bring it up." And the follower of Christ, who rears back in dismay with the thought, "Whose baby is this?"

By hallowing marriage the Church necessarily stigmatizes extramarital sex, and the resultant offspring becomes a "sin child." He is barred from holy orders.

But with the means of contraception now foolproof, cheap, and everywhere available, there need be no more bastards, for if a man is determined to commit the sin of adultery or fornication he will not add appreciably to his guilt—in fact he may even diminish it—by slipping on a condom just before entering his partner. Still, accidents will happen. But can there be a greater tragedy than the accidental, the unwanted child?

So the girl gets pregnant. She may be a schoolgirl, an adulterous wife and mother, an unmarried teacher, or career girl. Marriage is just not feasible. She is tempted to abortion—which is plain murder, and let no one kid you otherwise.

In this connection it gives me pleasure to recall the words of an old professor of mine at the Catholic University. In those days I thought—as I still think—that no one could possibly be more learned than Fr. Thomas Verner Moore, Doctor of Medicine, Doctor of Philosophy, psychiatrist, once a Paulist, then a Benedictine, and finally the founder of the first Carthusian community in America:

> The unborn child is fundamentally and essentially a
> human person and as such has the rights of a person even
> though he is utterly incapable of asserting and defending his
> rights. Why do we say that the unborn child is a human
> person? From the first moment of its fertilization the ovum
> commences an orderly process of growth and development
> which reaches its physical limits in the early adult years of the
> human being.
> One after another functions and powers unfold themselves
> as the physical basis for their manifestation is laid. In all the
> various processes of transformation and development the

> organism manifests a fundamental unity, so that this embryo
> becomes this adult human being by the organizing activity of
> one and the same living principle which determines growth
> and development in the embryo, and manifests intelligence
> and the power to control conduct in the adult. An intelligent
> individual is a person by reason of his fundamental capability
> of intelligence.
>
> The unborn child is fundamentally and essentially a
> person and has the rights of a person to life of which no human
> authority can deprive it. [14]

Nothing has since changed in either science or ethics to modify those facts. In a lengthy statement issued during November 1974, the Holy See once again put itself on record:

"The tradition of the Church has always held that human life must be protected and favored from the beginning, just as it is at the various stages of its development."

It traced the Christian stand against abortion—as opposed to the pagan Greek and Roman laxity—from the first century down to Vatican II and Paul VI, who had declared in December 1972 that the teaching of the Church regarding abortion "has not changed and is unchangeable." [15]

Dr. John T. Noonan, Jr., divides Catholics into two groups: educated Catholics who react to abortion with revulsion "even while they consider the rule against contraception to be almost unintelligible"; and poorly educated, merely nominal Catholics, with little regard for either the prohibition of contraception or the evil of abortion. They practice abortion "because it seems simpler, or because they have no access to contraceptive information." [16]

In defense of abortion, you may hear it argued that the human embryo is not immediately animated at conception by a rational soul but only after a certain state of development has been reached. Aristotle, St. Thomas, even Cardinal Mercier, postulated a succession of embryonic forms or souls—vegetative, sensitive, rational—in the development of the new life. According to the ancients, it took forty days for the male to become human, eighty to ninety for the female fetus.

But where there is controversy on such a vital subject, the Church always imposes the "safer" opinion—in this case, that the new creature is a human being and must be considered and respected as such from the first moment of its existence. Although they held to their opinion of a delayed ensoulment as a matter of private speculation, in practice St. Thomas and Cardinal Mercier would have followed the safer opinion.

A little over a year after the Supreme Court allowed the liceity of abortion under certain conditions, the country was evenly divided: 47 percent favored permitting abortion (within three months after conception), 44 percent opposed; 61 percent of the Catholics opposed it. [17]

Question: Is not the unwanted embryo an unjust aggressor against the mother?

Not at all. To be unjust, the aggressor must be conscious, aware of the injustice he is perpetrating. The embryo on the other hand is unaware of what is going on, so sublimely innocent that if he were aborted he would go straight to heaven. The sad thing is that the poor creature is completely helpless. Talk about cursing a deaf man, putting a hurdle in front of a blind man, stabbing someone in the back! Why not give this little fellow a chance? Let him be born, look him over, size him up, and then just wring his little neck if you still don't want him.

There is an alternative, you know. The Church has made provision for just such cases and I have known more than one girl who had her baby safely and in privacy. No one ever found out. These girls never even saw their children. They were immediately adopted into good Catholic homes. Any girl's pastor or confessor would be happy to advise her in the matter.

Of course the most effective way of easing the problem would be to remove all the social, religious, and civil disabilities of children born outside of marriage, as also to be more tolerant of prostitutes, adulterers, and fornicators, and to dilute or entirely discard the idea of "respectability": that I am more "respectable" than you, beloved reader, because while you may sin through human weakness, I sin merely through Christian hatred.

18

The Garden of Love

According to *U.S. News & World Report*,[1] the Catholic Church in America is losing ground on every front. Infant baptisms are down 32 percent from 1959: not so much fewer babies as fewer Catholic parents. Conversions: down 49 percent from 1959. Net gain in 1973 was only 5,011 in a total membership of 48,500,000. For a focus on that figure, back around 1948 I wrote a little pamphlet *Come On In!*, which included a postpaid application for instructions in the faith. These were then given by Capuchin seminarians using a correspondence course which I had prepared. Over the next fifteen years, more than 22,000 converts were thus instructed.

Students in Catholic colleges: down 7 percent from 1968. Students in Catholic schools: down 36 percent from 1964. Priests: down 5 percent from 1966. Seminarians: down 61 percent from 1964. Brothers: down 26 percent from 1966. Nuns: down 23 percent from 1965.

Attendance at Mass in 1972—61 percent; in 1973—48 percent. A 13 percent falloff in one year.

215

The gothic edifice could well symbolize the status of the Catholic Church in the 1970s. Whether it be Notre Dame, Chartres, Cologne, or St. Patrick's, New York—the style is seven or eight hundred years behind the times. It is out of date, an anachronism, a museum piece, bespeaking by its architecture an almost visible yearning for the era in which the gothic was contemporary, in which the church stood in the town square and exercised a vital influence in human affairs.

There was a day when these fanes were thronged almost constantly with worshippers. Oh, they still draw crowds on high holydays, when a successor of Matthew, the poor tax gatherer, or Andrew, the fisherman, sweeps into his cathedral with fanfare of trumpets, clad in six layers of silk and damask, topped with the Oriental miter, golden staff of office firmly clasped in a hand that is gloved and jeweled.

(A child's voice breaks a moment of dramatic silence: "Mommy, why is he wearing that funny hat?" Why, indeed? There are many who wonder.)

It used to be that a mere man needed all these "props" to support his outrageous claims on the fear, obedience, and assets of "the faithful." But now the swishing skirts and swinging tassels are void of all but aesthetic effect. They are high camp, appreciated mostly by interior decorators and male beauticians—and possibly by Hollywood.

Until just a few decades ago, God's sanction on illicit sex was dramatically shown forth by the supposed curse on masturbation (blindness, insanity, nervous exhaustion) and the very real pox on intercourse (syphilis and gonorrhea). Then came the medical and psychiatric liberation of masturbation. There was no curse on it after all. Next came penicillin. So neither was there a pox on fornication.

Finally came the pill, and for the first time in the history of Christendom, people could form the pattern of their sex lives with pregnancy a matter of choice and little fear of disease. The great penalty of bastardy had been withdrawn. Catholics everywhere held their breath—half-hopeful, half-fearful. Would the pope now write a jubilant encyclical, rejoicing at the release of his flock from the cautions, bans, denials, and prohibitions with which sexuality had hitherto been shackled? Would he free the Pilgrim People of God to express their love in carefree joy, now that God himself had cleared the way?

But no, when you have people by the crotch you really control

them and the human being finds it practically impossible to let go;
power never dissolves itself. So against the all-but-unanimous counsel
of his experts, Pope Paul VI decided to retain that control—thereby
making the Church finally irrelevant in this, our day and age.

And that is when the people started getting bored and losing
interest. Why should they bother trying to make converts when they
themselves no longer cared enough even to assist at Sunday Mass?
Why should parents have their baby baptized when they themselves
no longer bothered with religion? Why should any boy study for the
priesthood when it would only mean becoming the custodian of a
religious museum?

> So I turned to the Garden of Love
>   That so many sweet flowers bore.
> And I saw it was filled with graves,
>   And tombstones where flowers should be;
> And priests with black gowns were walking their rounds,
>   And binding with briars my joys and desires.[2]

Hearing of the fuss over the teaching of evolution in the high-
school science class, a concerned parent asked her teen-age daughter
for her idea of creation. The girl hesitated. Then she asked, "Do you
want the Church version or the real facts?"

In matters of sex the adolescents have long had a mask of propriety which they wear at home, at church, and in school. It is shaped to
what is expected of them. They give the conventional answers when
questioned on matters moral. But it is only a mask, for "the real facts"
as they see and intuite them are far otherwise.

Sadly, the adults, too, have recently learned to distinguish between "the Church version" and reality. How else is one to explain the
statistics on sexual morality and personal evaluation of religion cited
throughout this book?

It was Christianity that made Europe and America. And, to this
day, wherever our missionaries—priests and nuns—penetrate, they
do as they have always done. They dismantle the human personality
and rebuild it from the ground up, not exactly according to the
Gospel pattern, but rather according to the latest Vatican specifica-
tions and those of the canonists and theologians. Every feeling, every
belief, his self-image, his attitude toward his fellows, every duty,
every right, every impulse and reaction and reflection, every senti-

ment of community and distinction, is changed through and through, programmed with the neo-Catholic as a human computer.

We have seen how the parochial school operates. But the process starts in the cradle. All five senses are used from infancy in conditioning the emotions—the irrational side of human nature—to react mechanically according to program. The crucifix pressed to the lips of the child still in his crib: "Kiss Jesus!" Church bells, pipe organ, plainchant, and polyphonic choir for the ears. Incense for the nostrils. Vestments, flower-banked shrines, votive lights and candles for the eyes. There are rosaries, medals, and blessed palm to touch and handle. Holy Communion is received into the mouth, and the other six sacraments are sensibly perceptible. Emotional and intellectual formation of this type is not so much instruction as inoculation. It would require almost superhuman willpower to evade its effects.

In deference to Christ, there is a ritualistic obeisance to charity—love of God and neighbor—but the child or convert early learns that this is mostly a formality, for it is chastity that *really* matters, that is the Supervirtue and the hallmark of the Roman Catholic. The neophyte soon marks the breach between theory and practice, between what is taught by the priest as official Church doctrine and how it is followed by even eminent Catholics in everyday life: theory as distinct from actual practice on lying, cheating, slander, cruelty, thievery, drinking, perjury, avarice. Tammany Hall under "Boss" Tweed was largely a Catholic achievement, staffed by pious Irishmen, leading laymen, buying votes and extorting graft until the City of New York was well-nigh bankrupt. Cosa Nostra is another contribution of Catholics to the American community. Sitting through *The Godfather*, the sensitive Catholic had to cringe with embarrassment at the pontifical baptism as the camera kept swinging from the font to the machine gun.

In reassembling the human person as a Roman Catholic, the Church is careful to insert a feeling for modesty, a sense of shame, of guilt or self-satisfaction as the appropriate reactions to specified conduct, a generous dollop of smugness, and a readiness to give his neighbor marks for propriety or impropriety. These traits are not inborn; they are acquired. They must be taught and learned.*

For instance, when Christian missionaries first entered the South Pacific they found it a natural paradise, but far from being pleased,

*For modesty it would be hard to beat the French Sulpicians of the old school. There were no urinals in our seminary, built over fifty years ago. I am told that a hundred years ago the seminarians wore drawers in the bathtub and tucked their shirttails in with a paddle.

they were aghast. Except for a breechclout, the aborigines were
naked. This would never do; they must be taught shame for their
bodies. So the Christians put trousers on the men and shrouded the
women in muumuus. At first the women cut holes in them to cool
their breasts, so they had to be taught that their breasts were the
second most shameful part of the body and therefore must always be
kept covered.

In accordance with the Church's evaluation of chastity as the
Supervirtue, the pursuit of perfection by way of the three vows in
community with others of like mind eventually reduced itself to the
observance of chastity alone. When you think of how poverty for
Christ meant real destitution—he never knew where he was going to
sleep from one night to the next—compare that with the "poverty" of
the present-day Jesuit teaching at Georgetown. Poverty has become a
mere formality; when you meet a monk or a friar on a plane, he
generally has the "use" of about twice as much money as you have. It
is a fiction by which the corporation rather than the individual religious holds title to his possessions. He does not have ownership, but he
does have the use of his things—a distinction without much of a
difference.

Nowadays a vow of obedience means that the superior must be
careful never to ask a subject to do what that subject may not want to
do. Otherwise, the monk may quit, get married, and end up a university professor at $18,000 a year.

But with the Supervirtue, it's different. Chastity definitely has
not been allowed to become a formality, and any priest or brother
caught in or even only accused of sexual activity is in deep, deep
trouble, with a lot of explaining to do. If his explanation is unsatisfac-
tory, he will not even be allowed the courtesy of resigning: he will be
abruptly expelled.

Oddly, virginity (and I include celibacy) is an autophagous system. It is self-destructive. Here is the dilemma of Christian asceticism: If God is pleased by virginity, then the more virginity there is,
the better pleased he will be.

But the more virginity, the fewer children to grow up and
profess virginity, and hence the less pleased is God. Thus, the pleasure of God in virginity is subject to diminishing returns and is
therefore self-defeating. In the logical extremity, it cancels itself out
in a completely depopulated earth.

We Catholics may be stuck with St. Augustine's dark, Manichaean mistrust of sex, but we still should not try to ram that mistaken opinion down the throats of those around us. Nor should we, as did the Sacred Inquisition, call upon the State—"the secular arm"—to enforce our morality.*

Social neutrality does not necessarily betoken moral relativism.

During the first half of the thirteenth century, the heretical Albigensians were defeated in Toulouse by greedy noblemen who had been promised the heretics' land by the Church. St. Dominic and his friars had the secular arm burn them alive. For the first time apart from the Crusades, Western Christians showed themselves willing to exterminate human beings for the sake of power disguised as an idea, proclaiming: "Orthodoxy is my doxy, whereas heterodoxy is your doxy. Therefore, since mine is mine, whereas yours is only yours, I shall kill you." Might made right.

The Dominican Fathers had Albigensian corpses dug up and burned a generation after their death. They had the homes of Albigensians destroyed, with the understanding that the land should never again be built upon or even cultivated.

"When the castle of Montségur was captured and the [Albigensian] Crusade achieved its end, more than two hundred people who would not abjure their faith, most of them women, were herded into a palisade, the palisade was closed, and they were burned alive."[3] In principle, this was worse than Dachau.

Technically, of course, it was neither the Dominicans nor the Church that killed the poor heretics. They only fingered them for a servile State. But when they can get away with it, churchmen will still manipulate the State in the interests of "orthodoxy," i.e., making the population at large conform with Roman Catholic notions of morality by threat of fines and imprisonment. For instance, police estimate the gay population of New York, men and women, at 400,000, of whom at least 200,000 are most likely Catholic. For three years they had been working hard to have an antidiscrimination bill passed by City Council. Such a bill prohibiting any discrimination in employment, housing, or public accommodation, on account of sexual orientation was finally voted out of committee in April 1974. It was endorsed by the local bar association, two former mayors, the Commission on Human Rights, and several responsible public figures.

*Except when we act against abortion, for here we are defending our neighbor's (the human embryo's or fetus's) life.

The bill does not endorse or "promote" homosexuality (if that were possible), but it does help to end open discrimination. Gays are already at work in every area of American society. This legislation would simply remove the terror of being found out. As a spokesman for the Board of Education put it, "I would say there are a number of homosexuals in the school system, and I don't see any dangers coming from it."

Seattle, Minneapolis, Detroit, and East Lansing, Michigan already have such protective legislation for homosexuals and the Michigan Civil Rights Commission is about to extend these guarantees statewide.

"It simply takes away the crutch that now enables people to discriminate legally," said a gay attorney in San Francisco. "My parents run a restaurant, and they are racial bigots. When the Civil Rights Act passed, they just started serving blacks and that was that."[4]

Discrimination against gays is both uncharitable and unjust. Could anyone have predicted, then, that the great Archdiocese of New York would favor discrimination against at least 200,000 of its gay communicants? Wisdom would have suggested that regardless of their own opinion the regime would have just kept quiet: "If you can't do good, then at least don't do harm." But no, the Church of New York put herself on record as opposing civil rights for gays and favoring continued discrimination against them. There was a full-page ad in the archdiocesan paper, *The Catholic News*, pointing to a front-page editorial entitled "Menace to Family Life." It said that homosexuality is "an increasing threat to sound family life in our city today" and that enactment of the proposed law "will afford unrestricted opportunities to propagandize deviant forms of sexuality."*

Such rubbish is mortifying to the informed Catholic, advertising once again how little some priests know about sex. There is no possible way in which homosexuality can threaten family life, and you can no more propagandize homosexuality than you can propagandize blue eyes, curly hair, or high I.Q.'s. Further, it is neither infectious nor contagious, physically or morally.

Cardinal Cooke ordered the editorial read from the pulpits of the archdiocese that Sunday, but a spot check by local television news crews indicated that perhaps one out of four pastors "forgot." In some

---

*Because this particular issue is bound to become a collector's item, I wrote for a copy, enclosing my dollar, but it never came. One could only surmise that the circulation manager was ashamed of His Eminence.

parishes there were walkouts of fair-minded parishioners while the editorial was being read. His Eminence had his way; the legislation was defeated. It was an exemplary demonstration of clerical fascism.

You see the inquisitorial technique: the Church cannot herself control or punish the nonconformists, so she has the State do it for her.

—From 1970 on, Italy had permitted divorce, but only on the toughest terms in Europe: a five-year legal separation was required before the courts would grant a divorce mutually agreed upon by both husband and wife, while a seven-year waiting period was required in case of a contest.

Nevertheless, by petition, the opponents of divorce forced a referendum on repeal, run off in May 1974, and were thoroughly defeated. Actually, it was a defeat for the Italian hierarchy and the Vatican. The bishops had told Catholics that it was their duty to "defend the model of the family"—a clear directive to repeal divorce and thus prolong the imprisonment of thousands of Italians, Protestants and Jews included, in failed and unbearable marriages.

Most of the country's 190,000 priests and nuns worked hard for the cause, i.e., to limit their neighbors' civil liberty. The many civil libertarians among the clergy were promptly disciplined. After the balloting, the Holy Father expressed "his astonishment and pain" that Italians would be allowed the continued freedom enjoyed by all the rest of the world.

It was Mussolini who in 1929 established Catholicism as the official religion in Italy. Is this a good thing? True, the State squeezes money from Protestant and Jewish taxpayers (as well as Catholics) for the salaries of priests and bishops, but the vote on divorce ran 19,000,000 for, 13,000,000 against, which could mean at least 19,000,000 Italians grown restive at being tied to the apron strings of Holy Mother Church. It is just such clergy-dominated societies that breed anticlericalism.

In England, the Established Church claims a membership of 28,000,000, of whom only 2,600,000 are active enough to vote on parish affairs, and a mere 1,800,000 show up on Easter Sunday. In all of England, only 373 men were ordained in 1973, as against 636 in 1963. Whether the union of Church and State is the cause of the increasing apathy one cannot know, but the fact is that the Church of England is beginning slowly to move away from the State.[5]

So it is not altogether the vernacular mass or the reduction of mystery in the liturgy that is alienating the laity and the lower clergy. Their gradual secession is motivated in great part by the reaction of the hierarchy as by reflex against any extension of human freedom, moral or civil, especially in matters of sex. If it seems that right now we are caught up in a veritable explosion of sex, it is because the public have been for so long held down and have so much to catch up. There was the same reaction against Puritanism at the time of the Restoration in England. What was formerly bought and sold under the counter is now displayed openly on the racks. The stag movie was once shown to a closed circle at the firehouse or in a hayloft. Now it is a two-hour show open to all the adult public.

The strategy of the hierarchy follows a regular pattern. Take "smut": Catholics are taught that they are bound in conscience to avoid it—and that should be enough. But that is not enough: "We bishops must make it unavailable, and to do that, we'll have to have a law passed." But a civil law would also make it unavailable to Protestants, non-Christians, and the great nonreligious sector of the public who may find nothing very much wrong with "smut," who may even find it diverting and amusing. Thus, a law proscribing "smut" would be a substantial abridgment of their freedom. But do you think that that consideration would deter the bishops in the least? Certainly not.

Remember the Hays Office in Hollywood? The Legion of Decency? The National Organization for Decent Literature? All of them Catholic pressure organizations. The hierarchy persist in treating the laity like children who cannot be trusted to follow their conscience, who must not be allowed freedom of choice in moral matters, who must be forced to behave, constrained by police action if necessary. If they could work it, the bishops would happily have the pill banned by law, just for the sake of the Roman Catholic minority. Indeed, if anything could destroy the Church, it would be this un-Christlike suppression of freedom in personal sexual behavior.

The reason for the moral crisis of our day and the increasing alienation of the Catholic laity is sharply illustrated by the opposition of the Archdiocese of New York to civil rights for gays. Don't they realize that there is a gay in every family—an uncle, an aunt, a son or a daughter? There is a gay on every block? We all have gay friends and we respect them, and we cannot see any valid reason for singling them out as the stepchildren of the community.

But what is so clear to us, especially to those of us who are under thirty, is apparently obscure to the hierarchy. One is tempted to question their good faith, their motivation: are they blind or do they simply refuse to see? In either event their credibility has been diminished, their moral authority impaired, their prophecies of gloom become no longer "operative."

The old taboos are being more often challenged, coming increasingly under scrutiny, and the traditional explanations and "proofs" will no longer wash. But a taboo without reasonable support is no more than a scruple, a superstition. We can see that. In the preceding chapters you have watched me drive a Mack truck through one taboo after another—birth control, fornication, masturbation, sodomy, "bad thoughts and desires," "kinky" sex—and you have been in substantial agreement with my facts, logic, and conclusions. In fact you had had it all pretty well thought out for yourself; this book only brought it back to mind and articulated it for you.

What the world and his wife are asking themselves then is this: "If we can see it, why can't the bishops? They must be either fools or knaves. In either case they are out of touch, and if the Church does not even understand our problems, how can she possibly supply right answers?" Hence, the spreading apathy of today's young Catholics.

Because of the rapid advance in science and knowledge even just within the last few years—for instance, the pill, and sex changes —because of instantaneous communication by television and telephone, of accurate techniques in surveying public opinion and conduct, we Catholics are witnessing the breakdown of casuistry within the Church—and casuistry is the method by which Catholics have lived since the sixteenth century.

Thus, we still try to apply general norms to a concrete case. No one finds this entirely satisfactory, but at any rate we are used to it—until we once begin to realize how remarkable it is that modern living has so many situations in which such casuistry is impossible. How little life seems to fit theory. But then we see that it has to be the other way around: how little the old theories and principles apply to the problems of our day. But we can't change a concrete situation, so therefore we must adjust our theories and principles. And when we try that, we meet resistance. What then are we to do?

We must change the climate within the Church. Each of us must be an apostle: study the proofs and arguments as I have given them to you, and then be articulate. Learn the art of polite contradiction. Be a sexual liberal. Fight censorship and repression wherever you meet it.

We have a duty to propagandize, for the Gospel of Christ is essentially a leaven, an expanding force in human affairs, and we shall betray our whole vocation as Catholics if we treat the mistakes of our teachers as if they did not exist—especially when they have personal urgency such as those that touch on sexual matters.

The human being is happy in the long run only when he is giving himself to something outside himself, only when he is working for a cause into which he can pour himself with some assurance that he is building rather than destroying, or at least that he is not wasting his time.

Cain is the archetype of the unconcerned Catholic. "Where is Abel?" God asked him. "How should I know?" countered Cain. "Am I my brother's keeper?"

It happened once that some men sat together in a boat at sea, whereupon one of them got out an awl and began boring into the boat's bottom.

"Stupid one," cried the others, "what are you doing?"

"And what concern is it of yours?" he answered. "Is it not under my own seat that I am making a hole?"

Saul D. Alinsky, the community organizer, was vehement on the point:

> A major revolution to be won in the immediate future is the dissipation of man's illusion that his own welfare can be separate from that of all others. As long as man is shackled to this myth, so long will the human spirit languish. Concern for our private, material well-being with disregard for the well-being of others is immoral according to the precepts of our Judæo-Christian civilization, but worse, it is stupidity worthy of the lower animals. . . . The fact is that it is not man's "better nature" but his self-interest that demands that he be his brother's keeper. We now live in a world where no man can have a loaf of bread while his neighbor has none. If he does not share his bread, he dare not sleep, for his neighbor will kill him. To eat and sleep in safety man must do the right thing, if for seemingly the wrong reasons, and be in practice his brother's keeper. [6]

In moral theology as in many other areas, no one man is big enough to buck the tide. "You can't fight City Hall." It is next to impossible even for an organized group to overthrow an opinion that is "in possession." Debate between the Dominican and Franciscan schools, for instance, has seesawed through the centuries, each defending conflicting positions with never a clear-cut victory on either side.*

In geography, Christopher Columbus—one man—could make a significant discovery. In science, Galileo, Newton, Pasteur. In mathematics, Euclid, Descartes, Einstein. In music, Palestrina, and the priest Monteverdi. But in moral theology, the individual counts hardly at all. There is little scope for creative genius and no possibility at all of a spectacular discovery. Even the most eminent of contemporary theologians—people like Karl Rahner and Bernard Lonergan—if they diverge too notably from the commonly accepted opinion, risk having their writings ignored, their opinions rejected as "frivolous": "Some kind of screwball . . ."

That is very likely why so many of the theologians seem to copy from one another, for the Catholic churchman is suspicious as soon as he runs across a fresh insight, an original solution to an old problem. "Somebody rocking the boat?" It makes him uneasy. Control of the Church is, after all, in the hands of old men, and old men just don't like change; they become attached to the old ways. As for sex, to them it becomes more and more a necessary nuisance, of interest only to everyone else, and as their own powers wane they are inclined to wonder what all the fuss is about.

Certainly no Catholic approves of subverting dogma, for it is revealed truth. But moral theology is something else again. It admits of change, even reversal, and in working up a consensus, the technique of praising with faint damns can be useful. Thus in this matter of sexual relief, I take the onus of pushing the frontiers of moral theology to their outermost limit. Other theologians can then use this book as a launching pad for their own views. I have given the reviewers lots of scope to pretend conservatism by trimming back my admittedly far-out opinions: "Fr. Ginder is not quite correct in saying . . . There is much truth in Ginder's contention that . . . Indeed, I would have put it much stronger than Ginder . . ."

The more my opinions are discussed, the more they get around and a consensus may develop.

---

*Except for the dogma of the Immaculate Conception. The Franciscans won out there, but there was actually no very heated argument; the Dominicans certainly loved our Blessed Mother no less than the Franciscans. It was rather that the Dominicans could not see much validity in the Franciscan argument: *"Potuit, decuit, ergo fecit."*

(To help explain the meaning of "consensus": the bishop of a certain Greek-rite exarchate once gave his people the option of changing their celebration of Christmas from their traditional January 6 to December 25. The people of one parish voted 51 to 49 for a change. So, of course, when their pastor announced the change his parish split right down the middle and he lost half his congregation. He should have waited a year or so until he had built up a more substantial consensus.)

We must never forget that the Church is our mother. I will not say that we are her "children," for that is rather a patronizing term. No, we are her sons and daughters, all of us gathered into one family under the direction of our Holy Father and the bishops. We are in fact her grown sons and daughters—not infants, but adults. We cannot be expected, then, to yield unquestioning obedience nor with closed eyes and pinched nose to gulp down whatever is handed to us in the name of truth and moral guidance. We examine and test our orders from above and if it be necessary for our peace of mind, we ask why. Mindful, too, that truth is not created by papal fiat, we ask proofs and reasons for what we are expected to believe.

Bluntly, the hierarchy are a self-perpetuating oligarchy who would not be human if their decrees were not at least occasionally self-serving rather than altruistic.

It is not wicked or irreverent then to criticize the Church providing it be done in a constructive way. And when I write "Church," I prescind from the divine element. It is a community of men and women in various degrees of moral strength and frailty. It is men not angels who are God's ministers on earth, and human beings are too often proud, vain, arrogant, ambitious, avaricious, two-faced, domineering . . .

So if one thinks that the Church (churchmen) is following a mistaken policy, has been ill-advised in some affair, or is being betrayed by unworthy ministers, then for God's sake he should speak up. One does not drop out: rather, one stays in, and works and prays for an improvement. Besides, the Church has the mass and the sacraments. Where outside the Church could we have our sins forgiven and be nourished by the Bread of Life? Where else do we have the comfort of the mass?

Taking the Church, then, as our mother, let us compare the conscience of the adult with that of the child. The adult is self- rather than other-directed. As children we had no moral freedom; Mother made all our decisions for us. It was rather a comfortable way of life, like being an enlisted man in the Service. We never had to think, to form a judgment.

"Mother, may I go swimming?"—"Yes, child, but be home by five o'clock."

"Mom, Junior gave me this wristwatch. He says he found it."—"Give it back."

Many Catholics carry that juvenile relationship with the Church right on through life to the grave. Morally, they never grow up. They shirk responsibility for their own soul. Every question must be referred to some outside agent for an answer. They ply their confessor with questions. They get the pastor on the telephone. They even pester the nuns.

But normal development entails moral alongside physical maturity. During adolescence we begin exercising independence of judgment, making our own decisions, living our own life. This increasing assumption of responsibility should extend to matters of conscience. It always brings with it the anguish of occasional uncertainty. Where there is responsible moral freedom there is bound to be fear of a mistake. But just do your best, and don't be afraid of our Lord. When one compares Catholic paranoia with Protestant confidence in God, it is not hard to see which is the better.

Particular rules are easy to apply. It is the general principles that create difficulty, for one must appraise one's motivation and the degree of one's responsibility and freedom (force of habit, passion, emotional relationship, sobriety, opportunity, monetary incentive, and the like). Outside advice may be needed on occasion for an objective sizing up of the situation and to guard against self-deception.

But authority can hardly ever be more than a guide offering approximate, rather than absolute, certainty. It is comforting, however, to recall that approximate certainty is enough for prudent action.

In sum, the mature Catholic is not abject, servile, craven. He does not crawl before Church authority. Rather, he stands on his own two feet, his mind open to Church teaching, his heart ready to obey. But he also depends on common sense, practical judgment, and the "Code of Decent Behavior"—over all of which his conscience presides as supreme and final judge.

Keep trying to develop a personal religion, an immediate relationship with our Lord. Use the Church for the Holy Sacrifice, the sacraments, inspiration, and moral instruction; but keep your life centered on Christ. What matters is *His*, not the churchmen's, opinion of you. Keep deepening your fundamental option with an intense and unshakable loyalty to our Lord.

We should often ponder and appropriate the words of St. Augustine: "Love God and do as you please." As Bishop Bekkers wrote, they throw us back on our own conscience and comfort us with our own responsibility before God. They make us watchful. They put us on guard.

Whenever you find the claims made on behalf of the Supervirtue getting you down, think of these words from St. James:

"Talk and behave like people who are going to be judged by the law of freedom, because there will be judgment without mercy for those who have not been merciful themselves; but the merciful need have no fear of judgment."[7]

Finally, according to St. Thérèse of Lisieux: "He who expects justice from God will get justice, but he who expects mercy will find mercy."

Dixi et salvavi animam meam.

NOTES

Chapter 1

1. Alvin Toffler, *Future Shock*. (New York: Random House, 1971), p. 235.
2. *Observer*, London, May 26, 1974.
3. Toffler, *op. cit.*, p. 214.
4. Marc Oraison, *Morality For Our Time* (Garden City, N.Y.: Doubleday, 1968), p. 68.
5. Cf. John Ratté, *Three Modernists: Loisy, Tyrrell, Sullivan* (New York: Sheed, 1967), p. 210.
6. Coventry Patmore.
7. Robert C. Sorensen, *Adolescent Sexuality in Contemporary America* (New York: World, 1973), pp. 96-97.
8. *Ibid.*, pp. 131-32.
9. *Ibid.*, p. 197.
10. *Ibid.*, p. 416.
11. Sept. 23, 1974.
12. Sept. 16, 1974.
13. *The Advocate*, Los Angeles, *semper et passim*.
14. The Mattachine Society, Washington and New York.
15. Martin S. Weinberg and Colin J. Williams, *Male Homosexuals* (New York: Oxford, 1974), p. 248.
16. Victor J. Pospishil, *Divorce & Remarriage: Towards a New Catholic Teaching* (New York: Herder & Herder, 1967), pp. 84-85.
17. *The Critic*, Chicago, Feb. 1975, quoted in *National Catholic Reporter*, Kansas City, Mo., Jan. 10, 1975.

Chapter 2

1. Cf. Charles Malik, ed., *God & Man in Contemporary Islamic Thought* (Syracuse U. Press, 1972), *passim*.
2. Karl Rahner and Herbert Vorgrimmler, *Theological Dictionary* (New York: Seabury, 1965), p. 482.
3. Matt. 19: 12.
4. Rom. 7: 2-3, 1 Cor. 7: 39-40, 1 Tim. 5: 14.
5. H.A. Ayrinhac, S.S. and P.J. Lydon, *Marriage Legislation in the New Code of Canon Law* (New York: Benziger, 1933), p. 349.
6. Canon 1143.
7. Rev. 14: 4.
8. 1 Cor. 7: 7.
9. Cf. Charles E. Curran and Robert E. Hunt, *Dissent In and For the Church* (New York: Sheed, 1969), pp. 169-76.
10. G.G. Coulton, *Five Centuries of Religion* (Cambridge, 1929), I, p. 177.

11. These catechetical examples are cited by Robert P. O'Neil and Fr. Michael A. Donovan in their book *Sexuality and Moral Responsibility* (Washington: Corpus Books, 1968).

12. Donald Webster Cory, *Homosexuality: A Cross-Cultural Approach* (New York: Julian Press, 1956), p. 428.

13. Frank J. Sheed, *The Church and I* (Garden City, N.Y.: Doubleday, 1974), p. 223.

14. Dr. John Rock, *The Time Has Come* (New York: Knopf, 1963), pp. 87-88.

Chapter 4

1. *The Thomist,* July 1971, Vol. XXXV, No. 3, pp. 447-81.

2. William James, *The Varieties of Religious Experience* (New York: Macmillan, 1966), pp. 186-213.

3. St. Ignatius Loyola *Spiritual Exercises,* trans. Fr. Corbishley (Westminster, Md.: Christian Classics, 1973), pp. 60-63.

4. Hans Küng, *The Church* (New York: Sheed, 1967), pp. 203ff.

5. W.M. Bekkers, *God's People On the March* (New York: Holt, 1966), p. 123.

6. A good exposition of the fundamental option can be found in O'Neil & Donovan, *op cit.*, p. 55. Cf. also p. 36.

Chapter 5

1. John 15: 18-19.
2. Phil. 4: 13.
3. Ps. 40: 9.
4. John 15: 16.
5. *National Review Bulletin,* Oct. 18, 1974.
6. Henry C. Lea, *History of Sacerdotal Celibacy in the Christian Church* (London: Watts, 1932), pp. 2-3.

7. Joseph Crehan, S.J., *Father Thurston* (London: Sheed, 1952), p. 152.

8. Lea, *op. cit.*, p. 244.

9. *Ibid.*, pp. 560-61.

10. Rahner and Vorgrimmler, *op. cit.*, p. 73.

11. Jacques Leclercq, *Marriage and the Family,* trans. Thomas R. Hanley, O.S.B. (New York: Pustet, 1941), pp. 144ff.

Chapter 6

1. Tim. 5: 14.
2. *Jerusalem Bible* (Garden City, N.Y.: Doubleday, 1966), New Testament, p. 254.
3. Gal. 5: 21.
4. 1 Tim. 1: 10.
5. Eph. 5: 5.
6. *Ibid.*
7. Luke 15: 4-7.
8. Luke 15: 11-32.
9. Luke 7: 36-50.
10. Luke 18: 24.
11. Matt. 5: 19.
12. Matt. 5: 22.
13. Matt. 18: 34.
14. Matt. 10: 37-39.
15. Matt. 15: 19-20.
16. 1 Cor. 6: 9-10.
17. 1 Cor. 13.
18. Matt. 28: 18-20.
19. Matt. 18: 17.
20. Titus 3: 10.
21. 1 Cor. 4: 21.
22. Cf. *The Spanish Inquisition,* Harry Kamen (New York: North American Library, 1971), *passim.*
23. 1 Cor. 5: 9ff.
24. St. Paul is quoting Deut. 13: 6.
25. 2 Thess. 3: 6.
26. 1 Cor. 15: 33.
27. Eph. 5: 7.
28. Matt. 7: 1-5.
29. John 8: 7.
30. Luke 18: 10-14.

31. Matt. 23: 27.
32. Mark 12: 42.
33. Mark 7: 3.
34. Luke 5: 30.
35. 1 Thess. 3: 10.
36. Joseph Lortz, *The Reformation In Germany*, Vol. I, p. 86, citing a contemporary estimate by Johannes Agricola quoted by Karl Adam, *The Roots of the Reformation* (New York: Sheed, 1951), p. 22. The figure is almost incredible.

Chapter 7

1. E.R. Chamberlin, *The Bad Popes* (New York: Dial, 1969), *passim*.
2. Matt. 16: 18.
3. Matt. 28: 20.
4. John 14: 16.
5. John 16: 13.
6. 1 Tim. 3: 15.
7. F. Simons, *Infallibility and The Evidence* (Springfield, Ill.: Templegate, 1968), p. 80.
8. *Ibid.*, pp. 87-89.
9. John L. McKenzie. *Myths and Realities: Studies in Biblical Theology* (Milwaukee: Bruce, 1963), p. 6.
10. Hans Küng, *Infallible?* (Garden City, N.Y.: Doubleday, 1971), p. 114.
11. *Catholic Encyclopedia*, New York, 1913, Vol. XIV, p. 39.
12. Sam Wagenaar, *The Pope's Jews* (Freeport, N.Y.: Library Press, 1974), p. 133.
13. Patrick Granfield, quoted by Curran & Hunt in *op. cit.*, p. 76.
14. Hans Küng, *Truthfulness* (New York: Sheed, 1968), p. 136.

Chapter 8

1. There is an excellent survey of this development in *The Making of the Modern Mind*, by John Herman Randall, Jr., of Columbia Univer-

sity (Boston: Houghton Mifflin, 1954).
2. Xavier Rynne, *The Second Session* (New York: Farrar, Straus & Giroux, 1964), pp. 292-93.
3. *Time*, April 1, 1974.
4. For the basic history of the Third Reich, I rely on Bullock rather than Schirer, the historian rather than the journalist: *Hitler: A study in Tyranny*, by Alan Bullock (London: Odhams Press, 1952).
5. Matt. 22: 21.
6. In his *Myths & Realities*, pp. 3-37, Fr. John L. McKenzie is eloquent on this subject.
7. Quoted by Randall, *op. cit.*, pp. 442-43.

Chapter 9

1. Luke 11: 52.
2. *God's People On the March*, p. 121.
3. O'Neil & Donovan, *op. cit.*, pp. 122-23.

Chapter 10

1. Sorensen, *Adolescent Sexuality*, p. 138.
2. *Newsweek*, Nov. 11, 1974.
3. *Time*, April 1, 1974.
4. Matt. 19: 6.
5. Matt. 19: 8.
6. O'Neil & Donovan, *Sexuality & Moral Responsibility*, p. 45.

Chapter 11

1. Garry Wills, *Bare Ruined Choirs* (Garden City, N.Y.: Doubleday, 1974), pp. 224-25.
2. Fr. Joseph Sommer, S.J. *Catholic Thought On Contraception Through the Centuries* (Liguori, Mo.: Liguori Publications, 1970), pp. 28ff.—a concise thesaurus on the subject. I am deeply grateful to Fr. Sommer for his research.

3. *Ibid.*, pp. 49-50.
4. Sheed, *The Church & I* (Garden City, N.Y.: Doubleday, 1974), p. 241.
5. Sommer, *op. cit.*, pp. 52-53.
6. Hildebrand's book was *Marriage* (Munich: 1928). Others, developing the same theme: Matthias Laros, *Modern Marriage Questions. I. The Relations Between the Sexes* (Cologne: 1936); Norbert Rocholl, *Marriage As Consecrated Love* (Duelman: 1936); N. Zimmermann, *Both Sexes In the Sight of God* (Wiesbaden: 1936).
7. Sommer, *op. cit.*, p. 55.
8. Rock, *The Time Has Come*, p. 149.

Chapter 12

1. Matt. 26: 24.
2. Bishop Francis Simons, S.V.D., "The Catholic Church & the New Morality," in *Cross Currents*, VI, 4, Fall, 1966, pp. 439-40.
3. Garry Wills, *Bare Ruined Choirs*, p. 179.
4. *Ibid.*, pp. 183-86.
5. Abbott-Gallagher, *The Documents of Vatican II* (New York: Association Press, 1966), "The Church in the Modern World," No. 5, p. 204.
6. Bruce Vawter quoted by Herbert Haag, *Is Original Sin in Scripture?* (New York: Sheed, 1969), p. 11.
7. Dr. Frederick E. Flynn *quoted by* John Rock, M.D., *The Time Has Come* (New York: Knopf, 1963), pp. 62-63.
8. Michael F. Valente, *Sex: The Radical View of a Catholic Theologian* New York: Bruce, 1970), p. 73.
9. Samuel G. Kling, *Sexual Behavior & the Law* (New York: Pocket Books, 1969), pp. 77-78.
10. Hans Küng, *Infallibility?* (Garden City, N.Y.: Doubleday, 1971), p. 236.

11. Abbott-Gallagher, *Documents of Vatican II*, p. 29.
12. Curran and Hunt, *Dissent*, pp. 6-7.
13. *Ibid.*, pp. 43-44. *Cf.* also p. 85.
14. John 16: 13.

Chapter 13.

1. Weinberg, *Society & the Healthy Homosexual* (Garden City, N.Y.: Doubleday, 1973), p. 77.
2. *Fag Rag/Gay Sunshine*, Stonewall 5th Anniversary Issue, San Francisco, Summer, 1974.
3. Feb. 12, 1972.
4. *New York Times*, Dec. 16, 1973.
5. Weinberg and Williams, *Male Homosexuals*, pp. 153ff.
6. Curran and Hunt, *Dissent*, p. 65.
7. *Abbott-Gallagher, Documents, pp. 269-70: "The Church in the Modern World,"* No. 62.
8. *The Thomist*, July, 1971.
9. Gen. 13: 3; 18 : 20; Jer. 23: 14; Ez. 16: 49-50; Wis. 10: 8; Ecclus. 16: 8.
10. All through the discourse at the Last Supper: John 14, 15, 16.
11. *Ibid.*
12. *A New Catechism* (New York: Herder & Herder, 1967), pp. 384-85.
13. Rock, *The Time Has Come*, p. 63.
14. *The Thomist*, p. 475.
15. Valente, *Sex: The Radical View*, pp. 126-27.
16. National Office: 755 Boylston Street, Room 514, Boston, Mass. 02116.

Chapter 14

1. Xavier Rynne, *Letters from Vatican City* (New York: Farrar, Straus & Giroux, 1963), p. 248.
2. *Difficulties of Anglicans* (London: Longmans, Green, 1876), II, p. 248.
3. O'Neil & Donovan, *Sexuality & Moral Responsibility*, p. 12.

4. *Ibid.*, p. 18.
5. *Apud idem*, p. 20.
6. *Ibid.*, p. 30.
7. *Ibid.*, p. 31.

24. Wayland Young, *Eros Denied* (New York: Grove, 1964), p. 325.
25. O'Neil & Donovan, *op. cit.*, p. 96.

Chapter 15

1. In *Sexual Self-Stimulation*, by R.L.E. Masters (Los Angeles: Sherbourne, 1967), p. 222.
2. *Ibid.*, p. 228.
3. *The Kinsey Report* (Philadelphia: W.C. Saunders, 1948), p. 514.
4. Daniel Yankelovich, *The New Morality: A Profile of American Youth in the 70's* (New York: McGraw-Hill, 1974), p. 159.
5. *Ibid.*, p. 87.
6. *Ibid.*, p. 90.
7. *Newsweek*, Nov. 4, 1974, p. 69.
8. Edward Sagarin, in R.E.L. Masters, *op. cit.*, p. 169.
9. C.S. Field & F.A. Beach, *Patterns of Sexual Behavior* (New York: 1951), p. 187.
10. Edward Sagarin, in *op. cit.*, p. 170.
11. *Observer*, London, Jan. 1, 1967.
12. *"Regula tactus,"* Constitutions, Art. 32.
13. Robert C. Sorensen, *Adolescent Sexuality in Contemporary America: Personal Values & Sexual Behavior, Ages 13-19* (New York: World, 1973), p. 469.
14. *Cross Currents*, Fall, 1966, Vol. XVI, No. 4, p. 442.
15. O'Neil & Donovan, *Sexuality & Moral Responsibility*, p. 100.
16. Sorensen, *op. cit.*, p. 138.
17. *Esquire*, Dec. 1974, p. 124.
18. O'Neil & Donovan, *op. cit.*, pp. 102-3.
19. Sorensen, *Adolescent Sexuality*, p. 303.
20. *Ibid.*, p. 311.
21. *Ibid.*, p. 197.
22. *Ibid.*, p. 203.
23. *Ibid.*, p. 299.

Chapter 16

1. Wayland Young, *Eros Denied*, p. 139. Except for Swinburne's, the rest of these instances are cited from Young.
2. Alex Comfort, *The Joy of Sex* (New York: Simon & Schuster, 1972), pp. 7-8.
3. O'Neil & Donovan, *Sexuality & Moral Responsibility*, p. 124.
4. Young, *op. cit.*, p. 252.
5. Comfort, *Joy*, p. 250.
6. John Woodbury and Elroy Schwartz, *The Silent Sin: A Case History of Incest* (New York: North American Library, 1971), pp. 10-13.
7. *Observer*, London, April 28, 1974, p. 30.
8. *Christine Jorgensen: A Personal Autobiography* (New York: Bantam, 1973), p. 90.
9. *Ibid.*, p. 113.
10. *Ibid.*, pp. 117-18.
11. *Newsweek*, April 8, 1974, p. 74.
12. Jorgensen, *Autobiography*, p. 226.

Chapter 17

1. Ayrinhac-Lydon, *Marriage Legislation*, p. 1.
2. Victor J. Pospishil, *Divorce & Remarriage: Towards a New Catholic Teaching* (New York: Herder & Herder, 1967), pp. 84-85. Professor of theology at New York's Manhattan College, Msgr. Pospishil was for sixteen years head of the marriage court for the Byzantine Rite Catholic Diocese of Philadelphia.
3. *Ibid.*, p. 48.
4. Mark 10: 5-12.

5. Luke 6: 35.
6. 1 Cor. 7: 12.
7. Pospishil, *op. cit.*, p. 51.
8. *Ibid.*, pp. 108-9.
9. *Ibid.*, p. 102.
10. *Cross Currents*, Vol. XVI, No. 4, p. 443.
11. *Ibid.*, pp. 429-45.
12. Quoted by Leclercq-Hanley, Marriage, p. 223n.
13. *De genesi ad litteram*, IX, 7.
14. Moore, *Principles of Ethics* (Philadelphia: Lippincott, 1938), pp. 159ff.
15. National Catholic News Service, Nov. 29, 1974.

16. Noonan, *Contraception*, p. 6.
17. *National Review*, April 26, 1974, p. 458.

Chapter 18

1. May 20, 1974.
2. William Blake, *Songs of Experience.*
3. Young, *Eros Denied*, p. 167.
4. *Newsweek*, May 30, 1974.
5. *Time*, May 27, 1974.
6. Saul Alinsky, *Rules For Radicals* (New York: Random House, 1972), p. 23.
7. James 2: 12-13.

BIBLIOGRAPHY

Abbott, S.J., Walter M. and Msgr. Joseph J. Gallagher, *The Documents of Vatican II.* New York: Association Press, 1966.

Adam, Karl, *The Roots of the Reformation.* New York: Sheed, 1951.

Aertnys, C.SS.R., J. and C.A. Damen, C.SS.R., J.C.D., *Theologia Moralis.* Turin, 1944.

Alinsky, Saul D., *Rules For Radicals.* New York: Random House, 1972.

Altman, Dennis, *The Homosexual: Oppression and Liberation.* New York: Outerbridge, 1971.

Anchell, Melvin, *Sex and Sanity.* New York: Macmillan, 1971.

Armas, O.R.S.A., P. Gregoria, *La Moral de San Agustin.* Madrid, 1954.

Ayrinhac, S.S., H.A. and P.J. Lydon, *Marriage Legislation in the New Code of Canon Law.* New York: Benziger, 1938.

Barnett, Walter E., *Sexual Freedom and the Constitution.* Albuquerque: UNM Press, 1973.

Baum, O.S.A., Gregory, *The Credibility of the Church Today.* New York: Seabury, 1968.

————ed. *Ecumenical Theology Today.* Glen Rock, N.J.: Paulist-Newman, 1964.

————ed. *The Future of Belief.* New York: Herder & Herder, 1967.

Bekkers, Most Rev. W.M., *God's People On the March.* New York: Holt, 1966.

Bender, David L. and Gary E. McCuan, *The Sexual Revolution: Traditional Mores Versus New Values.* Anoka, Minn.: Greenhaven, 1972.

Boyd, Malcolm, ed., *The Underground Church.* New York: Sheed, 1968.

Brown, Norman O., *Life Against Death.* New York: Random House, 1959.

Bullock, Alan, *Hitler: A Study In Tyranny.* London: Odhams Press, 1952.

Callahan, Daniel, *The Catholic Case For Contraception.* New York: Macmillan, 1969.

A Catholic Commentary On Holy Scripture. New York: Nelson, 1953.

Cavanagh, John R., *The Popes, the Pill and the People.* Milwaukee: Bruce, 1965.

237

Chamberlin, E.R., *The Bad Popes*. New York: Dial, 1969.

Clayton, George, *Sex and the Youth Revolution*. New York: Manor, 1971.

Codex Juris Canonici. Rome, 1917.

Cogley, John, *Catholic America*. New York: Dial. 1973.

Comfort, M.B., Ph.D., Alex, *The Joy of Sex*. New York: Simon & Schuster, 1972.

Cooper, D.D., John M., *Religious Outlines For College*. Washington: CUA Press, 1949.

Copleston, S.J., Frederick, *A History of philosophy*. Garden City, N.Y.: Doubleday, 1962.

Cory, Donald Webster, *Homosexuality: A Cross-Cultural Approach*. New York: Julian Press, 1956.

Coulton, G.G. *Life in the Middle Ages*. Cambridge University Press, 1935.

Cox, Harvey, *The Secular City*. New York: Macmillan, 1966.

———— *The Seduction of the Spirit*. New York: Macmillan, 1973.

Crehan, S.J., Joseph, *Father Thurston*. London: Sheed, 1952.

Curran, Charles E., *Christian Morality Today: The Renewal of Moral Theology*. Notre Dame, Ind.: Fides, 1967.

————*Contraception: Authority & Dissent*. New York: Herder & Herder, 1969.

————and Robert E. Hunt, *Dissent In and For the Church*. New York: Sheed, 1969.

———— "Homosexuality and Moral Theology: Methodological and Substantive Considerations," article in *The Thomist* (Washington, D.C.), 3, July, 1971.

————*A New Look At Christian Morality*. Notre Dame, Ind.: Fides, 1970.

Davis, S.J., Henry, *Moral and Pastoral Theology*. New York: Sheed, 1936.

Denzinger-Bannwart, Carolus Rahner, S.J., ed. *Enchiridion Symbolorum*. Barcelona, 1960.

Derrick, Christopher, *Honest Love and Human Life: Is the Pope Right About Contraception?* New York: Coward, 1969.

Dictionnaire Apologétique de la Foi Catholique. Paris, 1931.

Draper, E., *Birth Control in the Modern World: The Role of the Individual in Population Control*. Gloucester, Mass.: Peter Smith, 1972.

Duprée, Louis, *Contraception and Catholics*. Baltimore: Helicon, 1964.

Edwards, John N., ed., *Sex and Society*. Chicago: Markham, 1972.

Feldman, David M., *Birth Control In Jewish Law*. New York: NYU Press, 1968.

Finch, Bernard E. and Hugh Green, *Contraception Through the Ages*. Springfield, Ill.: C.C. Thomas, 1963.

Ford, S.J., John C. and Gerald Kelly, S.J., *Contemporary Moral Theology*. Westminister, Md.: Newman, 1963.

Fraser, Ian M., *Sex As Gift*. Philadelphia: Fortress, 1968.

Freeman, Eugene and David Appel, *The Wisdom and Ideas of Plato*. New York: Fawcett World, 1970.

Friedenberg, Edgar Z., *The Vanishing Adolescent*. New York: Dell, 1959.

Fülöp-Miller, René, *The Jesuits*. New York: Putman, 1963.

Gasparri, Petrus Cardinalis, *Catechismus Catholicus*. Vatican City, 1933.

Gay, Peter, *The Rise of Modern Paganism*, New York: Knopf, 1966.

Genicot, S.J., Eduardus and I. Salsmans, S.J., *Institutiones Theologiae Moralis*. Buenos Aires, 1946.

Gide, André, *Corydon*. New York: French & European, 1965.

Ginder, Richard, *Thou Art the Rock*. Denver: Catholic Laymen of America, 1968.

Gleason, Robert V., *Situational Morality*. Albany, N.Y.: Magi Books, 1968.

Gregersen, E.A., *Sex, Culture and Society*. New York: Gordon, 1974.

Grisar, S.J., Hartmann, *Luther*. St. Louis: Herder, 1919.

Grisez, G., *Contraception and the Natural Law*. Milwaukee: Bruce, 1964.

Guttmacher, A.F., *Birth Control and Love*. New York: Macmillan, 1969.

Haag, Herbert. *Is Original Sin In Scripture?*. New York: Sheed, 1969.

Hales, E.E.Y., *Pio Nono*. Garden City, N.Y.: Doubleday, 1962.

Hall, Robert E., ed., *Abortion In a Changing World*. New York: Columbia U. Press, 1970.

Hamilton, Eleanor, *Sex Before Marriage*. New York: Bantam, 1973.

Hardon, S.J., John A., *Christianity in the Twentieth Century*. Garden City, N.Y.: Doubleday, 1972.

Häring, C.SS.R., Bernard, *Bernard Häring Replies*. Staten Island, N.Y.: Alba House, 1967.

———*What Does Christ Want?*. Staten Island: Alba House, 1968.

Hechinger, Grace and Fred M., *Teen-Age Tyranny*. New York: Fawcett World, 1970.

Hettlinger, Richard F., *Sexual Maturity*. Belmont, Cal.: Wadsworth, 1973.

Heer, Friedrich, *The Intellectual History of Europe*. New York: World, 1968.

Hitchcock, James, *The Decline and Fall of Radical Catholicism*. Garden City, N.Y.: Doubleday, 1972.

Höffding, Harald, *A History of Modern Philosophy*. New York: Dover, 1965.

Howlett, Duncan, *The Fourth American Faith*. Boston: Beacon, 1968.

Hoyt, Robert G., ed., *Issues That Divide the Church*. New York: Macmillan, 1968.

Hughes, Philip, *A Popular History of the Catholic Church*. New York: Sheed, 1960.

———*A Popular History of the Reformation*. Garden City, N.Y.: Doubleday, 1960.

Huxley, Julian, *Religion Without Revelation*. New York: North American Library, 1958.

Hyde, H. Montgomery, *The Other Love*. Boston: Little Brown, 1970.

James, Howard, *Children In Trouble: A National Scandal*. New York: McKay, 1971.

James, William, *The Varieties of Religious Experience*. New York: Macmillan, 1966.

Jan, Mary and Lawrence J. Losoney. *Sex and the Adolescent*. Notre Dame, Ind.: Ave Maria, 1971.

The Jerusalem Bible. Garden City, N.Y.: Doubleday, 1966.

Johnson, Cecil, *Sex and Human Relationships*. Columbus, Ohio: Merrill, 1970.

Jone, O. Cap., J.C.D., Heribert, *Moral Theology*. Westminster, Md.: Newman, 1947.

Jorgensen, Christine, *A Personal Autobiography*. New York: Bantam, 1967.

Joyce, S.J., George Hayward, *Christian Marriage*. New York: Sheed, 1933.

Kamen, Henry, *The Spanish Inquisition*. New York: North American Library, 1971.

Kanaby, Donald, *Sex, Fertility and the Catholic*. Staten Island, N.Y.: Alba House, 1967.

Kaufmann, Walter, ed., *Existentialism from Dostoevsky to Sartre*. Gloucester, Mass.: Peter Smith, 1969.

Kavanaugh, James, *The Birth of God*. New York: Trident Press, 1969.

Kelleher, Stephen J., *Divorce and Remarriage For Catholics?*. Garden City, N.Y.: Doubleday, 1973.

Kelly, George A., *Birth Control and Catholics*. Garden City, N.Y.: Doubleday, 1963.

Kelly, S.J., Gerald, *Medico-Moral Problems*. St. Louis: Herder, 1955.

Kellett, E.E., *A Short History of Religions*. Baltimore: Helicon, 1962.

Kling, Samuel G., *Sexual Behavior and the Law*. New York: Pocket Books, 1969.

Knight, C.S.Sp., Gordon F., *Rational Theology*. Pittsburgh: Duquesne U. Press, 1957.

Knox, R.A., *Enthusiasm: A Chapter in the History of Religion*. Oxford, 1951.

Küng, Hans, *The Church*. New York: Sheed, 1967.

————*The Council, Reform and Reunion*. Garden City, N.Y.: Doubleday, 1957.

————*Infallible?–An Inquiry*. Garden City, N.Y.: Doubleday, 1971.

————*Truthfulness: The Future of the Church*. New York: Sheed, 1968.

Kurts, Paul and Albert Dondeyne, eds., *The Catholic-Humanist Dialogue*. Buffalo: Prometheus Books, 1973.

Lea, Henry C., *History of Auricular Confession and Indulgences in the Latin Church*. New York: Greenwood, 1968.

————*History of Sacerdotal Celibacy in the Christian Church*. London: Watts, 1932.

Leclercq, Ph.D. LL.D., Jacques and Thomas R. Hanley, O.S.B., Ph.D., *Marriage and the Family*. New York: Pustet, 1941.

Lednicer, Daniel, ed., *Contraception: The Chemical Control of Fertility*. New York: Dekker, 1969.

Lewis, C.S., *The Problem of Pain*. New York: Macmillan, 1943.

Lo Bello, Nino, *The Vatican Empire*. New York: Pocket Books, 1969.

————*Vatican, U.S.A.* New York: Pocket Books, 1973.

Lortz, Joseph, *How the Reformation Came*. New York: Herder & Herder, 1964.

Mace, David R., *Abortion: The Agonizing Decision*. Nashville, Tenn.: Abingdon, 1972.

Malik, Charles, ed., *God and Man in Contemporary Islamic Thought*. Syracuse U. Press, 1972.

Marcus Aurelius, tr. G.M. Grube, *Meditations*. Indianapolis: Bobbs-Merrill, 1963.

Maritain, Jacques, *Reflections On America*. Staten Island, N.Y.: Gordian, 1973.

Marmer, Judd, ed., *Sexual Inversion: The Multiple Roots of Homosexuality*. New York: Basic, 1965.

Marshall, John, *Catholics, Marriage and Contraception*. Baltimore: Helicon, 1965.

————*The Infertile Period*. Baltimore: Helicon, 1967.

Martial, *Epigrams*. Oxford U. Press, 1903.

Masters, R.E.L., ed., *Sexual Self-Stimulation*. Los Angeles: Sherbourne, 1967.

McCaffrey, J., ed., *Homosexual Dialectic*. Englewood Cliffs, N.J.: Prentice-Hall, 1972.

McCarthy, D.D., D.C.L., John, *Problems in Theology*. Westminster, Md.: Newman, 1956.

McKenzie, S.J., John L., *Dictionary of the Bible*. Milwuakee: Bruce, 1965

———*Myths & Realities: Studies in Biblical Theology*. Milwaukee: Bruce, 1963.

McLuhan, Marshall and Quentin Fiore, *The Medium Is the Massage*. New York: Bantam, 1970.

Merkelbach, O.P., Benedictus Henricus, *Summa Theologiae Moralis*. Paris, 1947.

Miller, Merle, *On Being Different*. New York: Popular Library, 1972.

Moore, O.S.B., M.D., Ph.D., Thomas Verner, *Principles of Ethics*. Philadelphia: Lippincott, 1938.

Morris, Desmond, *The Naked Ape*. New York: Dell, 1969.

Muggeridge, Malcolm, *Jesus Rediscovered*. Garden City, N.Y.: Doubleday, 1969.

Müller, Alois, *Obedience In the Church*. Westminster, Md.: Newman, 1962.

Murray, S.J., John Courtney, *We Hold These Truths*. New York: Sheed, 1960.

Nabuco, Joachim, *Jus Pontificalium*. Rome, 1965.

National Institute of Mental Health Task Force on Homosexuality: Final Report and Background Papers. Washington: Govt. Ptg. Office, 1972.

Nestle, D. Eberhard, *Novum Testamentum Graece & Latine*. Stuttgart, 1932.

Neuner, S.J., Josef and Heinrich Roos, J.S., *The Teaching of the Catholic Church*, Karl Rahner, S.J., ed., Staten Island, N.Y.: Alba House, 1967.

The New American Bible. Paterson, N.J.: St. Anthony, 1970.

A New Catechism. New York: Herder & Herder, 1967.

Newman, John Henry, *An Essay in Aid of a Grammar of Assent*. Westminster, Md.: Christian Classics, 1973.

———*Apologia Pro Vita Sua*. Westminster, Md.: Christian Classics, 1973.

Noldin, S.J., H.A. and A. Schmitt, S.J., *Summa Theologiae Moralis*. Innsbruck, 1940.

Noonan, Jr., John T., *Contraception: A History of Its Treatment by the Catholic Theologians and Canonists*. Harvard, 1965.

Novak, Michael, ed., *The Experience of Marriage*. New York: Macmillan, 1964.

O'Neil, Robert P. and Michael A. Donovan, *Sexuality and Moral Responsibility*. Washington: Corpus Books, 1968.

Oraison, Marc, *Morality For Our Time*. Garden City, N.Y.: Doubleday, 1969.

Ostow, Mortimer, ed., *Sexual Deviations*. New York: Quadrangle, 1973.

Otto, Rudolf, *The Idea of the Holy*. Oxford U. Press, 1958.

Paris, O.P., G.M., *Synopsis Totius Summae Theologicae S. Thomae*. Naples, 1958.

Pascal, Blaise, *Pensées*. New York: Pantheon, 1965.

Perry, Rev. Troy D., *The Lord Is My Shepherd and He Knows I'm Gay*. Los Angeles: Nash, 1972.

Pincus, Gregory, ed., *The Control of Fertility*. New York: Academic Press, 1965.

Pius XI, *"Casti connubii."* Rome, 1930.

Pospishil, Victor J., *Divorce and Remarriage*. New York: Herder & Herder, 1967.

Principles to Guide Confessors in Questions of Homosexuality. Washington: National Catholic Conference, 1974.

Prümmer, O.P., Dominicus M., *Manuale Theologiae Moralis*. Barcelona, 1964.

Rahner, S.J., Karl, *Free Speech in the Church*. New York: Sheed, 1959.
———*Christian Commitment*. New York: Sheed, 1963.
———*Nature and Grace: Dilemmas in the Modern Church*. New York: Sheed, 1964.
———*Theological Investigations*. Baltimore: Helicon, 1961.
———and Herbert Vorgrimmler, *Theological Dictionary*. New York: Seabury, 1965.
Randall, Jr., John Herman, *The Making of the Modern Mind*. Boston: Houghton Mifflin, 1954.
Ratté, John, *Three Modernists: Loisy, Tyrrell, Sullivan*. New York: Sheed, 1967.
Reich, Charles A., *The Greening of America*. New York: Random House, 1971.
Reich, Wilhelm, *Sexual Revolution*. New York: Octagon, 1972.
Rembar, Charles, *The End of Obscenity*. New York: Simon & Schuster, 1969.
Rénan, Ernest, *Life of Jesus*. New York: Belmont-Tower, 1972.
Reuben, M.D., David, *Everything You Always Wanted To Know About Sex*. New York: McKay, 1969.
Richette, Lisa Aversa, *The Throwaway Children*. New York: Dell, 1973.
Riesman, David, with Nathan Glazer & Reuel Denney, *The Lonely Crowd*. New Haven, Conn.: Yale, 1967.
Rock, M.D., John, *The Time Has Come*. New York: Knopf, 1963.
Rosen, David H., *Lesbianism: A Study of Female Homosexuality*. Springfield, Ill.: C.C. Thomas, 1973.
Rosenfels, Paul, *Homosexuality: The Psychology of the Creative Process*. Roslyn Heights, N.Y.: Libra, 1971.
Ruitenbeek, Hendrik, *Homosexuality & Creative Genius*. Stamford, Conn.: Astor-Honor, 1965.
———*Sexuality and Identity*. New York: Dell, 1971.
Russell, Bertrand, *A History of Western Philosophy*. New York: Simon & Schuster, 1967.
Rynne, Xavier, *Letters from Vatican City*. New York: Farrar, Straus & Giroux, 1963.
———*The Second Session*. New York: Farrar, Straus & Giroux, 1964.

Sabetti, S.J., Aloysius and Timotheus Barrett, S.J. and Daniel F. Creeden, S.J., *Compendium Theologiae Moralis*. New York, 1969.
Schillebeeckx, O.P., E. *God and Man: Theological Soundings*. New York: Sheed, 1969.
Schoeps, Hans-Joachim, *The Religions of Mankind: Their Origin and Development*. Garden City, N.Y.: Doubleday, 1968.
Schopp, Ludwig and Roy J. Deferrari, ed., *The Fathers of the Church*, 66 vv. New York & Washington: SIMA, 1946—.
Segundo, S.J., Juan Luis, *Grace and the Human Condition*. New York: Orbis, 1973.
Selner, S.S., John Charles, *Teaching of St. Augustine on Fear as a Religious Motive*. Baltimore: St. Mary's Seminary, 1937.
Sheed, Frank, *The Church and I*. Garden City, N.Y.: Doubleday, 1974.
———*Is It the Same Church?*. Dayton, Ohio: Pflaum, 1968.
Sheridan, John D., *The Hungry Sheep*. New Rochelle, N.Y.: Arlington, 1974.
Siegle, Bernard, *Marriage Today: A Commentary on the Code of Canon Law in the Light of Vatican II and the Ecumenical Age*. Staten Island: Alba House, 1973.

Simons, S.V.D., Most Rev. Francis, "The Catholic Church and the New Morality," in *Cross Currents*, XVI, 4, Fall, 1966. Nyack, N.Y.

———*Infallibility and the Evidence*. Springfield, Ill.: Tamplegate, 1968.

Sommers, S.J., Ph.D., Joseph, *Catholic Thought on Contraception Through the Centuries*. Liguori, Mo.: Liguroi Publications, 1970.

Sorensen, Robert C., *Adolescent Sexuality in Contemporary America*. New York: World, 1973.

Speaight, Robert, *Teilhard de Chardin: A Biography*. London: Collins, 1967.

St. Augustine (tr. F.J. Sheed), *Confessions*. New York: Sheed, 1949.

Stearn, Jess, *The Sixth Man*. New York: Manor, 1971.

St. Ignatius Loyola (tr. Fr. Corbishley), *Spiritual Exercises*. Westminster, Md.: Christian Classics, 1973.

Stoller, Robert J., *Sex and Gender: On the Development of Masculinity & Femininity*. New York: J. Aronson, 1968.

Strachey, Lytton, *Eminent Victorians*. New York: Harcourt Brace, 1969.

Suenens, Cardinal Léon-Joseph, *Love and Control*. Westminster, Md.: Newman, 1961.

Swicegood, Thomas L.P., *Our God Too*. New York: Pyramid, 1974.

Tanquerey, S.S., A., *Synopsis Theologiae Moralis*. Paris, 1933.

The Thomist. July, 1971. Vol. XXXV, No. 3. Washington.

Turner, William, *History of Philosophy*. Boston: Ginn, 1929.

Todd, John M., *Martin Luther*. Westminster, Md.: Newman, 1964.

Toffler, Alvin, *Future Shock*. New York: Random House, 1971.

Tyler, Edward T., ed., *Birth Control: A Continuing Controversy*. Springfield, Ill.: C.C. Thomas, 1967.

Valente, Michael F., *Sex: The Radical View of a Catholic Theologian*. New York: Bruce, 1970.

Vawter, C.M., Bruce, *A Path Through Genesis*. New York: Sheed, 1956.

Vermeersch, S.J., Arthurus, *Theologiae Moralis Principia, Responsa, Consilia*. Rome, 1945.

Vizzard, Jack, *See No Evil: Life Inside a Hollywood Censor*. New York: Pocket Books, 1971.

Voltaire, J.H. Brumfitt, ed., *Candide*. Oxford U. Press, 1968.

———tr. Peter Gay, *Philosophical Dictionary*. New York: Harcourt Brace, 1962.

Van Gagern, Frederick, *Marriage Partnership*. Westminster, Md.: Newman, 1966.

———*New Views on Sex, Marriage and Love*. Paramus, N.J.: Paulist-Newman, 1968.

Von Hildebrand, Dietrich, *Teilhard de Chardin: A False Prophet*. Chicago: Franciscan Herald, 1968.

———*Trojan Horse in the City of God*. Chicago: Franciscan Herald, 1967.

Wagenaar, Sam, *The Pope's Jews*. Freeport, N.Y.: Library Press, 1974.

Wall, Otto A., *Sex and Sex Worship*. Washington: McGrath, 1920.

Ward, Maisie, *Unfinished Business*. New York: Sheed, 1964.

Watts, Alan W., *Myth and Ritual in Christianity*. Boston: Beacon, 1968.

Weigel, S.J. Gustave, *Faith and Understanding in America*. New York: Macmillan, 1959.

Weinberg, Dr. George, *Society and the Healthy Homosexual*. New York: St. Martin, 1972.

Weinberg, Martin S. and Colin J. Williams, *Male Homosexuals*. New York: Oxford, 1974.

Whelpton, P.K. and others, *Fertility and Family Planning in the United States*. Princeton, N.J.: Princeton U. Press, 1966.

Williams, Colin J. and Martin S. Weinberg, *Homosexuals and the Military: A Study of Less Than Honorable Discharge*. New York: Harper & Row, 1971.

Wills, Garry, *Bare Ruined Choirs: Doubt, Prophecy and Radical Religion*. Garden City, N.Y.: Doubleday, 1974.

Wilson, Paul, *Sexual Dilemma: Abortion, Homosexuality, Prostitution and the Criminal Threshold*. New York: Optimum Books, 1971.

Woodbury, Ph.D. and Elroy Schwartz, *The Silent Sin: A Case History of Incest*. New York: North American Library, 1971.

Yankelovich, Daniel, *The New Morality: A Profile of American Youth in the 70's*. New York: McGraw-Hill, 1974.

Young, Wayland, *Eros Denied*. New York: Grove, 1964.

INDEX

Binding
With
Briars

So I turned to the Garden of Love
   That so many sweet flowers bore.
And I saw it was filled with graves,
   And tombstones where flowers should be;
And priests with black gowns were walking their rounds,
   And binding with briars my joys and desires.

WILLIAM BLAKE (1757-1827)

Binding With Briars

Sex and Sin in the Catholic Church

RICHARD GINDER

PRENTICE-HALL, INC., Englewood Cliffs, N.J.

*Binding With Briars: Sex and Sin in the
Catholic Church* by Richard Ginder
Copyright © 1975 by Richard Ginder

Printed in the United States of America
Prentice-Hall International, Inc., London
Prentice-Hall of Australia, Pty. Ltd., Sydney
Prentice-Hall of Canada, Ltd., Toronto
Prentice-Hall of India Private Ltd., New Delhi
Prentice-Hall of Japan, Inc., Tokyo

10   9   8   7   6   5   4   3   2   1

Library of Congress Cataloging in Publication Data

Ginder, Richard.
  Binding with briars.

  Bibliography: p.
  Includes index.
  1. Sexual ethics. 2. Sex and religion.
3. Catholic Church—Doctrinal and controversial
works—Catholic authors. I. Title.
HQ59.G56   261.8'34'17   75-11610
ISBN 0-13-076299-7

Deiparæ

FOREWORD

I am a Roman Catholic priest. My diocese is Pittsburgh. I am in good standing and celebrate the Holy Sacrifice every day.

Among my other qualifications: I was a Basselin Fellow with three years of philosophy and four of theology at the Catholic University of America. As associate editor for twenty years, I wrote a highly controversial column, "Right Or Wrong," for *Our Sunday Visitor*, in those days the most widely circulated Catholic periodical in the world, with close to a million subscribers.

I founded and for twenty-four years edited *The Priest*, a kind of trade journal for the Catholic clergy. I founded and for eleven years edited *My Daily Visitor* for shut-ins. For thirteen years I edited *The Catholic Choirmaster*. I have written altogether one hundred twenty-four pamphlets with a total sale of twenty-six million copies. I have spoken and my musical compositions have been performed on all four of the major radio networks and on CBS-TV.

I am a Fellow of the American Guild of Organists, a published author and composer, with a master's degree in philosophy and the equivalent, a licentiate, in sacred theology. For three years I taught at St. Charles College and St. Mary's Seminary, Baltimore.

I have been working on this book for twenty-five years: reading, taking notes, analyzing my own inner experience and comparing it with that of others. The seed was planted in 1949 when I first realized my sexual identity. Gradually, with the passing years, the embryo developed into a fetus, until finally last year I entered into labor. Here is the child. During all that time I was never allowed to express myself on this subject in either *The Priest* or *Our Sunday Visitor*. I was always overruled.

But once I started writing, I felt the book taking on a life of its own. It began to unfold and grow almost of itself as I thought through this whole matter of sexuality in its relationship to religion. I began the book a conservative and ended a liberal.

While writing the very first chapters, I still accepted the classical morality with which I had been inoculated: drunkenness is not much of a sin, lying is only a venial sin, and to enjoy marijuana is no sin at all; theft can usually be rationalized on grounds of need or occult compensation,* cursing and profanity are generally venial for lack of advertence, whatever you do on the Sabbath is okay so long as you get to mass—BUT that second glance at a provocative billboard is a mortal sin.

(Not, as Alex Comfort hints in *The Joy of Sex*, that we Catholics aren't playing sex as often as the rest of the world; it's just that we aren't getting nearly as much fun out of it because of what Dr. Comfort calls our "guilt hangup.")

Writing this book has forced me to rethink the whole subject of morality—rather, not to rethink but for the first time in my life to think it all the way through. As I pondered the different aspects of the subject, making them explicit in my mind, framing them in words for the reader, the classical morality on sex became increasingly implausible. I kept having to modify what I had hitherto considered my "absolutes."

If it strikes the reader that I give rather disproportionate space to the homosexuals, it is because Gay Liberation is the cutting edge of sexual liberation. If the "respectable" elements of the American community can ever come to tolerate sodomy and to welcome the gays as their peers in every way, then, *a fortiori*, they will concede anything at all to the heterosexuals. It is the gays who are the shock troops, in the front lines, on the barricades.

In dogma I remain an open-minded conservative. With Plato, Aristotle, St. Augustine, and St. Thomas, I still believe in a spiritual and "detachable" soul, in a particular judgment, and in the communion of saints. The Holy Father is the visible head of Christ's Church on earth, and the bishops in communion with him are successors of the apostles, each ruling his diocese by divine right. As a priest I have the power to forgive sins and consecrate the body of the Lord. I am not about to yield one period or comma of the Nicene Creed. I love my priesthood and my Church. I love God and I love all his creatures:

*Secretly taking one's due.

men and women, boys and girls, cats and dogs, snakes and spiders—*sed aliter et aliter*, "one one way and another another."

As for moral theology, that is something else again. My opinions may have to travel underground in the Church until popular sentiment is ready to accept them. But if you find my arguments and proofs probable, even though not conclusive, then the Church says you may form your own conscience accordingly.

For several years I was official censor of books for the Diocese of Pittsburgh. Nevertheless, it is with prayer and no little trepidation that I submit my analysis, hoping that it may bring some degree of comfort, however slight, to the reader. All my life has been a preparation for the writing of this book.

——Richard Ginder

CONTENTS